women

war

peace

**The Independent Experts' Assessment
on the Impact of Armed Conflict on Women
and Women's Role in Peace-building**

by

Elisabeth Rehn & Ellen Johnson Sirleaf

CONTENTS

CONTENTS

CONTENTS

Mayan women voted in 1999 in a constitutional referendum
that included proposals from the Guatemalan peace accords.

As Executive Director of UNIFEM I have witnessed the impact of conflict on women in many countries. In the "Valley of Widows" in Colombia, I met women who had lost their husbands and their land — everyone and everything important to them had been destroyed by civil war and drug lords. I have been to Bosnia where women described abduction, rape camps and forced impregnation, and to Rwanda where women had been gang raped and purposely infected with HIV/AIDS. Stories like these were repeated again and again, in different languages, in different surroundings: East Timor, the Democratic Republic of the Congo, Guatemala. Only the horror and the pain were the same. Clearly the nature of war has changed. It is being fought in homes and communities — and on women's bodies — in a battle for resources and in the name of religion and ethnicity. Violence against women is used to break and humiliate women, men, families, communities, no matter which side they are on. Women have become the greatest victims of war — and the biggest stakeholders of peace.

I was prepared to find bitterness and hatred among the women who had experienced such horrific violence and loss, and pervasive trauma, but in many places I found strength. I met women who had transcended their sorrow and discovered in themselves the courage and will to rebuild their lives and communities. Many believed the only way to stop the cycle of violence was to make security and justice key issues on the agenda for a new, more equitable society. A few years ago in South Africa I lit UNIFEM's peace torch alongside African women; it was sent to other conflict areas and then to Beijing to open the Fourth World Conference on Women in 1995. The women wanted peace, but they also wanted to be shapers of the peace process in their countries, to use their own suffering and transform it into a force that would build a more secure future for humanity.

That is the deeper story I want the world to know: that despite what they have experienced, many of the women I met have been able to rise to the challenge of building a sustainable peace, recognizing that the security and satisfaction of one side can never be based on the frustration or humiliation of the other. They were women like those in East Timor who created collectives to provide each other with emotional support as well as employment schemes to keep their families and villages going. They instituted literacy classes — at the end of the war 90 per cent of rural women were illiterate — and demanded a role in political elections. In Sudan women from the North and the South took the initiative to come together across ethnic and religious divides to talk about building peace. In Ghana women refugees from Liberia learned construction skills through a UNIFEM-supported programme and built a safer camp for themselves and their families. In Afghanistan women met in secret to organize while the Taliban was in power. They developed maps of streets and neighbourhoods where underground homeschools for girls or medical help or jobs could be found, and shared them at weddings and birthdays.

We cannot expect women to do all this alone. Their efforts must be recognized, valued and supported. To build peace and contribute to the rebuilding of their countries, women need resources, skills, authority. Despite the work they have done on the ground, they are not at the peace table when warring factions sit down to negotiate. No one is held accountable for the enormous crimes committed against women. Although women are feeding their families and have taken in orphans, there are countries where they cannot inherit property or own land to farm. Their needs and their work are not systematically supported in the programmes developed by international agencies. Their rights are not enshrined in constitutions or protected by legislation. All this must change.

Women's peace-building and reconstruction efforts must be supported, not only because it is the right thing to do, but also because most nations consumed by conflict need the strength of their women. The women are the ones who hold their families and communities together during the worst of the fighting, even while on the run from armies. They keep a measure of stability during times of chaos and during displacement. Now as peace accords are negotiated and countries are rebuilt, those contributions must be recognized.

I appointed Elisabeth Rehn and Ellen Johnson Sirleaf to conduct an independent assessment of women, war and peace so that people throughout the world would know and understand not only what women have suffered but what they have contributed. Many who read this report will already know what has happened to women in Bosnia, East Timor or Afghanistan, but I believe we have not recognized how pervasive violence against women is during conflict and how great the need for protection and assistance. We know a little about women building peace, but we have not yet recognized women as a force for reconstruction. New responses are vital if we want this century to banish the worst brutalities of the previous one. We must invest in the progress of women from war-affected countries.

For helping to make this assessment possible, my deepest appreciation goes to the bilateral donors and foundations that have supported UNIFEM's programme on women, peace and security. I would like to thank the Conflict and Humanitarian Affairs Department (CHAD) of the Department for International Development of the United Kingdom (DFID-UK) for its programme support. Thanks also go to the Governments of Belgium, Denmark, Italy, Japan, Luxembourg, the Netherlands and Sweden and to the United Nations Foundation for support of initiatives in specific countries, and to the Government of Switzerland and DFID-UK for their ongoing support of *Progress of the World's Women*.

I also wish to acknowledge the support of several people within the United Nations system: Louise Fréchette, Deputy Secretary-General of the United Nations; Mark Malloch Brown, Administrator of the UN Development Programme (UNDP); Jean-Marie Guéhenno, Under-Secretary-General, Department of Peacekeeping Operations (DPKO); Kieran Prendergast, Under-Secretary-General of the Department of Political Affairs (DPA); Kenzo Oshima, Under-Secretary-General, Office for the Coordination of Humanitarian Affairs (OCHA) and Emergency Relief Coordinator; Thoraya Ahmed Obaid, Executive Director of the UN Population Fund (UNFPA); Sergio Vieira DeMello, High Commissioner for Human Rights; Ruud Lubbers, High Commissioner for Refugees; and Carolyn McAskie, Deputy Emergency Relief Coordinator. Throughout this project the UN system cooperated as one to support the visits of the independent experts and to ensure that the voices of women would be heard. I firmly believe that the authoritative analysis presented here will help create the political will to move forward, to promote the skills, strengths and leadership of women as they work for peace.

Noeleen Heyzer
Executive Director
UNIFEM

We were not strangers to war when UNIFEM asked us to carry out this independent assessment on the impact of armed conflict on women and women's role in peace-building. Elisabeth remembers the sound of World War II planes overhead. She witnessed the long rows of corpses and body parts as the mass graves of Srebrenica were exhumed. Ellen was one of only four government ministers who escaped assassination after the Liberian coup of 1980. As former Defence and Finance Ministers, and as Presidential candidates, we understand the world of politics, and we have a keen sense for ripe political moments. This is such a moment. This is an opportunity to improve protection for women in armed conflict and to strengthen women's contributions to peace processes and to rebuilding their communities.

Over the course of one year, during 2001 and 2002, we travelled to many of the world's conflicts. Focusing on the impact of armed conflict on women and women's role in peace-building, we visited 14 areas affected by conflict: Bosnia and Herzegovina; Cambodia; Colombia; the Democratic Republic of the Congo; East Timor; the Former Yugoslav Republic of Macedonia; the Federal Republic of Yugoslavia, including Kosovo; Guinea; Israel; Liberia; the occupied Palestinian territories; Rwanda; Sierra Leone; and Somalia. In all of these areas we saw how the militarization of society breeds new levels of violence and how impunity for these crimes becomes endemic. We saw a continuum of violence that shatters women's lives before, during and after conflict.

In retrospect, we realize how little prepared we were for the enormity of it all: the staggering numbers of women in war who survived the brutality of rape, sexual exploitation, mutilation, torture and displacement; the unconscionable acts of depravity; and the wholesale exclusion of women from peace processes.

We prepared for each visit by researching the background of the conflict and developing a set of questions to guide interactions, although we often found that a less rigid approach elicited better answers to our questions and provided more information. Due to the ongoing danger for women in many conflict zones, we did not film or record our meetings with women's organizations and individuals, but instead took extensive notes. Our meetings were informal and off the record in an effort to make women as comfortable as possible discussing what were extremely distressing events and issues.

We collected first-hand data and testimonies by meeting with women victims and survivors of conflict, including refugee and internally displaced women; activists; women leaders and women's groups; international and national non-governmental organizations (NGOs); the media; religious organizations; eminent leaders from civil society; and women and girls directly involved in armed conflicts and peace processes. We met women in their offices and homes, at health clinics, in refugee camps, on the street, in bars and restaurants.

We also met with representatives of United Nations agencies, at headquarters and in the field, along with host governments, opposition groups and peacekeeping and humanitarian personnel to find out what they are doing for women and how they are approaching gender issues.

In addition to field-based interviews and information collection, we relied on research and analysis from human rights groups and civil society, independent reports and UN documents. These provided useful analyses and raised policy issues that underscored what women themselves identified as priorities. While our goal was to focus on the testimonies of women we met during our visits, we wanted to demonstrate that their experiences are not country-specific, but global. Many of the trends we saw are universal phenomena, which is why we included a number of examples from places we could not visit.

In our report, we introduce you to many of the women we met, whose names have been changed in order to protect them from reprisals: Chantal from a UN High Commission for Refugees (UNHCR) transit camp in Goma, the Democratic Republic of the Congo; Lam, a 15-year-old Vietnamese girl in a women's shelter in Phnom Penh, Cambodia; and a prize-winning journalist from Colombia who fled her country after receiving death threats. We share their stories to show the reality of war for women and to give a human face to the struggle for security. We have concluded that the standards of protection for women affected by conflict are glaring in their inadequacy, as is the international response. Only by ending impunity for crimes against women in war can nations be rebuilt. Gender equality in this context means enabling women as full citizens: as voters, as candidates, as decision-makers. It means supporting women's centrality to reconstruction – to reforming the constitution, the electoral system, and the policies and resources that support development. Without women's representation – without half the population – no country can truly claim to be engaged in democratic development and participatory governance.

This glimpse of bitter reality is shadowed by the deadly nexus of HIV/AIDS and armed conflict for women. It is fuelled by the economies of war, relief and reconstruction. Women do not receive what they need in emergencies, for development, peace-building or reconstruction. Their entreaties for education and health care go largely unanswered. In short, women and their organizations need more resources. At all levels – from the grass roots to the international — women's organizations continue to be insufficiently recognized and supported.

But our report also shows many ways in which women in conflict situations are being supported. A large number of United Nations agencies and many international and local NGOs are protecting women and supporting their role in peace-building. We maintain, however, that this excellent work needs to be amplified exponentially.

We are proud to pay tribute in this report to the courageous peacekeepers and humanitarian workers on the front lines and to showcase new models of protection for women in a peacekeeping environment. We are encouraged that civilian police are working to protect women from domestic violence and, in some cases, to prevent it. We are gratified to see peace operations support HIV/AIDS awareness. But we were also appalled by reports of flagrant violations against women by those with the duty to protect them. We support fully Secretary-General Kofi Annan's position that there must be zero tolerance and full accountability for these crimes. We take note of the recent report of the UN Office for Internal Oversight (OIOS) on sexual exploitation and efforts by the humanitarian community to strengthen measures for protection from sexual exploitation and abuse in humanitarian crises.

We direct our findings to those with the power and resources to make a difference. Indifference is not an option. In representing women's experience of war we have paid attention to causes and consequences. But for each woman, the challenges, obstacles and opportunities are different. We accept full responsibility for our conclusions — their merits and their shortcomings. They do not necessarily represent the position of UNIFEM, whose courage we salute in commissioning this long overdue assessment. We pay special thanks to Noeleen Heyzer, UNIFEM Executive Director, for her courage in creating the political space for the assessment and for skillfully shepherding it to completion. We also owe thanks to Jennifer Klot, Adviser on Governance, Peace and Security at UNIFEM, for identifying the need for this report and her inspired leadership of the secretariat.

We are indebted to the experts who provided research specifically commissioned for this assessment. Radhika Coomaraswamy, the UN Special Rapporteur on violence against women, helped us understand the nature of sexual violence and exploitation in armed conflict. Angela M. Wakhweya, Catherine A. Rielly, Monica Onyango and Gail Helmer at the Center for International Health at Boston University conducted valuable research on the intersection of gender, HIV/AIDS and conflict, and Professor Donna Sullivan of New York University School of Law provided much needed guidance on the pursuit of justice and accountability for gender-based war crimes in post-conflict reconstruction. We also owe thanks to Victoria Brittain for her touching and insightful contributions.

We have relied enormously on the guidance of our Advisory Group, composed of eminent women and men from all regions of the globe whose expertise includes peace support operations, humanitarian assistance, human rights and peace-building. Their encouragement, support, knowledge and sheer intelligence have been invaluable to our work. In this regard, our thanks go to Rafeeuddin Ahmed, Winnie Byanyima, Isha Dyfan, Asma Jahangir, Stephen Lewis, Jane Holl Lute, Luz Mendez, Faiza Jama Mohamed, Maha Muna, Milena Pires, Maj Britt Theorin and Stasa Zajovic. We would also like to thank the many experts — too numerous to name — who offered advice, information and encouragement.

We are grateful for the support of the secretariat staff at UNIFEM, Aina Iiyambo, Sumie Nakaya, Felicity Hill, Gaella Mortel and Liliana Potenza, and for the input of Carol Cohn and Karen Judd. We thank Maarit Kohonen, seconded from the Office of the High Commissioner for Human Rights (OHCHR), who helped get this initiative off the ground and provided much substantive input. Saudimini Siegrist of the United Nations Children's Fund (UNICEF) provided insight and expertise. Pam DeLargy of the United Nations Population Fund (UNFPA) joined our field mission to West Africa and worked closely with the secretariat, contributing analysis and insights. Joyce Mends-Cole of the Office of the United Nations High Commissioner for Refugees (UNHCR) assisted with several of our field visits and commented on drafts. Our security adviser, Heljo Laukkala, was a great help during our visits. We express our deepest respect and appreciation to the courageous humanitarians in the field who went far beyond the call of duty to help us in so many ways.

We would also like to thank the United Nations Development Programme (UNDP), the Department of Peacekeeping Operations (DPKO) and the Department of Political Affairs (DPA) for their direct support of our work and the United Nations Relief and Works Agency for Palestine Refugees in the Near East (UNRWA) for facilitating our visits to camps in the West Bank and Gaza.

Finally we thank the women who inspired this report, who have committed their lives to peace and justice, for which they have waited too long.

Elisabeth Rehn and Ellen Johnson Sirleaf
October 2002

KEY RECOMMENDATIONS

Towards the full implementation of Security Council Resolution 1325, the Independent Experts call for:

1. An international Truth and Reconciliation Commission on violence against women in armed conflict as a step towards ending impunity. This Commission, to be convened by civil society with support from the international community, will fill the historical gap that has left these crimes unrecorded and unaddressed.

2. Targeted sanctions against trafficking of women and girls. Those complicit must be held accountable for trafficking women and girls in or through conflict areas. Existing international laws on trafficking must be applied in conflict situations and national legislation should criminalize trafficking with strong punitive measures, including such actions as freezing the assets of trafficking rings. Victims of trafficking should be protected from prosecution.

3. Strengthening of United Nations field operations for internally displaced women and of those bodies that support a field-based presence. Protection officers from all relevant bodies, including the Office of the High Commissioner for Refugees (UNHCR), the Office of the High Commissioner for Human Rights (OHCHR), the Office for the Coordination of Humanitarian Affairs (OCHA), the United Nations Children's Fund (UNICEF) and the International Committee of the Red Cross (ICRC), should be deployed immediately if a state cannot or will not protect displaced populations or is indeed responsible for their displacement. Resources should be made available for this purpose.

4. Psychosocial support and reproductive health services for women affected by conflict to be an integral part of emergency assistance and post-conflict reconstruction. Special attention should be provided to those who have experienced physical trauma, torture and sexual violence. All agencies providing health support and social services should include psychosocial counselling and referrals. The United Nations Population Fund (UNFPA) should take the lead in providing these services, working in close cooperation with the World Health Organization (WHO), UNHCR, and UNICEF.

5. All HIV/AIDS programmes and funding in conflict situations to address the disproportionate disease burden carried by women. Mandatory gender analysis and specific strategies for meeting the needs of women and girls should seek to prevent infection and increase access to treatment, care and support.

6. Gender experts and expertise to be included at all levels and in all aspects of peace operations, including technical surveys and the design of concepts of operation, training, staffing and programmes. To this end, a Memorandum of Understanding should set out the roles and responsibilities among the Department of Peacekeeping Operations (DPKO), the Department of Political Affairs (DPA), the United Nations Development Fund for Women (UNIFEM) and the Division for the Advancement of Women (DAW).

7. A review of training programmes on and approaches to the gender dimensions of conflict resolution and peace-building for humanitarian, military and civilian personnel. United Nations entities active in this area should lead this process with support provided by the Special Advisor on Gender Issues and Advancement of Women and the Task Force on Women, Peace and Security with a view to developing guidance on training policy and standards.

8. The Secretary-General, in keeping with his personal commitment, to increase the number of women in senior positions in peace-related functions. Priority should be given to achieving gender parity in his appointment of women as Special Representatives and Envoys, beginning with a minimum of 30 per cent in the next three years, with a view to gender parity by 2015.

9. Gender equality to be recognized in all peace processes, agreements and transitional governance structures. International and regional organizations and all participating parties involved in peace processes should advocate for gender parity, maintaining a minimum 30 per cent representation of women in peace negotiations, and ensure that women's needs are taken into consideration and specifically addressed in all such agreements.

10. A United Nations Trust Fund for Women's Peace-building. This Trust Fund would leverage the political, financial and technical support needed for women's civil society organizations and women leaders to have an impact on peace efforts nationally, regionally and internationally. The Fund should be managed by UNIFEM, in consultation with other UN bodies and women's civil society organizations.

11. UNIFEM to work closely with DPA to ensure that gender issues are incorporated in peace-building and post-conflict reconstruction in order to integrate gender perspectives in peace-building and to support women's full and equal participation in decision-making; and for UNFPA to strengthen its work in emergency situations in order to build women's capacity in conflict situations. UNIFEM and UNFPA should be represented in all relevant inter-agency bodies.

KEY RECOMMENDATIONS

12. The Secretary-General to appoint a panel of experts to assess the gaps in international and national laws and standards pertaining to the protection of women in conflict and post-conflict situations and women's role in peace-building.

13. Increased donor resources and access for women to media and communications technology, so that gender perspectives, women's expertise and women's media can influence public discourse and decision-making on peace and security.

14. The Secretary-General to systematically include information on the impact of armed conflict on women and women's role in prevention and peace-building in all of his country and thematic reports to the Security Council. Towards that end, the Secretary-General should request relevant information from UN operations and all relevant bodies.

15. The systematic collection and analysis of information and data by all actors, using gender specific indicators to guide policy, programmes and service delivery for women in armed conflict. This information should be provided on a regular basis to the Secretariat, Member States, inter-governmental bodies, regional organizations, non-governmental organizations (NGOs) and other relevant bodies. A central knowledge base should be established and maintained by UNIFEM together with a network of all relevant bodies, in particular DPA.

16. The Security Council to formulate a plan for the least diversion for armaments of the world's human and economic resources. Sixty years after being assigned the task, the Security Council should implement Article 26 of the United Nations Charter, taking into account the Women's Peace Petition which calls for the world's nations to redirect at least 5 per cent of national military expenditures to health, education and employment programmes each year over the next five years.

17. The UN Development Programme (UNDP), as a leading agency in the field of security sector reform, to ensure that women's protection and participation be central to the design and reform of security sector institutions and policies, especially in police, military and rule of law components. UNDP should integrate a gender perspective into its country programmes.

18. Operational humanitarian, human rights and development bodies to develop indicators to determine the extent to which gender is mainstreamed throughout their operations in conflict and post-conflict situations and ensure that gender mainstreaming produces measurable results and is not lost in generalities and vague references to gender. Measures should be put in place to address the gaps and obstacles encountered in implementation.

19. Gender budget analysis of humanitarian assistance and post-conflict reconstruction to ensure that women benefit directly from resources mobilized through multilateral and bilateral donors, including the Consolidated Appeals Process, the Bretton Woods Institutions and donor conferences.

20. Establishment of macroeconomic policies in post-conflict reconstruction that prioritize the public provision of food, water, sanitation, health and energy, the key sectors in which women provide unpaid labour. Special attention should be paid to the consequences for women of decentralization policies.

21. A lead organization to be designated within the United Nations for women's education and training in conflict and post-conflict situations. This lead organization, together with the United Nations Educational, Scientific and Cultural Organization (UNESCO), UNHCR and UNICEF, should ensure that all education programmes for displaced persons provide for women as well as girls.

22. The Security Council, the General Assembly and the United Nations Economic and Social Council (ECOSOC) to give serious consideration to the above recommendations and adopt relevant decisions to operationalize them. The Secretary-General should thereafter formulate an implementation plan addressing each of the recommendations contained in those decisions and submit an annual report to the Security Council and all relevant bodies on the progress made and obstacles encountered in implementation.

peace-for whom & when?

As we write this, in the summer of 2002, it is hard to imagine a world without war. Every day we hear reports of new conflicts and old grievances, of escalating tension and violence. During our missions to conflict situations, we met generations of women and girls who have known nothing other than war. Many were gripped by fear and anger; others had learned to dull their feelings with a quality of silence that often follows catastrophe. Having lost so many pieces of their lives to war, women shared their experiences with us hoping that we would make the difference that would bring them some stability, some safety, some shelter, or even some food. They hoped that their voices would be heard and their triumphs celebrated; that we would showcase, through their lives, every reason that women must be considered full citizens and must have a stake in deciding their own future — and that finally, the world would listen.

We are humbled by our experience over the past year. We spent long hours with women who refused to give up hope for peace, and who turned to us to make their claims. How could we possibly improve their lives? In part, the answer will depend on the serious-ness with which the testimony, analysis, hopes and vision of these ordinary but extraordinary women — survivors, leaders and heroines — are both received and acted upon.

Women are victims of unbelievably horrific atrocities and injustices in conflict situations; this is indisputable. As refugees, internally displaced persons, combatants, heads of household and community leaders, as activists and peace-builders, women and men experience conflict differently. Women rarely have the same resources, political rights, authority or control over their environment and needs that men do. In addition, their caretaking responsibilities limit their mobility and ability to protect themselves.

While an estimated one hundred million people died in war over the last century,[1] men and women often died different deaths and were tortured and abused in different ways — sometimes for biological reasons, sometimes psychological or social. While more men are killed in war, women often experience violence, forced pregnancy, abduction and sexual abuse and slavery. Their bodies, deliberately infected with HIV/AIDS or carrying a child conceived in rape, have been used as envelopes to send messages to the perceived "enemy." The harm, silence and shame women experience in war is pervasive; their redress, almost non-existent. The situation of women in armed conflict has been systematically neglected.

Contemporary conflicts have caused economic upheaval — and they have been created by it. The exploitation of natural resources has created "economies of war" where armed groups and other power brokers thrive on the instability of conflict in order to gain control of valuable resources and land. Along with the deepening violence women experience during war, the long-term effects of conflict and militarization create a culture of violence that renders women especially vulnerable after war. Institutions of governance and law are weakened and social fragmentation is pronounced. Until the state's security and legal infrastructure are rebuilt, women's security is threatened inside and outside of the home, and they are subject to the rule of aggression rather than the rule of law. Under constant threat of attack by family members, rogue elements, ex-

combatants, criminals, women spend their days searching for water, food and firewood and caring for children, the sick, the elderly and their extended families. Even though women provide these unpaid services in times of peace, their burden is intensified during conflict since the peacetime infrastructure is often destroyed: Wells may have been poisoned, trees for firewood destroyed, fields burnt and clinics vandalized.

This report does not claim the universal innocence of women, nor does it argue that women are inherently more peaceful, or that men are more warlike. Grappling with the concept of gender avoids these stereotypes, and leads to an examination of the different roles assigned to men and women in making war and peace. Conflict can change traditional gender roles: Women may acquire more mobility, resources and opportunities for leadership. But the additional responsibility comes without any diminution in the demands of their traditional roles. Thus, the momentary space in which women take on non-traditional roles and typically assume much greater responsibilities — within the household and public arenas — does not necessarily advance gender equality.[2]

We have grappled with the dilemma of describing the atrocities experienced by women in war in a way that will not ascribe to women the characteristics of passivity and helplessness. Women are everything but that. But as with all groups facing discrimination, violence and marginalization, the causes and consequences of their victimization must be addressed. If not, how will preventive measures ever focus on women? How will the resources and means to protect women be put in place? How will the UN system, governments and non-governmental organizations (NGOs) be mobilized to support women? We dwell on this point because, so far, not enough has been done.

The glaring gaps in women's protection expose the systematic failures of the humanitarian community to reach women. Although women have benefited from humanitarian assistance more generally, their specific needs are largely neglected, particularly in relation to physical and psychosocial care, economic security, HIV/AIDS and displacement. Women continue to have the least access to protection and assistance provided by the state or international organizations.[3]

In Afghanistan, for instance, women have not entered a new era yet, despite the many symbolic photographs in the media of women removing their burqas. Afghan women are neither secure nor safe. In fact, they have not removed their burqas in significant numbers and, for many women, this is less important than the violence and exclusion they experience in Afghanistan's political, economic and social reconstruction. The status of Afghan women is as precarious as the stability of their country's transition to peace. But in one essential way, the media did get it right: When women are safe, so are nations. When women feel secure, peace is possible. The power of this message undoubtedly lends new significance to the contributions of Afghan women — past, present and future — to their nation's development. And it reminds us of the risks they face as they try to rebuild their nation and their lives.

Women were taking risks in every place we visited. They were putting communities and families back together, providing healing and recovery services and organizing solidarity networks across ethnic, class and cultural chasms. Through women, we saw alternative ways of organizing security and of building peace. We saw women's resistance to war — expressed through theatre, public demonstrations and civil disobedience. We watched women educate each other, write, publish news, lobby for ceasefires and outline the contours of peace agreements. Women often spoke to us about the challenges of working with men to build peace and resolve conflicts and of overcoming male identification with militarism and war.

WHY AN INDEPENDENT EXPERT ASSESSMENT?

As the nature of warfare has changed, the Security Council has recognized that international peace and security are advanced when women are included in decision-making and when they contribute to peace-building. In October 2000 the first UN Security Council Resolution on Women and Peace and Security was passed unanimously.[4] Resolution 1325 emerged from the leadership of supportive governments, the advocacy of a coali-

tion of NGOs and technical assistance from the United Nations Development Fund for Women (UNIFEM) and other gender advocates in the UN system. The Resolution set a new threshold of action for the Security Council, the UN system and for all governments.

Resolution 1325 is a watershed political framework that makes women — and a gender perspective — relevant to negotiating peace agreements, planning refugee camps and peacekeeping operations and reconstructing war-torn societies. It makes the pursuit of gender equality relevant to every single Council action, ranging from mine clearance to elections to security sector reform.

This Independent Expert Assessment was designed in response to Resolution 1325, as one effort to continue to document and analyse the specific impact of war on women and the potential of bringing women into peace processes. This Assessment is also a direct response to the call from Graça Machel, the United Nations Secretary-General's Expert on the Impact of Armed Conflict on Children, for a report on the gender dimensions of conflict and its relevance to international peace and security.[5]

We were commissioned to undertake this independent study by UNIFEM and we undertook it in the belief that what is presented here will provide the United Nations and the international community with the information they need to implement Resolution 1325.

The women's movement has already seized the opportunity provided by this Resolution with vigour. It is evident that even in the most unlikely places, including refugee camps and clinics, women are organizing on the basis of Resolution 1325. The Resolution has trickled down to the grass roots because it has given political legitimacy to a long history of women's peace activity. The Security Council has heard testimony from women who described their efforts to overcome the deadly hold warlords had on their countries by providing education, housing and alternative income to war-affected women. In turn women's organizations and networks at all levels are paying more attention to Security Council actions and have invested resources and time in publicizing

Resolution 1325. They, and we, are genuinely hopeful that this expression of political commitment will translate into concrete resources, political access, and protection and assistance for women.

THE ECONOMIES OF WAR

Over the course of the 20th century civilian casualties in war climbed dramatically from 5 per cent at the turn of the century, to 15 per cent during World War I, to 65 per cent by the end of World War II, to more than 75 per cent in the wars of the 1990s.[6] This shift was accompanied by a changing demographic landscape of war-torn societies seen mostly in terms of a declining male population, changing household size and composition, and increased migration. Conflict causes an overall increase in female-headed or child-headed households; women and children are among the majority of displaced in refugee camps and conflict zones. Often displaced men set up new households in cities, abandoning their wives and families who remain in rural areas. In these situations, women search not just for a minimal level of economic security but for an acceptable social status in a society where lone women are far more at risk than their male counterparts.[7]

Violence will not abate while weapons are easier to acquire than a bag of maize. Weapons in the community translate into violence against women in the home and on the street. For women, more guns do not mean more security. Through women's eyes, we found a broader notion of security — one that is defined in human, rather than in military terms. Yet those with the power to define security see the equation differently. Current global military spending has returned to Cold War levels. The United Nations and all its Funds and Programmes spend about US$10 billion each year, or about $1.70 for each of the world's inhabitants,[8] compared with military expenditures of approximately US$139 per person worldwide — roughly eighty times more.[9] In the 1990s at least US$200 billion was spent by the international community on seven major interventions: Bosnia and Herzegovina, Cambodia, El Salvador, Haiti, the Persian Gulf, Rwanda and Somalia. The Carnegie Commission on Preventing Deadly Conflict estimates that a preventive approach would have saved the world US$130 billion.[10]

Women in war zones throughout the world talked to us about the weapons flowing into their communities. They told us how militarization affected their sons, their husbands, their brothers — that it turned them into different people. They complained that their men were cold, cut off or explosive and often violent, relying heavily on alcohol to block out the pain and trauma of what they had seen and done. Cynthia Enloe, a professor at Clark University, USA, has frequently explored this issue: "When a community's politicized sense of its own identity becomes threaded through with pressures for its men to take up arms, for its women to loyally support brothers, husbands, sons and lovers to become soldiers, it needs explaining. How were the pressures mounted? What does militarization mean for women's and men's relationship to each other? What happens when some women resist those pressures?"[11] And what about the men who resist the social pressures and name-calling and do not choose to align their identity or masculinity with war fever? Militarization often forces men into committing acts of violence or into imprisonment if they do not wish to fight. Militaries rely not on men per se but on men who behave in certain ways.

UN AGENCIES, WOMEN AND WAR

Women do not receive the humanitarian assistance they need. We saw over and over again that need is not, in fact, what determines a woman's access to assistance, protection and support. Her nationality, ethnicity, age, marital status, family situation and even her place of residence are far more likely determinants. Overall levels of assistance to women in conflict, and especially humanitarian aid, are related strongly to the media interest in a conflict's duration, the country's trauma, its natural and mineral resource base and its geopolitical relevance. Described by Oxfam as "one of the most brutal inequalities in the world today," the disparity in resources mobilized across conflict situations is becoming ever more pronounced.

The agencies and staff of the United Nations

have both the opportunity and the challenge to address the impact of war on women and women's roles in building peace. As we travelled to different countries, we saw courageous and dedicated UN staff working to prevent conflict, deal with its aftermath and assist countries to re-build. Yet it is indisputable that, despite numerous UN resolutions passed by consensus by governments from around the world, the UN system still needs to improve staff capacity, organizational practices and systems, and high-level commitment to more effectively address the gender dimensions of war and peace.

This Independent Expert Assessment complements the study undertaken by the UN Secretary-General as called for in Resolution 1325. That study will provide far greater detail about the work of the UN system. Nevertheless, during our visits, we saw the challenges that the UN system confronts when its tries to honour the commitments made by governments to gender equality and women's rights; and we saw the lost opportunities from having inadequate resources, coordination and focus on protecting women and promoting their role in peace-building.

A number of agencies are well positioned to strengthen their work in the area of women, peace and security. The General Assembly has encouraged UNIFEM to expand its work in this area.[12] In the early 1990s, UNIFEM developed the African Women in Crisis (AFWIC) programme, which called attention to women's psychosocial and trauma needs in the aftermath of war and supported African women leaders to build activist peace networks. It has since created similar programmes in almost every region in the world, and now supports women's efforts to advocate for peace in Colombia, Southern Africa and South Asia, as well as women's leadership in re-building war-torn countries from Afghanistan to Sierra Leone. But, despite its best efforts, UNIFEM needs additional strengthening to be able to play a more effective advocacy role and to pilot innovative ways of addressing women's protection and assistance issues.

UNIFEM is an innovative and catalytic fund with a budget of just over US$30 million a year, so its efforts on behalf of women have necessarily been limited. The larger UN agencies must get on board and, here too, we have seen great potential and great need. In some areas, the United Nations Population Fund (UNFPA) is filling this gap by providing essential services to women, such as reproductive health care, psychosocial support, HIV/AIDS awareness and other crucial forms of assistance. The Office of the United Nations High Commissioner for Refugees (UNHCR), the World Food Programme (WFP) and a wide range of NGOs and faith-based organizations are on the front lines responding to women's needs. But even when these needs are understood by the humanitarian community, the gap between ideology and practice is often very large. Full-scale delivery for women is simply not possible in the absence of appropriate programme and policy guidance, expertise and resources.

Women were taking risks in every place we visited. They were putting communities and families back together, providing healing and recovery services and organizing solidarity networks across ethnic, class and cultural chasms.

It goes without saying that the first step in removing obstacles to women's protection is identifying what they are. UNHCR has noted that women are likely to suffer from a range of discriminatory practices in conflict situations, from receiving smaller food rations to being denied custody, inheritance and property rights. Not only do women carry the emotional and physical burden of caring for the whole family under difficult conditions but, in the process, they are more exposed to violence and often become victims of inadequate diets and infectious disease. Ironically, women's role as caregivers may affect their ability to receive assistance. By standing in a queue to collect food or water, a woman may forfeit the chance to receive medical attention. Girls may be kept out of school to help with domestic chores — a practice that helps to explain the three-to-one ratio of school attendance between refugee boys and girls.

Given the present institutional arrangements for women's protection, we have concluded that a system-wide recommitment and implementation plan must address the situation of women in conflict. Overhauling humanitarianism costs money. It requires expertise. And it means, according to Charlotte Bunch, Executive Director of the Center for Women's Global Leadership, "not just looking at what have been called 'women's issues' — a ghetto, or a separate sphere that remains on the margins of society — but rather moving women from the margins to the center by questioning the most fundamental concepts of social, [legal and political] order so that they take better account of women's lives."[13]

THEMES ADDRESSED IN THIS REPORT

It is crucial that women's voices are heard and their work on the ground is recognized, valued and supported. Decisions should be made with them, not for them. To move this agenda forward, both operational and political action are needed. This nexus goes to the heart of the debate. Humanitarian and human rights concerns do not compromise military and political decision-making; they are intrinsic to it. This is the human security equation. In setting out this equation, our report addresses ten central themes:

1. **VIOLENCE AGAINST WOMEN**: The magnitude of violence suffered by women before, during and after conflict is overwhelming. The glaring gaps in women's protection must be addressed. Unless resources are specifically dedicated for women's protection and unless the requisite technical and operational capacity is mobilized, women will continue to be neglected.

2. **DISPLACEMENT**: The gender dimensions of displacement are overwhelmingly neglected. The international community has a responsibility to protect women who are forced to flee their homes. It must help women to rebuild their lives, protect them and their children, and prevent the violence and exploitation often associated with displacement.

3. **HEALTH**: Sometimes even basic health care is lacking for women in conflict situations. Attention to reproductive health in emergencies

has to be institutionalized as part of the response. The knowledge and skills already exist, and experience shows what can be achieved with sufficient resources and political will, and with the participation of women in planning.

4. **HIV/AIDS**: Wherever a woman lives with conflict and upheaval, the threat of HIV/AIDS and its effects are multiplied. Women are more susceptible to infection than men, yet often have little control over their sexuality. At the same time they are forced by conflict conditions to trade sex for money, food, shelter and any other number of necessities. Education, protection and access to treatment are essential for people in conflict zones if the rates of infection are to be reduced.

5. **PEACE OPERATIONS**: A gender perspective must inform all aspects of mission planning and operation, beginning with the very concept of the operation. Currently, gender concerns are often isolated in the form of a single staff person or small unit lacking sufficient seniority and resources. Women in the local community may have little contact with missions and believe that their needs are not taken into account. Violations committed by peacekeepers, United Nations and other humanitarian personnel are inexcusable. The Secretary-General's call for zero tolerance for those who commit such crimes must be honoured and stronger investigative and disciplinary mechanisms must be put in place.

6. **ORGANIZING FOR PEACE**: Women organize for peace in their communities and at the national and regional level, but they are rarely a part of the official peace process. Formal negotiations that exclude half the population from the political process have little hope of popular support. Women's activism must be supported and their political demands acknowledged at every step, from peace negotiations to post-conflict elections and the restructuring of society.

7. **JUSTICE AND ACCOUNTABILITY**: The impunity that prevails for widespread crimes against women in war must be redressed. Accountability means being answerable to women for crimes committed against them and punishing those responsible. In addition, from the International Criminal Court to regional, national and traditional justice

systems, gender must be taken into account and women must have full access to the rule of law.

8. MEDIA AND COMMUNICATIONS: The media supplies information for good or ill; it presents images of women that resound throughout communities in complex ways, especially during conflict and post-conflict periods, when tensions are high. Post-conflict reconstruction depends on honest and truthful reporting about all parties and communities. In order to achieve this, women must be involved in developing information and media outlets, and stories about them must go beyond stereotypes of women as victims or sexual objects.

9. PREVENTION: Information from and about women in conflict situations has not informed preventive actions. This is as much a problem of expertise as one of organizational shortcomings. Information from and about women must be collected, analysed, and made available in a way that is politically meaningful. The beneficiaries of disarmament, demobilization and reintegration programmes must not be limited to male combatants. Female combatants and the wives, widows and other dependents of ex-fighters must be included explicitly so that they are invested in rebuilding a new society and ending the cycle of violence.

10. RECONSTRUCTION: In the aftermath of conflict, when nations begin to rebuild they must provide for women's specific needs. Water, food and energy must be provided in a safe environment. Training and education are essential. Access to land, resources and jobs must be guaranteed.

CONCLUSION

September 11, 2001 altered the world in many ways. But what remained unchanged after the events of September 11 is as important as what changed. Across the world 30,000 children under the age of five died of preventable diseases on September 11, September 12, and every day since;[14] the plague of HIV/AIDS has marched on; and decision-making on matters of peace and security remains male dominated.

We hope this report will do more than set an agenda for action; we hope that it will bring new information and new issues to substantive research, policy and political agendas. We hope that it will bring a new perspective to the issues already on these agendas. But we also hope that it will help strengthen the standards for women's protection. We will measure the success of our work by the commitment it generates, of both resources and political will, from the Security Council to the Organisation for Economic Cooperation and Development (OECD), from the General Assembly to the Group of 8 industrial nations (G8), from the non-governmental to the governmental. We will measure progress through the strengthened capacity of civil society and of women's organizations working in conflict situations. We are convinced that new modalities

> **How will the resources and means to protect women be put in place? How will the UN system, governments and NGOs be mobilized to support women? We dwell on this point because, so far, not enough has been done**

are needed and that the present institutional arrangements to protect women in war and to support their leadership are inadequate. Accountability must be established. Without it nothing will change. And there are budgetary implications to this agenda. Denying them amounts to denying the agenda itself.

Women have not given up hope of transformation — that hope drives their determination to throw off the mantle of victimization. That women are surviving horror and rebuilding war-torn societies in ingenious and creative ways is indeed worth celebrating and documenting. That women have no choice but to do so, and that their under-resourced peace-building efforts are not acknowledged or funded, is yet another layer of injustice.

Much of the material that follows will make you uncomfortable; it might even make you weep. But reducing the women we met to mere tragedy is not our goal. We hope the graphic detail of injustices inflicted upon the bodies and lives of women fills every reader with a determination for change. Anger is inevitable after witnessing the needlessness and waste of war, and what it deliberately and inevitably does to women in every region of the world. Our anger multiplied our determination to make these women heard, and to believe that the Security Council would rise to the challenge it set the international community through its October 2000 Resolution on Women and Peace and Security, by listening, reflecting and taking action. The international community can only gain from what women have to offer, and will continue to miss opportunities for peace and democracy if it persists in systematically excluding them.

Our purpose is to expose women's invisibility — as victims, as survivors and as peace-makers and leaders. We believe this is the first step in addressing the opportunities for and obstacles to improving progress for women affected by war.

An ethnic Albanian woman in the Former Yugoslav Republic of Macedonia shows her bruises from a beating by security forces, 2001.

THE
INDEPENDENT
EXPERTS'
ASSESSMENT
ON

violence against women

Violence against women in conflict is one of history's great silences. We were completely unprepared for the searing magnitude of what we saw and heard in the conflict and post-conflict areas we visited. We knew the data. We knew that 17 per cent of displaced households surveyed in Sierra Leone had experienced sexual assaults, including rape, torture and sexual slavery.[1] That at least 250,000–perhaps as many as 500,000–women were raped during the 1994 genocide in Rwanda.[2] We read reports of sexual violence in the ongoing hostilities in Algeria, Myanmar, Southern Sudan and Uganda. We learned of the dramatic increase in domestic violence in war zones, and of the grow-ing numbers of women trafficked out of war zones to become forced labourers and forced sex workers.[3]

But knowing all this did not prepare us for the horrors women described. Wombs punctured with guns. Women raped and tortured in front of their husbands and children. Rifles forced into vaginas. Pregnant women beaten to induce miscarriages. Foetuses ripped from wombs. Women kidnapped, blindfolded and beaten on their way to work or school. We saw the scars, the pain and the humiliation. We heard accounts of gang rapes, rape camps and mutilation. Of murder and sexual slavery. We saw the scars of brutality so extreme that survival seemed for some a worse fate than death.

On every continent we visited, in refugee camps, bars, brothels, prisons and shantytowns, women survivors shared their stories with us. They told us about their struggles to heal from the physical violence and the enduring psychological pain. And the numbers simply could not begin to capture the anguish that permeated the life of each survivor whom we met.

And yet we saw something else as well. Time and again, we met women who had survived trauma and found the courage and the will to recommit to life. They were struggling to rebuild community and remake their lives.

In Freetown, Sierra Leone we entered a ramshackle building on a lush hillside. The house was made up of small rooms that became flooded and mud-filled in the rainy season, the young girls who lived there told us. Photographs of the girls hung on the walls, with their names and positions in the cooperative written on the bottom in coloured marker: "Miriama, co-chairperson" "Esther, member." There were many hand written signs as well, with slogans like, "Condom is for protection from AIDS — Use it" or "Respect Yourself and Protect Yourself."

The girls were all sex workers. They belonged to different religions and ethnic groups, but they all had one thing in common: They had been separated by force from their families during the war. Most had been abducted and forced to stay with the rebels until they escaped or until the cease-fire was signed. They had been raped repeatedly. Many had seen their parents and siblings killed by armed groups. After the war, some had tried to go back to their villages only to find their houses burned and their families gone. Like many other young girls without family or livelihood, they made their way to the city and began earning a living on the streets. We talked to one girl, very small and shy, who was only about 4 1/2 feet tall, perhaps 80 pounds — and pregnant. She was 14 and told us she had been in the bush for several years with the rebels. They forced her to cook for them and raped her regularly.

The girls were matter-of-fact about what they had suffered, and continued to suffer. They had little hope of recapturing even a semblance of their former world. Many will be physically and emotionally scarred for the rest of their lives, which in too many cases will be painfully short, since they often have unprotected sex because men will pay more for it that way.

It is impossible to ignore the desperation of these girls, but at the same time we were moved by their efforts to support and protect each other. Out of nothing they had created a community. They had a "housemother," a woman with a child who cooked for them, and GOAL, an Irish humanitarian organization, provided literacy classes three days a week.

THE CONTINUUM OF VIOLENCE

Violence against women during conflict has reached epidemic proportions. Civilians have become the primary targets of groups who use terror as a tactic of war. Men and boys as well as women and girls are the victims of this targetting, but women, much more than men, suffer gender-based violence. Their bodies become a battleground over which opposing forces struggle.[4] Women are raped as a way to humiliate the men they are related to, who are often forced to watch the assault. In societies where ethnicity is inherited through the male line, "enemy" women are raped and forced to bear children. Women who are already pregnant are forced to miscarry through violent attacks. Women are kidnapped and used as sexual slaves to service troops, as well as to cook for them and carry their loads from camp to camp. They are purposely infected with HIV/AIDS, a slow, painful murder.

Certainly the picture of violence against women during conflict is not monochromatic. Women are not always victims. They actively work to improve their situation, and they often actively support one side or another in conflict. Given that many conflicts arise out of social and economic inequality, it is not surprising that women take sides in an effort to better their lives, or to protect themselves and their families. Women become combatants, provide medical help, protect and feed armed groups. But this can put them at even greater risk if they are caught by the opposing side. In South Kivu, in the Democratic Republic of the Congo (DRC), researchers told us that women in the area had been buried alive by local villagers, ostensibly because they were believed to be witches, but in reality because they were suspected of providing food and medicine to armed groups that the villagers did not support.

The extreme violence that women suffer during conflict does not arise solely out of the conditions of war; it is directly related to the violence that exists in women's lives during peacetime. Throughout the world, women experience violence because they are women, and often because they do not have the same rights or autonomy that men do. They are subjected to gender-based persecution, discrimination and oppression, including sexual violence and slavery. Without political rights or authority, they often have little recourse. The United Nations Declaration on the Elimination of Violence Against Women defines this violence as "any act of gender-based violence that results in, or is likely to result in, physical, sexual or psychological harm or suffering to women, including threats of such acts, coercion or arbitrary deprivation of liberty, whether occurring in public or in private."[5]

Because so much of this persecution goes largely unpunished, violence against women comes to be an accepted norm, one which escalates during conflict as violence in general increases. Levels of domestic violence and sexual abuse rise sharply.[6] Militarization and the presence of weapons legitimize new levels of brutality and even greater levels of impunity. Often this escalating violence becomes a new "norm" which continues into the post-conflict period, where chaos adds to the many frustrations that were not solved by war. The 1999 mass rape of women in East Timor occurred at the time of the referendum on independence, as pro-Indonesian militia vented their fury before escaping to West Timor.[7]

No woman is exempt from violence and exploitation.[8] During conflict women and girls are attacked because they are related to political adversaries, because they are political leaders themselves, or simply because they were at home when the soldiers arrived. One UN official we spoke to in Goma, in eastern DRC, said violence against women had become pervasive in the area, where as many as eight foreign armies and at least as many militia groups have patrolled the countryside. "People are living through an extraordinary drama here in eastern Congo," he told us. "From

The girls were all sex workers. Most had been abducted and forced to stay with the rebels until they escaped or until the cease-fire was signed. They had been raped repeatedly. Many had seen their parents and siblings killed by armed groups.

Pweto down near the Zambian border right up to Aru on the Sudan/Uganda border, it's a black hole where no one is safe and where no outsider goes. Women take a risk when they go out to the fields or on a road to a market. Any day they can be stripped naked, humiliated and raped in public. Many, many people no longer sleep at home, though sleeping in the bush is equally unsafe. Every night there is another village attacked, burned and emptied. It could be any group, no one knows, but always they take women and girls away."

During conflict, women and girls experience violence at the hands of many others besides armed groups. Women are physically and economically forced or left with little choice but to become sex workers or to exchange sex for food, shelter, safe passage or other needs; their bodies become part of a barter system, a form of exchange that buys the necessities of life. Government officials, aid workers, civilian authorities and their own families have all been complicit in using women in this way.

Police and other civilian officials often take advantage of women's powerlessness even when they are in custody. Women have been raped and tortured as a form of interrogation. In many instances, sex workers are routinely arrested and forced to have sex with police officers. In Freetown the girls we met in the sex workers' collective told us that the police went after them regularly: "They catch us and take our money away and then put us in jail. Then we have to pay even more money to get out and they also force us to have sex with them in the jail. When the police get you, it's a lost night and you have no money to even eat the next day."

While the arrival of peacekeeping personnel has the obvious advantage of providing the local population with an increased sense of security, it may also have some negative repercussions. Sexual violence against women and prostitution, especially child prostitution, may increase with the influx of relatively well-off personnel in situations where local economies have been devastated and women do not have options for employment.[9] In Kisangani and Goma in the DRC, members of local communities told us that peacekeepers were buying sex from young girls. A local woman told us that girls "just lie down in the fields for the men in full view of people as they are not allowed into the camps." In Kinshasa, according to an official we spoke to, women line up at the hour most humanitarian workers go home, hoping a male worker will choose them.

We heard similar stories in the Balkans and about conditions in Cambodia after peacekeepers arrived. Radhika Coomaraswamy, the United Nations Special Rapporteur on Violence against Women, has expressed concern at reports of peacekeepers' involvement in violence against women, and has called on the UN to take measures to prevent it and to punish it when it arises.[10] In response, the Department of Peacekeeping Operations has assured the Special Rapporteur that they take her allegations seriously, and that specific allegations will be investigated and appropriate action taken.

TRAFFICKING, SEXUAL SLAVERY AND EXPLOITATION

Trafficking and sexual slavery are inextricably linked to conflict. Women are trafficked out of one country into another to be used in forced labour schemes that often include forced prostitution. They are pushed into marriage with members of opposing groups either directly, through abduction, or in order to protect their families.

They are abducted by armed groups and forced to accompany them on raids and to provide everything from food to sexual services. Many sexual slaves are also used for dangerous work like de-mining contested areas, forced to risk their lives to make a field or a hillside safe for soldiers.

In East Timor Kirsty Gusmao, the wife of President Xanana Gusmao, told us the story of Juliana dos Santos, who was kidnapped by an Indonesian army officer when she was about 14 years old. She was taken to a camp in West Timor controlled by militia groups and the Indonesian Army. Eventually she married an Indonesian in the camp and bore a child. Kirsty Gusmao campaigned vigorously to have dos Santos and her child returned to her home and her family and, in the process, the girl became a symbol in East Timor of the terrible price women had paid for their country's independence. Gusmao's efforts ultimately failed. Arrangements were made for dos Santos to meet with her family at the border, but on the appointed day she arrived surrounded by a group of armed men and said she did not want to go home.

Trafficking is also on the rise.[11] The breakdown of law and order, police functions and border controls during conflict, combined with globalization's free markets and open borders, have contributed to create an environment in which the trafficking of women has flourished. Although it is difficult to document definitively, most experts believe the majority of trafficked persons are women.[12] Trafficking worldwide grew almost 50 per cent from 1995 to 2000,[13] and the International Organization for Migration (IOM) estimates that as many as 2 million women are trafficked across borders annually.[14] The annual profit from this trade is estimated at somewhere between US$5 and US$7 billion. Traffickers often use routes through countries that have been engulfed by conflict, since border controls and normal policing are reduced. These countries also become sources of trafficked women, either through abduction or because poverty and danger force women to seek work at any cost. The connection between armed conflict and trafficking in women is becoming increasingly apparent as criminal networks involved in the trade of arms and drugs expand to include trafficking in people. Trafficked women may become workers in illegal factories, or virtual slave labour for wealthy families in the countries to which they are brought. A large number of trafficked women and girls are forced into prostitution; many are barely adolescents. In Cambodia a 1995 survey indicated that about 31 per cent of the sex workers in Phnom Penh and 11 provinces were between the ages of 12 and 17.[15]

We met Lam, a 15-year-old Vietnamese girl, in a women's shelter in Phnom Penh. Her grandmother had sold her for $200 to a brothel owner who was visiting Lam's home village near Ho Chi Minh City. Lam had no idea that she had been sold or that she was expected to become a prostitute until she arrived at a hotel in Phnom Penh with 10 other Vietnamese girls, and a man was brought into her room. "I hid under the bed, but he pulled me out. The owner was Vietnamese, he gave me food and condoms, but never any money." After about a month, Lam managed to escape and found a police officer who brought her to the Cambodian Women's Crisis Centre (CWCC) where we spoke with her.

In Southeast Asia, young girls such as Lam are bought for as little as $50 and sold for up to $700 to organizations that ship them to Western developed nations. The ones who are not sent to developed countries are sold to local brothels. The director of the CWCC told us that Lam's story is not unusual. The Human Rights Task Force on Cambodia estimates that nationwide, 44 per cent of trafficked children under 18 were sold by intermediaries, 23 per cent by family members, 17 per cent by boyfriends, 6 per cent by an employer and 6 per cent by unknown persons.[16] Typically women are forced to service 20 to 30 men every day. Condoms are rarely available.

In Colombia, where a civil war has gone on for decades, the trafficking of young girls and women has risen dramatically. According to *Fundación Esperanza,* an anti-trafficking organization, perhaps as many as 50,000 women are being trafficked annually out of the country. *Fundación,* which was set up in 1996, works closely with the IOM and the Colombian Ministry of Justice to train government officials in recognizing and stopping trafficking.[17] *Fundación,* also tries to help women who want to return to Colombia, but it is not easy. "The pimps will threaten to tell their families," a spokesperson for the World Health Organization (WHO) told us. "There are certainly families that close their eyes to where the money the woman sends home is coming from."

Southeast Europe is also a source of trafficked women as well as a major transit route for traffickers. According to the UN mission in Bosnia and Herzegovina (UNMIBH), 60 per cent of the

The extreme violence that women suffer during conflict does not arise solely out of the conditions of war; it is directly related to the violence that exists in women's lives during peacetime.

women trafficked through these areas are between the ages of 19 and 24, and are from both rural and urban areas. Seventy-five per cent leave home with a false job offer. The rest are kidnapped or agree to be sex workers, but are then forced into sexual slavery. There have been reports of women being stripped naked and forced to walk on a table or platform while brothel owners bid for them. "The stories are monstrous, and the problem is probably even more serious than we know," Macedonia's Public Prosecutor told us.

We met three Ukrainian girls in the UNMIBH office in Sarajevo who had been rescued by a team of local and UN police from a brothel/bar where they were being kept against their will. One, Larissa, said she had been promised work as a dancer, but instead was brought to the brothel with the two other girls. A Danish police officer in the UNMIBH anti-trafficking team visited the bar and inquired about the girls, but the bar owner forced them to say they were fine. Nevertheless, the officer returned to investigate and eventually helped set up a raid on the bar. Since there is no witness protection programme in Bosnia and

Herzegovina, most women will not testify against traffickers because of their fear of reprisals, especially when they are sent back to their home countries. The girls agreed to help identify UN personnel who might be exploiting or trafficking women because, Larissa told us, "We wanted to help the UN as they helped us." Like these three girls, we appreciate the difficulties facing the United Nations, and acknowledge the serious efforts being undertaken to address the problem of trafficking in the Balkans. A follow-up investigation into allegations that UN personnel are involved in trafficking in the Balkans has been unable to substantiate the charges.

The effects of both sexual slavery and trafficking are profound, especially for young girls. A Bosnian girl who was a sexual slave to Bosnian Serb paramilitary soldiers told the International Tribunal for the former Yugoslavia (ICTY), "I think for the whole of my life, all my life, I will feel the pain that I felt then."[18] Torn from their homes, women and girls are brutalized by their kidnappers and then often rejected by their families. In Sierra Leone we met many young girls who spent months searching for their family members after escaping from Revolutionary United Front soldiers, only to be turned away in disgrace if they did manage to find someone. Some felt they had no choice but to return to their abductors; others went to Freetown and became sex workers.

In 2001 in Macedonia IOM helped 346 trafficked women and girls between the ages of 13 and 41 return to their homes. Each was cared for in a shelter provided by the Macedonian Government. They were offered English and computer classes, as well as counselling and gynaecological and medical care. Local NGOs have worked with the IOM to reintegrate women into their communities. If a woman chooses not to return, the IOM provides financial support for six months. The IOM director in Belgrade told us he plans to open a similar shelter to assist "the thousands, not hundreds, of women and children who are trafficked through Serbia each year." The Office for the High Commissioner for Human Rights (OHCHR) has issued guidelines on human rights and trafficking in persons that offer wide-ranging multidisci-plinary recommendations for all relevant actors in the field. These include law enforcement response; research, analysis and evaluation; access to remedies; and the obligations of peacekeepers, civilian police, humanitarian and diplomatic personnel.[19]

DOMESTIC VIOLENCE

Domestic violence is common during peacetime, but until recently the fact that it increases during or after conflict was generally overlooked. Many things contribute to the increase in domestic violence — the availability of weapons, the violence male family members have experienced or meted out, and the lack of jobs, shelter, and basic services.[20] "Men who have witnessed and perpetrated violence during war seem to continually act violently to their families," reported one Cambodian woman. "My husband was a Khmer Rouge soldier. I think this has made him broken in some important human way."[21] Psychotherapist Dusika Popadic of the Belgrade Incest Trauma Centre voices similar concerns: "It is early to draw any conclusions," she said. "I only know that the war brought an endless amount of ultimate confrontation with violence of all sorts... I know that war trauma breaks something in people's perceptions of themselves."

Recent research indicates that many combatants have difficulty making the transition to peacetime nonviolent behaviour after returning home.[22] In the United States in 2002 four Special Forces soldiers at Fort Bragg in North Carolina killed their wives within a period of six weeks. Three of the four had recently returned from overseas duty in Afghanistan, although some commentators believe it is not the experience of conflict but the culture of violence and masculinity that permeates military forces that causes soldiers to be violent in civilian life.[23] In Israel recent studies indicate that domestic violence is increasing, perhaps because of increased militarization, and studies in Cambodia in the mid-1990s indicated that many women - as many as 75 per cent in one study - were victims of domestic violence, often at the hands of men who had kept the small arms and light weapons they used during the war.[24]

In the occupied Palestinian territories women told us that some men who were detained by Israelis were using the same interrogation tactics against their wives and family members that were used on them in prison. Since the second Intifada began, Israeli restrictions on movement have led to unemployment and overcrowded living conditions created when homes are bulldozed. These in turn may have contributed to increased levels of domestic violence, incest, rape and suicide, according to one study.[25] At the Bisan Centre, an NGO in Ramallah that runs a hotline on domestic violence, a social worker told us, "We have no safe house, but we listen and advise. Ours are very small societies in which everyone's families are linked. It is hard to imagine reporting these things to the police."

Legal protections for women experiencing violence have expanded in recent years, in large part due to the efforts of women's advocates. Forty-five countries now have legislation protecting women against domestic violence, but many of these laws are not regularly enforced, especially during periods of conflict.[26] Serbia has only recently upgraded its laws on family violence, according to Brankica Grupkovic, Serbia's Assistant Minister for Internal Affairs. "Family violence was not covered in our laws until recently," said Grupkovic, "and although in our legislation there is a declaration of equality, there was no enforcement mechanism. Now, under heavy lobbying from women's groups, some amendments to the criminal code have been passed that deal with violence in the family."[27] In Cambodia women's NGOs are working with lawyers to revise the draft law on domestic violence that is expected to come into force in 2003. Posters telling stories in cartoon style, and proclaiming, "Domestic violence is against the law," are being distributed. "After five years of work, people have begun to understand that domestic violence is not a private issue," said Hor Phally, Director of the Project Against Domestic Violence.

UN authorities are also beginning to recognize the problem in conflict and post-conflict situations. As Special Representative of the Secretary-General (SRSG) in East Timor, Sergio Vieira de Mello launched a nationwide campaign against domestic violence there in January 2002, calling the campaign "a concerted effort, with the support of all political and civil society leaders of East Timor, alongside law enforcement officials, to put an end to the abhorrent practice [of domestic violence] that is still, unfortunately, prevalent in East Timor and many other countries of the world."[28]

CHILDREN BORN OF RAPE AND SEXUAL EXPLOITATION

Sexual exploitation in all its forms, including forced pregnancy, reverberates through generations, most specifically in the children who are born of such exploitation. Forced pregnancy was used as a form of ethnic cleansing in Bosnia and Herzegovina and Rwanda, and has occurred in Bangladesh, Liberia and Uganda as well. In Bosnia, many women were imprisoned until the children were born to ensure that the pregnancy was not terminated. In many other conflict zones women who have been raped repeatedly and become pregnant have little choice but to continue with the pregnancy. In Liberia and Sierra Leone thousands of babies were born to women and girls who had been abducted and forced to accompany combatants into the bush, where many gave birth without medical help. Up to 20,000 women are believed to have been raped during the fighting in Kosovo, and many of them bore children. In one month alone, January 2000, the International Red Cross estimated that 100 babies conceived in rape were born in Kosovo, and that many other women gave birth to children born of rape but decided not to identify them as such.[29]

In addition many children result from the liaisons of peacekeepers or other international personnel who are not subject to the UN code of conduct. For example Liberia registered more than 6,000 children fathered by peacekeepers from the Economic Community of Western African States Monitoring Group (ECOMOG) between 1990 and 1998, many of whom had been abandoned by both their fathers and their mothers and lived on the streets. In Sierra Leone, when a group of ECOMOG peacekeepers were leaving the country at the end of their tour of duty, women who had borne babies during relationships with the soldiers lined the route to the airport. In many cases children born of these relationships do not have citizenship rights; Liberia's constitution is one of the few to recognize them.[30]

The children born of sexual exploitation and their mothers need social services, medical and psychosocial attention and economic support. But in many countries the children have become a symbol of the trauma the nation as a whole went through, and society prefers not to acknowledge these needs. In some cases the children are growing up in orphanages or on the streets, although in many countries a large proportion of women have accepted the children and are raising them. In East Timor 23-year-old Lorenca is raising her son, conceived when she was raped by militia in a refugee camp. "I have to accept the baby," she said. "Because of the war, that's what happened."[31]

TOWARDS ENDING IMPUNITY

Although the existing international legal framework clearly prohibits and criminalizes violence against women, Gay J. McDougall, the former Special Rapporteur on Contemporary Forms of Slavery, recommends that it "must better reflect the experience of women and the true nature of the harms to them, particularly during armed conflict." She calls for the "further development of the legal framework through consistent, gender-responsive practice."[32] The UN Human Rights Committee reaffirmed this view by establishing that the right to gender equality is not merely a right to non-discrimination, but one that requires affirmative action. In March 2000 the Committee called on States to take special measures to protect women from rape, abduction or other forms of gender-based violence.[33] In its Resolution 1325 on Women and Peace and Security, the Security Council makes the same call.

And yet the reality is that protection and support for women survivors of violence are woefully inadequate. Their access to protection, services and legal remedies is limited in many ways. The upheaval of war itself makes it nearly impossible for women to seek redress from government entities. But cultural and social stigmas, as well as a woman's status in society, also affect her ability to protect herself or seek protection. When a woman's virtue is linked to her virginity, for example, survivors of rape and other forms of sexual violence become unmarriageable, or are rejected by their husbands, and become a financial burden and a source of lingering shame to their families. In many cases, families force their daughters into marriage with whoever will have them — including the same men who attacked them. According to the International Rescue Committee (IRC), 25 per cent of the marriages of displaced Burundian women in one refugee camp were compelled by shame or by fear of reprisals or further attack.[34]

Survivors of violence need safe places to go for help. They need medical support, resources, protection and security. Some work is being done, but much more is needed. In Bosnia and Herzegovina, Kosovo and Serbia, we met dozens of local NGOs who were providing telephone hotlines, shelters, advocacy campaigns and policy research. One group, Medica Zenica, has a mobile clinic that offers obstetrical and gynaecological services to women in remote villages and displaced persons camps. It also trains local institutions in methods of caring for traumatized women. But such informal, ad hoc efforts need to become routine and institutionalized.

These and other projects around the world, such as training for law enforcement officials in Cambodia and Croatia, and political and legal advocacy in Liberia, are aided by UNIFEM's Trust Fund in Support of Actions to Eliminate Violence Against Women. But further effort is needed by both international and national groups. States must adopt special legislation incorporating human rights, and humanitarian and international criminal law into their own legal systems. Greater specificity is needed in codifying war crimes against women and in recognizing the distinct harm that results from violations like forced pregnancy. Procedures and mechanisms to investigate, report, prosecute and remedy violence against women in war must be strengthened. Otherwise, the historic refusal to acknowledge and punish crimes against women will continue.

I

RECOMMENDATIONS

ON VIOLENCE AGAINST WOMEN THE EXPERTS CALL FOR:

1. An international Truth and Reconciliation Commission on violence against women in armed conflict as a step towards ending impunity. This Commission, to be convened by civil society with support from the international community, will fill the historical gap that has left these crimes unrecorded and unaddressed.

2. Targeted sanctions against trafficking of women and girls. Those complicit must be held accountable for trafficking women and girls in or through conflict areas. Existing international laws on trafficking must be applied in conflict situations and national legislation should criminalize trafficking with strong punitive measures, including such actions as freezing the assets of trafficking rings. Victims of trafficking should be protected from prosecution.

3. Domestic violence to be recognized as systematic and widespread in conflict and post-conflict situations and addressed in humanitarian, legal and security responses and during training in emergencies and post-conflict reconstruction.

4. The UN, donors and governments to provide long-term financial support for women survivors of violence through legal, economic, psychosocial and reproductive health services. This should be an essential part of emergency assistance and post-conflict reconstruction.

Displaced woman and child, Rwanda, 1994

women forced to flee

I was an organizer and educator of peasant groups in Magdalena Medio, the heart of the oilfields in northern Colombia. I was in the office when a videotape was delivered to me. I saw on the tape a colleague of mine being tortured and killed. The message was clear: If I continued with my activities, I'd be next. I ran to the police and asked for their protection but they told me there was nothing they could do. I was afraid for my own life, and for my co-workers. I fled to Bogotá.

— Maria, a community organizer

Maria was living with friends on the outskirts of Bogotá, Colombia when we met her. She had become one of the approximately 40 million people — an estimated 80 per cent of whom are women and children — who have fled their homes because of armed conflict and human rights violations.[1] Approximately 12 million of these displaced persons are refugees, which means they have crossed an international border. Some 25 million have been forced to flee but remain within their own nations and are considered "internally displaced persons."[2]

Armed conflict, political violence and civil unrest forcibly uproot hundreds of thousands of civilians every year. Communities are being torn apart by the routine tactics of war. Intimidation, terror, murder, sexual violence and armed forces drive people out of their homes, leaving them without food, shelter or health care. This is often not an indirect effect of war but a careful calculation by combatants. As UN Secretary-General Kofi Annan said in his report to the Security Council on protection for humanitarian assistance to refugees and others in conflict situations, "the forced displacement of civilian populations is now often a direct objective, rather than a by-product, of war."[3]

During our visits we met with many women who shared with us the horrors that had led to their displacement. The circumstances are unique in each country, but the stories are similar. In places such as Bosnia and Herzegovina, Colombia, the Democratic Republic of the Congo (DRC), East Timor, Liberia, Sierra Leone, Somalia and in the occupied Palestinian territories — whose people constitute the longest-standing and largest refugee population — women have been forced from their homes and exposed to indiscriminate violence while searching for a safe haven.

In a refugee camp in Guinea we met Rebecca, a 45-year-old mother. Three years earlier, two of her seven children had disappeared in the scramble to escape from rebel troops. "In 1998 we ran away from our town near Bo [Sierra Leone]," she told us. "A group of rebels caught us and murdered my husband. They made me take off all my clothes and lie on the ground. I was sure they were going to kill me, but one of the rebels was a boy from my village, and he asked the others to leave me alone."

As with all aspects of war, displacement has specific gender dimensions. Women are more likely than men to end up as displaced persons and to become the sole caretakers for children. Women and girls have to learn to cope as heads of household, often in environments where, even in peacetime, a woman on her own has few rights. And having fled, they may find themselves vulnerable to attacks and rape while they are escaping and even when they find refuge. They may become trapped between opposing factions in areas where there is no humanitarian access, as was the case in the DRC.[4] In a hostile environment, without access to basic services, women are expected to provide the necessities for themselves and their families. After talking to women in many different countries, we learned that this may mean being forced to provide sexual services in return for assistance or protection. Other times women may have no choice but to become sex workers in order to support their families.

A refugee is a person who, as a result of well-founded fear of being persecuted for reasons of race, religion, nationality, membership in a particular social group or political opinion, is outside the country of his [or her] nationality and is unable, or owing to such fear is unwilling, to avail himself [or herself] of the protection of that country.

1951 Geneva Convention on the Status of Refugees, Article I.A.(2)

Internally Displaced Persons are persons or groups of persons who have been forced or obliged to flee or leave their homes or places of habitual residence, in particular as a result of, or in order to avoid the effects of, armed conflict, situations of generalized violence, violations of human rights or natural or human made disasters, and who have not crossed an internationally recognized State border.

Guiding Principles on Internal Displacement

THE RESPONSIBILITY TO PROTECT

In accordance with international law, the obligation to protect forced migrants lies first and foremost with the government of the state in which the displaced persons are living. Armed opposition groups also have legal and moral responsibilities not to assault civilians or subject them to human rights abuses and to protect the rights of the displaced people in the territories under their control.[5] These rights, however, are regularly violated. Humanitarian agencies can only assist displaced people if the host country allows them access. Some armed opposition groups may refuse access, afraid that their human rights violations will be exposed, even if a government has promised help to people in need.[6] The question of who provides protection and assistance, and when, is one that is hotly debated.

In September 1999 Secretary-General Kofi Annan proposed a new course, calling upon the international community to intervene to protect civilians threatened by war. He argued that survival in the 21st century will depend on a broader definition of national interest — one that unequivocally supports basic human rights.[7] In September 2000 the Secretary-General expanded upon this theme and challenged the governments of the world to reject the narrow interpretation of sovereignty that has prevented the international community from providing assistance unless a government asks for it: "If humanitarian intervention is, indeed, an unacceptable assault on sovereignty, how should we respond to a Rwanda, to a Srebrenica — to gross and systematic violations of human rights that affect every precept of our common humanity?"[8]

In response to the Secretary-General's challenge, the Canadian Government assembled an independent panel of experts in September 2001 which supported the position that the international community must act to protect civilians if a state cannot, will not, or is the perpetrator of "conscience-shocking events crying out for action" such as "large scale loss of life or large scale ethnic cleansing, whether carried out by forced expulsion, acts of terror or rape."[9]

INTERNALLY DISPLACED PERSONS: WHOSE RESPONSIBILITY?

During the last decade and a half, the nature of displacement has shifted dramatically. The growing number of internally displaced persons, who generally do not have access to international aid, has creating what is being called a "crisis of displacement." There are many reasons for the surge in internal displacement. Because of border closings, many people who would have become refugees are trapped inside a country at war. The breakdown of the rule of law and of democratic governance has led to national and regional conflicts and economic chaos. Basic services like water and electricity are disrupted and food supplies are cut off. People fear the violations of international human rights and humanitarian law that have become endemic to many of these wars. Under such conditions, people flee wherever they can. More often than not, they end up somewhere within their own country, although many displaced people can be internally displaced at one stage, then become refugees and then return to their native country again. In many cases, the same conflict will create refugees and internally displaced persons. After the referendum for independence in East Timor in 1999, violence and armed conflict forced nearly two-thirds of the total population from their homes: Of an estimated 850,000 East Timorese, more than 200,000 fled or were forced across the border into West Timor, but an even larger number, around 300,000, were uprooted from their homes but remained within the country.[10]

As of 2001 an estimated 13.5 million people were displaced internally in various nations in Africa, 4.5 million in Asia and the Pacific, 3.6 million in Europe, 2.2 million in the Americas and 1.5 million in the Middle East.[11] While refugees are entitled to assistance and protection under international law, the internally displaced have no institutional or legal mechanism for receiving international assistance.[12] The key legal document safeguarding refugee rights is the 1951 UN Convention Relating to the Status of Refugees and its 1967 Protocol. Under the Convention, states are expected to cooperate with the United Nations High Commission for Refugees (UNHCR), which provides protection and assistance in partnership with governments, regional organizations and non-governmental organizations (NGOs).

The situation for internally displaced persons is less clearly defined. Although international humanitarian law guarantees all civilians the right to protection and assistance, the fact is that humanitarian agencies can only assist internally displaced people if the host country allows them access. In addition, since there is no single agency within the United Nations mandated to provide for internally displaced persons, it can take time to raise the funds, and set up and coordinate the aid programmes they need.

Ultimately, many internally displaced people must fend for themselves, or rely on poorly run, often dangerous camps that are not always under the protection of international agencies. Many of the internally displaced disappear into cities, doubling up with family or friends, or struggling to survive on their own. Some, like a group of displaced farmers in Luanda, Angola, have banded together in empty buildings or fields, and receive some food and medical aid. In the Kivu province of the DRC, civilians have fled into nearby forests to escape various armies and militias. In 2000 it was estimated that out of 200,000 people who had fled their homes because of unrest, only 60,000 were in areas where aid workers could reach them.[13] The others struggle to survive in the forests of south Kivu. According to humanitarian workers, these people are destitute: "They don't have anything human except the shape of a body. The feet are inflated, with several wounds, an empty look … [there are] a lot of cases of mortality in the forest for lack of health care."[14]

In Colombia an estimated 1.5 million people have been displaced internally by a conflict that has been going on for decades; nearly 80 per cent are women and children. Many of them go to towns or cities hoping to escape armed groups — despite the fact that these groups are based in cities as well as rural areas.[15] Human rights organizations that we met with in Colombia told us that the paramilitaries were responsible for the majority of forced displacements. The Colombian Government has recognized this as well, according to the Global IDP Project, which states, "according to the government, in 2000, paramilitaries were responsible for 71 per cent of forced displacement."[16]

For those internally displaced who have access to camps, provisions are minimal. There are rarely organized methods for distributing food or shelter, and families must devise their own ways to earn money to get these necessities. When we visited Kinshasa, a woman told us that as many as 100 girls from a camp for the internally displaced, des-

perate for money to buy food, would go "to a certain point on the river, every evening at 5 p.m., and bathe naked so that men can choose them." And in an Indonesian camp for the internally displaced, Masmudeh, who is among the more than 1 million internally displaced persons in the country, said she and her two children had been living since 1997 without basic services or any way to support themselves: "There is not enough money here to buy things that people need like soap. We can't plant any food to sell or eat. I want to go back to Sambas but I can't until it's safe."[17]

In response to the vast numbers and needs of internally displaced persons, the UN Secretary-General in 1992 appointed a Special Representative on Internally Displaced Persons, Dr. Francis M. Deng, to develop a framework to protect their rights. In collaboration with a team of international legal experts, Deng developed the Guiding Principles on Internal Displacement.[18] One of the hallmarks of the principles is that they call for specific recognition of the needs of women. They acknowledge the situation of female heads of households; emphasize women's physical and psychosocial needs; reaffirm their need for access to basic services; and call for their participation in education and training programmes. Over the past five years, humanitarian agencies have promoted the Guiding Principles and used them as a framework for providing assistance and protection to the internally displaced. In addition, a number of countries with internally displaced populations, including Burundi, Colombia and Georgia, have indicated their willingness to use the Principles and to adapt national laws to reflect them.[19] Yet, when it comes to the vast majority of the internally displaced, the Guiding Principles are not implemented. In our view, these Principles are a useful tool that must be adhered to and implemented by all states. Beyond that, these Guiding Principles should be enshrined in a binding international instrument, although many of its elements are already covered in international humanitarian and human rights law.

The lack of binding principles has led to a situation described in a study by the United States General Accounting Office in 2001 as one in which officials lack "knowledge and techniques regarding protection considerations and assistance activities in the field." The study also found that 79 per cent of the 48 countries surveyed reported that they had not taken any action to set up and manage camps for internally displaced persons, or to prevent attacks on women, "such as ensuring that vulnerable female-headed households are not isolated to remote areas in the camp."[20] The Secretary-General, with the support of other relevant agencies, has created within the Office for the Coordination of Humanitarian Affairs (OCHA) an Internal Displacement Unit that has called for increased attention to protection issues, including rapid deployment of protection officers in displacement situations, but there has been little response.

Because there is no framework that guarantees the right of the international community to step in and help the internally displaced, donor nations continue to operate on a case by case basis, largely based on political and economic interests. The indecision about how to increase protection for internally displaced people is exacerbating the crisis.

In addition, it has been extremely difficult to raise money for internally displaced persons through international channels.[21] In March 2000 UNHCR said that as a matter of policy it would provide more aid to the internally displaced, but the number of IDPs that it assisted actually declined, from 5 million in 2000 to 4 million one year later, because it did not have the funds to meet the need.[22]

VIOLENCE AGAINST WOMEN IN CAMPS

Camps for displaced people offer help in desperate situations. But camps can become extremely dangerous places for women. The majority of women we met, whether refugees or internally displaced, told us that they did not feel safe in camps and did not have access to basic necessities. In most camps there are not enough protection officers or female staff. Domestic violence increases, and women and girls face sexual violence and discrimination in the distribution of everything from food to soap to plastic sheeting.

Despite the fact that policies to prevent violence against women are in place, they are not being implemented. It has been particularly shocking to learn that even some humanitarian workers are contributing to violence against women. In April 2002 UNHCR and Save the Children-UK issued a report in which the authors cited numerous stories of sexual violence and exploitation committed by peacekeepers and humanitarian workers in camps in Guinea,

The impact of sexual exploitation is devastating. The teenage pregnancy rate in the camps is estimated at 50 per cent. Girls are dropping out of school. And, on a continent that has been ravaged by HIV/AIDS, these girls and women are at grave risk of infection and have little or no hope of receiving proper preventive care.

Liberia and Sierra Leone. More than 1,500 people were interviewed, and most told similar stories: "If [a girl] refuse[s]," said one woman, "when the time comes for the supply of food items, you will be told that your name is not on the list." A man in Sierra Leone told interviewers: "If you do not have a wife or a sister or a daughter to offer the NGO workers, it is hard to have access to aid." The report describes an incident in which a group of peacekeepers banded together to have sex with a child; many girls were forced to sell themselves for a few cents, enough to buy only a handful of peanuts.[23]

The United Nations Office of Internal Oversight Services (OIOS) was asked by UNHCR to conduct an investigation into the allegations in the UNHCR/Save the Children-UK report. OIOS could not substantiate any of the 12 cases in the consultants' report, or any allegations against UN personnel. They also looked into 43 additional cases of alleged sexual abuse and were able to substantiate 10 of these cases. The report confirmed that conditions in the camps and in refugee communities in the region make refugees, especially young women, vulnerable to sexual and other forms of exploitation.

In our visits to the same area, we met girls, the majority between 13 and 18 years old, who said that they too were forced to exchange sex for all manner of aid, including cooking oil, wheat, medicine, transport, loans, educational courses or skills training. In Guinea, we spoke with an international aid worker who admitted that some women were required to have sex with humanitarian workers to obtain what was theirs by right.

The impact of sexual exploitation is devastating. The teenage pregnancy rate in the camps is estimated at 50 per cent.[24] Girls are dropping out of school. And, on a continent that has been ravaged by HIV/AIDS, these girls and women are at grave risk of infection and have little or no hope of receiving proper preventive care.

Women can be subject to many other types of violence in camps. They may be attacked by militia or members of different ethnic groups. And they risk abuse from their own relations. Domestic violence is a severe problem in many camps. Increased spousal battering and marital rape often reflect the stress that displacement inflicts on the family unit.[25] In Macedonia a man said to us, "You need to understand. I am so stressed because of the war. It is inevitable that I beat my wife. That's just life." In Angola displaced men and women attribute increasing rates of domestic violence to boredom, frustration and alcohol consumption.[26] At the Gihembe refugee camp in Rwanda, Congolese women gathered around us during a meeting and talked about the domestic violence they saw everywhere:

"There can be conflict in the household. For instance, if I sell part of the camp rations to get food for a younger child, the husband will blame me if he is hungry, or he will take a young wife in the camp," Ephrace, a farmer, told us.

"The violence we have here only arises because of the way we are living in promiscuity and poverty," added Suzanne, an older woman wrapped in a thin faded cotton cloth. But a third woman said the problem was not only in the camps. When she spoke of what she wanted for the future, the group of 60 or 70 women sitting on their wooden benches all nodded vigorously. "Once our children are educated, the girls will know they do not have to submit to violence in order to have a husband," she said.

Generally, there is no legal redress for victims of domestic violence living in camps; many countries simply do not recognize it as a crime, and humanitarian groups administering camps have not always insisted on the necessity of dealing with the problem. According to the Women's Commission for Refugee Women and Children, there are no effective guidelines for UNHCR staff specifically on how to respond to domestic violence,[27] although the agency is in the process of revising its Guidelines on Sexual and Gender-based Violence, and will incorporate a clearer statement on domestic violence. In the meantime, some staff reportedly have refused to do anything about domestic violence, considering it a "private" family matter.

UNHCR first issued its Guidelines on the Protection of Refugee Women in 1991, but as our visits and various other reports indicate, these Guidelines have not always been effectively implemented and do not deal with current conditions.[28] According to the Women's Commission, the greatest success of the Guidelines has been in raising broad awareness among staff and implementing partners to women's specific needs and strategic interests. But "overall, implementation of the Guidelines was found to be uneven and incomplete, occurring on an ad hoc basis in certain sites rather than in a globally consistent way."[29] The Guidelines are also in the process of being revised. In addition UNHCR's Agenda for Protection addresses the protection concerns of refugee women, which include safety and security, equal access to humanitarian assistance, registration and documentation, gender-sensitive application of refugee law and procedures and trafficking in women and girls.

UNHCR has initiated several programmes to address the violence against women in recent years. In its Burundian refugee camps inside Tanzania, the agency hired two sexual and gender-based violence assistants and two Tanzanian lawyers to address all cases of violence against women, including domestic violence. It has also hired an international security liaison officer to train police in the camps.[30] In Kenya UNHCR is helping the government to provide mobile courts that travel from camp to camp.[31]

Some camps have set up committees of camp residents to address violence. In Ngara, in western Tanzania, a sexual and gender-based violence (SGBV) project was established in 1999 by the aid agency Norwegian People's Aid (NPA).[32] UNHCR is also working with the Government of Tanzania to provide better police protection in refugee camps,[33] and is recommending that all humanitarian agencies place more female staff in camps. The agency is considering other actions as well, both broad and specific: These include reviewing humanitarian assistance to determine whether it meets minimum requirements and basic needs; improving the monitoring of aid once it is delivered; increasing support to girls most at risk; improving ways of distributing aid; informing all staff of the code of conduct; and creating channels for refugees to lodge complaints. According to Ruud Lubbers, the High Commissioner for Refugees, UNHCR has prohibited all sexual relations between humanitarian workers and recipients.[34]

A number of these actions come in direct response to the UNHCR/Save the Children-UK report on sexual abuse in the Mano River camps. In addition, the Inter-Agency Standing Committee (IASC), which brings together the humanitarian community, including UN Agencies, the Red Cross movement and NGOs, under the chair of the United Nations Emergency Relief Coordinator, established a Task Force in March 2002 on Protection From Sexual Exploitation and Abuse in Humanitarian Crises. The Task Force adopted a Plan of Action outlining steps toward implementing a "zero-tolerance" policy of sexual exploitation and abuse by humanitarian workers. The Plan of Action includes core principles that must be incorporated into agency codes of conduct; situation analysis and assessment of vulnerability to sexual exploitation among displaced groups; improved camp governance that empowers women and children, including in the distribution of food and other assistance; the development of accountability measures and mechanisms; and avenues for reporting abuse and seeking legal, judicial and community-based recourse. The Task Force committed all its members to provide services such as psychosocial support, health care and safety and security measures, and articulated the need for improved monitoring and supervision.

However, at the same time that UNHCR is attempting to institute greater protection and support for women in camps, it is suffering from an overall drop in donor funds to the UN, which has meant a debilitating shortfall in assistance to refugees. The agency has been faced with budget cuts even while the need for aid has been growing. In mid-2002, UNHCR experienced a 20 per cent cut in its budget. The impact of this reduction is being felt in every corner of the globe.[35] "Our biggest problem right now is food," a refugee woman in a Guinean camp told us in January 2002. "We get 13.5 kilos of bulgur wheat. That is supposed to last for 45 days, but sometimes we do not receive anything for 55 or 60 days. Everyone is so hungry." We heard the same story in many camps. We visited Somalia in 2001 and conditions were dire then. In 2002, some 25,000 Somali refugees living in Djibouti were at risk of malnutrition, and the World Food Programme (WFP) reported that supplies were "rapidly running out."[36] According to UNHCR there is a strong link between falling levels of assistance to refugees and their increasing vulnerability and exposure to forced sex work and sexual exploitation.[37]

Many other organizations beside UNHCR have taken on the task of improving services to women and children. The United Nations Population Fund (UNFPA) is focusing on reproductive health care while the United Nations Children's Fund (UNICEF) continues to provide services in the areas of health care, education, nutrition and sanitation. In Sierra Leone, UNICEF is providing services to girls who are victims of sexual abuse and violence, and has launched a national sensitization campaign on rape. UNIFEM has also been working in this area, providing funding to local groups working in camps through the Trust Fund for the

Elimination of Violence Against Women. In places like East Timor, it has worked with local women's groups to provide rape counselling, and to help repatriate women kidnapped across the border.

But the efforts of the various agencies remain scattered and many policies to strengthen protection for displaced women have not had an impact yet. Training has been haphazard; policies are often unevenly implemented; funding has been minimal. The challenge is for the international community to fill the gap between what needs to be done and what is actually being accomplished.[38] The IASC has accepted that this is a major challenge, and the mandate of the Task Force on Protection from Sexual Exploitation and Abuse has been extended through 2003 to ensure advice on and monitoring of the implementation of the Plan of Action. According to one UNHCR staff person, "Refugee women and children bear a disproportionate share of the suffering [but] their needs still do not receive a commensurate portion of the agency's attention and care. We have a beautiful policy on [refugee women]. We have guidelines. We have everything ... But all this is only as good as the implementation. The mere enunciation of a policy is not sufficient."[39]

URBAN DISPLACEMENT

Johanna is a 24-year-old Sierra Leonean, living in the Guinean capital of Conakry, who told a typical story of life as an urban refugee. She and her 16-year-old brother fled the fighting in Sierra Leone and arrived in Conakry in 1997. "When we got here, they arrested us, accusing us of being rebels," she said. Johanna and her brother were eventually sent to a refugee camp, but when the camp was attacked by Revolutionary United Front (RUF) rebels, the two ran away to Conakry again. "I met a very nice lady who offered me work as a domestic worker and a place to stay. I was glad to have shelter and to be able to earn money to support my brother. But then the worst happened: Her husband used to come to my bedroom and rape me at night. This went on for four months. I threatened to tell his wife if he did not stop. I did not want to lose my job. He threatened to kill me

if I ever told his wife or reported him to the authorities." Johanna felt she had no choice but to tell his wife that she could no longer work for the family.

She left to live with her brother in a makeshift camp with other refugees, and started selling doughnuts on the street, until one day the police asked to see her permit. "Of course I did not have one," said Johanna. "So they took all my money and the doughnuts. I had to start all over again. But I was lucky I was not thrown in jail, as happens to so many other refugees who have no documentation. I was planning to be an accountant before the war broke out. One day when the war is over, I will return to school to fulfil my dream."

In recent years, many displaced people like Johanna and her brother have fled to cities where they live with virtually no assistance or protection. Some hope to avoid violence in camps. Others are in search of jobs, training, medical help and access to other services. Human Rights Watch conducted a survey of urban refugees living in Nairobi and Kampala in April 2002 and during random visits to refugee neighbourhoods found that approximately half were women, despite the popular belief that most urban refugees are men.[40]

Finding shelter is a major concern for those displaced in urban areas. Urban refugees and displaced persons often end up homeless, trying to survive by living and working on the streets, or they crowd together in the homes of local residents. In Kisangani, in the eastern DRC, we met with a group of women whose village homes had been destroyed by Ugandan and Rwandan soldiers. They told us that 170 families, 110 headed by women, had set up home in a building that was formerly a government office. But they were forced out by the Congolese Rally for Democracy (RCD), the rebel group that controls Kisangani, just before a visit by UN Secretary-General Kofi Annan. At the time we met them, a month and a half after the visit, the women had not been allowed back into the building, which remained empty, and were living on the streets.

Women without shelter face constant danger and are always at risk of sexual violence and harassment. One young woman told Human Rights

Watch that she had left the Kakama UNHCR refugee camp to go to Nairobi hoping to get medication for tuberculosis. She slept in the streets and was attacked soon after she arrived, gang raped, stabbed and left for dead.[41] In Nairobi and Kampala some women camp outside UNHCR or NGO offices in the hopes of being protected.

Most urban refugees have little or no documentation. Many flee their homes without identification papers — or, if they come from rural areas, they may never have had any. Without papers, they are often unable to receive even minimal protection and assistance. In Kampala, UNHCR provides shelter and food to only 275 people out of an urban refugee population estimated at approximately 50,000. The Government of Uganda generally requires urban refugees to show documentation that they are supposed to be in the city or to sign an agreement stating they are self-sufficient and will not rely on public assistance. Often they are advised to go to a camp rather than try to get help in the city, but many refuse.[42]

In Pakistan, Afghan refugees in urban areas have similar problems. At least 200,000 Afghans fled to Pakistan after September 2001, hoping to escape U.S. military action. But Pakistan was already hosting an estimated 2 million Afghan refugees. According to UNHCR, the majority of the new arrivals chose not to go to camps but went to urban areas, where they received almost no assistance. Many young girls have been forced into early marriage because their families cannot afford to care for them, or hope they will be safer if they are married. Many suffer physical harm as a result of early sexual activity.[43]

LONG-TERM DISPLACEMENT

Long-term displacement leads to a host of problems. Even in those places where peace agreements have been signed, families who have lost everything in flight find it hard to start over. Each new generation born into displacement reaps the bitterness of their parents and grandparents on top of the difficulty of living in crowded conditions with few services. In Angola and the occupied Palestinian territories long-term displacement has destroyed the future of several generations. In both the Balkans and Colombia displaced women report that their children are not allowed to attend local schools because of the stigma attached to being homeless. Estimates indicate that 85 per cent of internally displaced children in Colombia do not receive even primary education.[44] The hope is to return home, and repatriation is the preferred option of host countries.[45] But that may not be possible. Violence goes on for years in some cases and landmines may make agriculture nearly impossible. Many women are afraid to face the people they fled from, who have not been punished and continue to live in the villages and communities the women want to go back to. We

According to UNHCR there is a strong link between falling levels of assistance to refugees and their increasing vulnerability and exposure to forced sex work and sexual exploitation.

will never forget the horror on the face of Aminata, a woman we met in Guinea, as she described how RUF rebels in Sierra Leone forced her to dance in front of her husband as they killed him. Her voice rose in hysterics as she contemplated returning, "I can't go back, they'll kill me, there's no one to help me, I am alone."

We heard similar stories in the Balkans and among survivors of the Rwandan genocide. One woman from Srebrenica described the war criminals still at large back home, "How can I go back when I can see them sitting in cafes drinking coffee and watching us? Who is going to protect me?"

Even if safety was not a concern, many widows and female heads of household have no way to support themselves if they return home. Because women in some countries cannot inherit land or other property from either their husbands or their parents, unless they have sons they have no way to hold on to property that might help support them.

When returning home is impossible, the only hope for life outside a camp may be to seek asylum in another country. The Geneva Convention establishes principles for asylum, such as not forcing someone to return to a territory where she or he is afraid of being persecuted.[46] But the definition of persecution falls short of recognizing gender-based persecution. Each country has its own laws and policies that make entry into the country and application for asylum difficult, and many of them are punitive. Asylum-seekers, women and children included, are frequently imprisoned while they go through the legal process of applying for residency.[47]

Large numbers of refugees are vulnerable in their countries of first asylum. Third country resettlement is at times the only viable solution for some refugees. But it largely depends on both the West keeping its doors open and UNHCR fulfilling its gatekeeper role by identifying and referring to competent national authorities an appropriate number of resettlement cases.[48]

Almost all nations make it harder for women and children to seek asylum than for men. Even at the first step, interviewers and interpreters are often men who have little experience in understanding the special needs of women asylum seekers. Some countries register a male head of a refugee household without providing any residency protection to the family. If the man abandons the family or is otherwise not present, the wife will have a hard time proving that she and their children are legally in the country.[49]

Among children, it appears to be easier for boys to enter a country than girls. In November 2000 the United States brought 4,000 "lost boys" from the Sudan to the U.S., helping them to escape years of violence and deprivation. Not one girl was included in the effort although hundreds were roaming the countryside with no homes, no food and little hope of a safe haven. There were many girls in the same camps as the boys who were taken to the U.S., but the girls were left out of the resettlement effort. "There was little water to drink, we survived on leaves and wild fruit. Some of the girls were eaten by lions," said one girl who had travelled on foot with her mother, first to Ethiopia, then back to Sudan, and then south to Kenya. The journey continued for years. At some point she lost her mother and struggled on alone, eventually arriving at a camp.[50] Yet there is no programme to identify these girls and increase their chances of third

country resettlement. UNHCR has recently developed a "Women at Risk" programme which is aimed at providing resettlement opportunities to women who suffer from a wide range of protection problems including expulsion, *refoulement* and other security threats, such as sexual harassment, violence, abuse, torture and different forms of exploitation.[51] This programme could be expanded to include refugee girls and women who seek asylum.

The United Nations must take seriously its mandate to protect displaced people. It must recognize the gender dimensions of the great tragedy that envelops people swept up in violent conflict who are forced to flee their homes. It must help women to rebuild their lives, protect them and their children, prevent the sexual exploitation of them and their daughters. It must move to provide aid and assistance to the ever-growing number of internally displaced people.

RECOMMENDATIONS

1. Strengthening of United Nations field operations for internally displaced women and of those bodies that support a field-based presence. Protection officers from all relevant bodies, including the Office of the High Commissioner for Refugees (UNHCR), the Office of the High Commissioner for Human Rights (OHCHR), the Office for the Coordination of Humanitarian Affairs (OCHA), the United Nations Children's Fund (UNICEF) and the International Committee of the Red Cross (ICRC), should be deployed immediately if a state cannot or will not protect displaced populations or is indeed responsible for their displacement. Resources should be made available for this purpose.

2. Governments to adhere to the UN Guiding Principles on Internal Displacement, and incorporate them into national laws to ensure protection, assistance and humanitarian access to internally displaced persons within their territory.

3. Refugee and internally displaced women to play a key role in camp planning, management and decision-making so that gender issues are taken into account in all aspects, especially resource distribution, security and protection.

4. Women to be involved in all aspects of repatriation and resettlement planning and implementation. Special measures should be put in place to ensure women's security in this process and to ensure voluntary, unhindered repatriation that takes place under conditions of safety and dignity, with full respect for human rights and the rule of law.

5. All asylum policies to be reformed to take into account gender-based political persecution. Women, regardless of marital status, should be eligible for asylum and entitled to individual interview and assessment procedures.

A mother with the body of her son, five months old, who died of malnutrition in a camp in Angola, 2002.

war &
women's
health

On a hot Saturday afternoon in January, we travelled about an hour out of Liberia's capital city of Monrovia to visit a camp of displaced people who had fled, not for the first time, from fighting in Lofa province. Compared to the well-organized camps for Sierra Leonean refugees near the city, this camp for Liberians was chaotic. A large water bladder provided by a non-governmental organization (NGO) was the only source of clean water. There were no health care services, no shelter; in fact, there were hardly any services at all. The people were frightened.

There had been fighting nearby recently and they wanted to move closer to Monrovia for safe-

ty. A delegation had been sent to the capital to appeal to the authorities for permission to relocate, but so far there had been no response. Then, the night before we arrived, fighting broke out again, even closer to the camp. In a panic, the people had packed up their small shelters and their remaining possessions. When we arrived, most were sitting on the ground in the open air, frightened and desperate to get away.

We gathered together a group of women and asked them what was happening. "We are from Lofa, where there is fighting between the government and the rebels," said Lina, a dignified woman of about 50. "This is the fourth time many of us have moved since the fighting started. We have appealed to the government for safety, but they don't care about us because they think we are supporters of the rebels. If we supported the rebels, why would we be running from them?"

Lina was a trained nurse who had worked in a clinic in the north until the fighting started. She was articulate and well educated, an unusual person to find in this group of poverty-stricken rural people. Most educated Liberians in her position would have found their way to the capital or to another country by this time, but she had stayed here where people needed her. It was clear that the other women trusted her and looked to her to speak for them. Yet she was tired and discouraged.

"We came here two weeks ago," she told us, "and we have received hardly any help at all — only a bit of food and that water. There are hundreds of people — men, women and children. They are exhausted, sick and unable to take any more fighting. They tremble when they hear the mortars at night, and we all fear that this area will be attacked at any time. I am the only one to nurse all these people — there's not even a midwife. There are so many women who are pregnant and no one else to help with them. If there is a problem, they will just have to die here because I have no supplies, no transport and no way to help. I don't know how anyone can look at these women and not help them, not let them be in a safe place."

Young women, many with babies in their arms, gathered around, nodding in agreement as Lina spoke. When we asked why so many were pregnant, they laughed. "How could we avoid it? Do you think anyone would want to give birth here?" they asked. They were with their husbands or boyfriends; they had no access to contraceptives and, in their situation, no power to refuse sexual relations. Some said that children were the only good things they had, their only happiness. But others said that it was a bad time to have children and they would have preferred to wait until they were settled. As more and more women gathered around, we asked their ages. They were much younger than they looked. The months of hunger

and living on the run had aged them. They had been abandoned by their government and by the international community. They were the cast-offs of a long and complicated conflict that few journalists bothered to cover any more.

We asked Lina what she needed. "Everything!" she replied. "I need soap and cotton and antibiotics and aspirin. Children here have diarrhoea, infections and lice. Men have old wounds that are infected, or burns or other problems. Women have venereal problems, injuries from walking, burns and miscarriages. Old people have so many problems. We have people who are seriously mentally ill, who don't even know who or where they are. I don't have anything except the small amounts of medicine that an NGO left here a week ago. But at least I try to keep records of births and deaths. I do that for history."

At a far corner of the camp, next to a ditch, a young mother of newborn twins sat in front of a makeshift hut of twigs and cloth. She looked about 17 years old and was sitting on a straw mat, with her family gathered around her. She had one tiny baby lying on her legs and another at her left breast. Her right breast was swollen to the size of a basketball. She grimaced with pain when she touched it. Her husband explained that she had given birth to the twins a week before, just as they arrived in the camp; she now had a breast infection and her milk was contaminated. He said that Lina had told her not to feed with that breast, but when she didn't nurse, the breast was even more painful. "We need antibiotics, but we have no money and no way to get to the town even if we could buy medicine. There is no transport and they won't let us past the checkpoint." A colleague from a Liberian NGO gave the husband some small bills from his pocket. "I don't know if they can make it through to Monrovia," he told us, "but maybe they can bribe someone."

The situation of the people in that camp in Liberia was about the worst we had seen in all our visits to war-affected areas. They were people with nothing — and with no international or local groups to help them. They had absolutely no rights and were at the mercy of a war they did not understand. We wished we had brought medicines or food and had the power to do more than tell the world about them. We wanted to linger, to learn more, to understand how this could happen, but the government official with us insisted that we leave by 5 p.m. Our UN security officer was puzzled by his insistence and seemed to think that the official knew or feared that something was going to happen.

Evidently he was right. The next day we learned that the camp had been attacked only two hours after we left. No one knew what had happened to the hundreds of people who had been trapped there, and no one from the international community was allowed to go there. We never found out if Lina and the others were able to get to safety. We cannot imagine how the young girl with twins could have been able to move quickly enough to escape. The faces of the women we met haunt us.

Since that January day, tens of thousands more Liberians have fled the fighting, which has moved closer and closer to Monrovia. The neat camps supported by the Office of the United Nations High Commissioner for Refugees (UNHCR), once filled with refugees from Sierra Leone, have been abandoned, their residents crossing back into their own country. Some of the displaced Liberians we met have scattered to the woods. Others have crept into the city to live on the streets. Many have perished. There is no better example today of the horror and absurdity of war. How can this happen in the 21st century?

Armed conflicts have been major causes of disease, suffering and death for much of human history. The fatalities, injuries and disabilities suffered on the battlefield are obviously direct effects of conflict. But there are also health consequences from the breakdown of services and from population movements. The diverting of human and financial resources away from public health and other social goods contributes to the spread of disease. These indirect consequences of war may remain for many years after a conflict ends. Both the experience of conflict itself and the impact of conflict on access to health care determine the physical health and the psychological well-being of women and girls in very particular ways. Women are not only victims of the general violence and lack of health care —

they also face issues specific to their biology and to their social status. To add to the complexity of the picture, women also carry the burden of caring for others, including those who are sick, injured, elderly or traumatized. This in itself is stressful and often contributes to illness.

THE GENERAL IMPACT OF ARMED CONFLICT ON HEALTH: WOMEN ARE NOT EXEMPT

The exact number of deaths and injuries due to war is unknown since chaotic conflict situations make it difficult, if not impossible, to monitor death and injury rates. A few examples, however, show the harm that war brings. In December 1998, when the civil war in Congo restarted, a third of Brazzaville's population — about a quarter of a million people — fled into the forests. They remained trapped for several months, with no access to international aid.

> The camp was attacked only two hours after we left. No one knew what had happened to the hundreds of people who had been trapped there, and no one from the international community was allowed to go there. We never found out if Lina and the others were able to get to safety. We cannot imagine how the young girl with twins could have been able to move quickly enough to escape. The faces of the women we met haunt us.

In May 1999 surveys and data collection from people returning to the capital allowed officials to document the health consequences of the war. Death rates were more than five times what would be considered an emergency.[1] Earlier studies in the 1980s in Ethiopia, Mozambique and Sudan came up with similar findings: During periods of conflict, the mortality rates of internally displaced persons (IDPs) in each country ranged between 4 and 70 times the rates for non-displaced persons in the same country.[2]

In 2000 alone, conflict is estimated to have directly resulted in 310,000 deaths, with more than half taking place in sub-Saharan Africa. If the commonly held ratio is accurate — nine indirect deaths for every direct death caused by conflict — then approximately 2.8 million people died in 2000 of some conflict-related cause.[3] Arguably the figure is much higher. When the direct fatalities are estimated by age and sex, children and adolescents account for a significant proportion of the deaths. The highest mortality rates are among men aged 15 to 44, but a quarter of direct mortality is among women. The greatest number of deaths of women is among those aged 15 to 29; some 25,000 women in this age group died directly of conflict in 2000.[4]

The International Rescue Committee has estimated that between August 1998 and April 2001, there were 2.5 million excess deaths (i.e., above the number normally expected) in the five eastern provinces of the Democratic Republic of the Congo (DRC), where armed groups have been fighting each other as well as attacking civilians. Only 350,000 of these deaths were directly caused by violence; the majority stemmed from disease and malnutrition. One in eight households had experienced at least one violent death; 40 per cent of these deaths were of women and children. There were more deaths than births in many of the areas studied and, in one area, 75 per cent of the children died before they reached the age of two.[5] This is a terrible indictment of the warring factions and of the international community, which has virtually ignored the conditions in the eastern DRC.

Damage to Health Systems

Civil wars often result in severe damage to health services since health facilities and personnel may become targets. In Rwanda, over half the health workers were killed during the genocide, the health infrastructure was destroyed and administrative capacities were disrupted.[6] In the DRC "years of war have devastated the health system, and the effects on the well-being of the population are cataclysmic," according to the Minister of Health.[7] It is estimated that no more than 8 per cent of blood used for transfusions is being screened, either because facilities have been destroyed or the resources are not available. In Bosnia and Herzegovina, 40 per cent of physicians, 60 per cent of dentists and 30 per cent of nurses left the country during the war and have not returned.[8] In circumstances such as these, it is impossible to provide even the most basic health support without massive aid from the international community.

In many conflicts, health workers have become targets. In El Salvador and Nicaragua, dozens were kidnapped or assassinated. In the occupied Palestinian territories ambulances and medical personnel have been stopped at military checkpoints by Israeli forces, leaving a significant proportion of the civilian population without emergency services.[9] As a result, pregnant women experiencing complications have not been able to get critically-needed hospital care.

Sanctions can also undermine health systems. In Iraq after the Gulf War basic care for the entire population declined because of damaged infrastructure and the sanctions, which affected the distribution of food and medical supplies. Women's access to gynaecological care decreased dramatically. In Serbia during the sanctions period, the mortality of women aged 25 to 44 was significantly higher than in previous years, mainly due to urogenital diseases and endocrine disorders such as diabetes. Normally these diseases can be treated with relative ease, but in the case of Serbia, the necessary medical supplies became expensive and took long periods to be cleared.[10]

A study of economic embargoes in Cuba, Haiti, Iraq, Nicaragua, South Africa and Yugoslavia found that economically vulnerable groups, particularly children under five and women, suffer most from the deterioration in the health sector caused by sanctions.[11]

Infectious Diseases

"I don't know what we would do here if measles broke out or if there was a cholera epidemic. There's just no capacity to handle the situation, not enough transport, not enough health workers. We just pray for good luck."

—NGO worker in Somalia

Historically, war and displacement have always been associated with epidemics and the spread of disease from one area to another. The highest rates of death and illness among displaced populations stem from diseases such as measles, diarrhoea, pneumonia, malaria, cholera, meningitis and tuberculosis, with malnutrition playing an important role in many cases.[12]

The flight of half a million Rwandans in 1994 across the border into North Kivu, DRC (then Zaire) overwhelmed the resources of humanitarian groups trying to help. During the first month of the influx, almost 50,000 refugees died. This was almost entirely due to epidemics of diarrhoeal diseases caused by poor sanitation and inadequate water supplies. The highest death rates were among children under five and women.[13] In Afghanistan current tuberculosis infection rates as high as 325 per 100,000 indicate a serious problem. Women make up 67 per cent of all registered cases, compared to 37 per cent of cases worldwide.[14] This is undoubtedly due to the conditions under which women have been living during the past years — kept inside crowded dwellings, unable to move about freely outdoors and lacking access to health care.

Injuries and Wounds

Civilian casualties from injuries and wounds can be very high during guerrilla warfare and when small arms and landmines are used. Women and children are often the most exposed to these dangers, especially if they are primarily responsible for gathering fuel or water. Most of the civilian casualties of the 23-year war in Afghanistan have been a direct result of ballistic or landmine injuries. In 1995 long before the current fighting, Afghanistan had the highest population-based rates of landmine injuries and the highest mortality, even in comparison with such heavily mined countries as Bosnia, Cambodia and Mozambique.[15] Although the numbers are not well-documented, women are much less likely than children and men to have access to treatment and to rehabilitation and prostheses. In Angola women and girls who have lost limbs from mine injuries have faced social isolation and economic loss. In Sierra Leone the brutal fighters of the Revolutionary United Front (RUF) chopped off the arms and legs of many women, leaving them unable to farm or to care for their families.

Environmental Harm

Exposure to chemical warfare or the environmental effects of conflict can harm health directly and for long periods of time. In the case of nuclear testing, preparation for war has exposed many to radiation, causing a dramatic increase in cancer and other health problems; women's reproductive health is especially susceptible to the effects of radiation. Women living downwind from Pacific islands where nuclear testing has occurred have given birth to what they describe as "jellyfish babies" with transparent skin and no bones. Unfortunately politics has often prevented scientific research in this area.

Causality has not yet been proven but there is some indication that the Gulf War exposed both civilians and combatants to harmful substances. There appeared to be an increase in miscarriages and pregnancy complications among women in the Gulf States during the two years after the war, possibly due to chemical residues from weapons that leaked into the food chain or because of smoke pollution from the Kuwaiti oil fields — although the increase may also have been related to stress.[16] Women soldiers deployed to the Gulf War theatre reported a higher than average incidence of abnormal Pap smears as well as a cluster of problems including fatigue, joint pain, hair loss, irritability, memory difficulties and insomnia.[17]

Mental Health and Stress-Related Disease

Armed conflict traumatizes both combatants and civilians — on a daily basis and sometimes for the rest of their lives, long after the war is over. Numerous studies of the psychological state of refugees, war-affected populations and ex-combatants show that the experience of violence makes a deep impression on the human psyche. People's responses differ according to their own personalities, the levels and types of violence they experience and their cultural interpretations of the conflict, yet it is increasingly clear that if left untreated, the psychological impact of war can severely diminish the quality of life and even threaten a whole society. War-affected populations suffer high rates of anxiety, depression and post-traumatic stress disorders. Those who have been tortured may require intensive therapy in order to carry on with their lives. Refugees who leave their communities and countries also experience what one specialist calls "cultural bereavement," a grieving for home, language or traditions.[18] Those who are granted asylum in countries with very different cultures from their own experience social isolation and high levels of depression.[19]

Studies of combatants indicate that increased exposure to combat is a predictor of severe wartime violence,[20] which may contribute to the atrocities committed in some long conflicts. Once combatants are inured to extreme violence, it is difficult for them to revert later on to more normal, healthy attitudes towards conflict resolution. There seems to be a pattern of increased homicide rates after wars, which does not bode well for societies that have suffered years of atrocities, often at the hands of very young combatants.

In the countries we visited, we were overwhelmed by the depth and intensity of women's psychosocial needs. In eastern DRC, one international aid worker told us, "What we are confronting here — and in so many conflict zones where we work — is the need for a massive psychosocial programme of trauma counselling, which we are utterly unprepared for. It will have to be very long-term, with very skilled people, and I don't know whether the will is there for something so ambitious, never mind the resources." A social worker in the West Bank echoed the same concern: "Every single one of us, including the carers, needs extensive psychological help. Where is it ever going to come from?"

SPECIFIC EFFECTS OF CONFLICT ON WOMEN'S HEALTH AND WELL-BEING

In the past few years, there has been growing attention paid to gender issues as they affect and are affected by humanitarian programmes. Agencies such as the World Food Programme (WFP), UNHCR and the United Nations Children's Fund (UNICEF), as well as the many NGOs involved in emergency relief, have begun to think more carefully about the gender impact of their interventions. Yet studies of the health effects of conflict have rarely focused on women

(with the exception of reproductive health), and most of the data on conflict mortality and morbidity (illness) are not broken down by gender. Women are seldom mentioned as a special group, but are lumped together with children as "vulnerable groups." Yet women have particular experiences and exposure to circumstances that affect their health. They also have patterns of access to health care that are different from those of children and men.

Malnutrition

Famine and the resulting malnutrition and disease killed thousands during the 20th century. Most of these deaths were the fault of humans, not nature. Almost always, civil conflict and human rights abuses either paved the way for famines, such as those in Biafra in the 1960s and the Horn of Africa in the mid-1980s, or prevented food aid from reaching starving communities, as happened in Angola more recently. Women and children die at extremely high rates in such circumstances. Even in relatively affluent regions, war can lead to malnutrition, as it did in Bosnia in the early 1990s, where the death rate in one Muslim enclave reached four times the pre-war rate, mainly from severe malnutrition.[21] Because of women's physiology, they are vulnerable to vitamin and iron deficiencies that affect their health and energy levels as well as their pregnancies. Iron deficiency anaemia is a serious health condition for women of reproductive age and can be fatal for pregnant women. A study among Somali refugees indicated that up to 70 per cent of women of reproductive age were anaemic, probably caused by a lack of iron in the diet or by malaria, which depletes the body's iron stores.[22]

A recent nutritional survey in Afghanistan showed a 9.8 per cent rate of scurvy (vitamin C deficiency) among women of child-bearing age,[23] caused by lack of fruits and vegetables, which in turn may be related to the poor status of women and the preferential feeding of men and boys. An epidemic of konzo, a type of paralysis, occurred among women and children in Mozambique during the last year of the war there, caused by eating insufficiently cooked bitter cassava, which has a high cyanide content.

Unable to farm their usual crops because of the war, rural people began to depend on the bitter cassava as a food source.[24]

Reproductive Health

Women's reproductive health problems during conflicts may range from having no sanitary supplies for menstruation to life-threatening pregnancy-related conditions, from lack of birth control to the effects of sexual violence. In the past two decades, women have also had to deal with the deadly spread of HIV/AIDS.

Menstruation needs: It is obvious that refugee and displaced women between the ages of 10 and 50 need a way to handle their menstruation, yet strangely it is only in the past few years that humanitarian agencies have begun to include sanitary supplies in the package of relief items provided in emergencies. Without such supplies, girls have to stay home from school, mothers cannot take their children to health facilities and women may miss work or training. Providing clean cotton rags or modern sanitary products allows women to move about freely during their menstruation, instead of sitting at home or in their tents, isolated from others. Nevertheless, a 2000 UNHCR study found that despite headquarters' directives, many of its own staff were not providing sanitary supplies in camp settings.

Pregnancy and delivery: Pregnancy and delivery can be dangerous for women in the best of circumstances. In poor countries, maternal mortality is nearly 40 times the rate in the industrialized nations.[25] In countries suffering conflict, women are at even greater risk since they generally cannot get prenatal support or emergency obstetric care.

In the DRC approximately 42,000 women died in childbirth in 2001.[26] One woman in 50 dies giving birth in Angola.[27] In Afghanistan years of poverty, neglect of health facilities and policies restricting women's movement were catastrophic for women's health. Because the country lacks basic delivery and emergency obstetric services, maternal deaths are among the highest in the world.

Conflict can have indirect consequences as well.

In Eritrea the recent war with Ethiopia caused a redeployment of scarce health resources to the front lines, resulting in declines in maternal health care in areas far from the conflict. During flight and acute emergency periods, spontaneous abortions (miscarriages) can increase precipitously from the physical and mental stress; women who suffer miscarriages require immediate assistance to save their lives and protect their fertility.

Lack of access to appropriate medical care may not be the only cause of poor pregnancy outcomes. The exposure to trauma and violence itself may have an effect on pregnancy. When a community in Southern Sudan experienced a high number of miscarriages, the villagers blamed it on the fighting. A nurse told investigators that the unremitting smoke and noise from heavy artillery in 1991 could have made women miscarry, and women fleeing aerial bombing had suffered back pain followed by miscarriage.[28] A study in Santiago, Chile, on the relationship between pregnancy complications and sociopolitical violence in 1985-1986 suggests that the Sudanese villagers may be right. Chilean women who lived in neighbourhoods with high levels of violence, including bomb threats, military presence and demonstrations, were five times more likely than women in other neighbourhoods to experience pregnancy complications such as preterm contractions, rupture and haemorrhage.[29]

Unwanted pregnancies: Unplanned and unwanted pregnancies present serious problems for women in any circumstance and can be particularly stressful for those who are displaced and separated from their families and support systems. Women who have been using family planning to postpone or avoid pregnancy in their home communities should be able to continue when they become refugees. In fact, their needs may be even greater. Women and couples who did not use family planning deserve the chance to start doing so should they choose. Yet family planning has only recently become a regular part of health services in relief situations, and even now these services are not always available.[30]

Ensuring that family planning is a standard

part of emergency programmes is easy. Finding ways to help victims of "forced pregnancy" is much more difficult. The strategy of forcibly impregnating women as part of an ethnic cleansing campaign has occurred in recent conflicts in Bosnia and Herzegovina, East Timor, Kosovo, Rwanda and Sudan. Tens of thousands of women in these areas (and elsewhere) suffered the trauma of being raped repeatedly and impregnated by the rapist. The health and psychosocial needs of women who have endured these attacks are intricately entwined and require particularly sensitive responses.

Bosnian women who were sexually violated and intentionally made pregnant faced terrible choices. Some, who were able to get services early enough, chose abortion. Others continued their pregnancies and abandoned their babies at birth without ever seeing them. Of the few who kept their babies, many experienced family rejection and social isolation. Kosovar women also faced such choices. Rape is such a stigma that many resorted to abortion just so the men in their families would not know they had been raped. Many women we spoke to described an implicit understanding between men and women that amounted to a sad charade: The men never asked what had happened to the women and the women never offered to tell.

In Sierra Leone many women were raped by armed groups intent on sowing terror wherever they went and still others were forced into sex work to support themselves and their families. Abortion is illegal in Sierra Leone and most women have no choice about whether to continue with an unwanted pregnancy. One 14-year-old sex worker, who was three months pregnant, told us she would have ended her pregnancy but did not have enough money to pay for an abortion, which was available "underground." The cost was $100 — more than the average annual income of most Sierra Leoneans and more money than the girl had seen throughout her whole life.

Adolescent pregnancy and other risks: Young people who have lost family guidance and community support because of conflict are particularly vulnerable to engaging in risky behaviour as well as to sexual exploitation. In Colombia, violence and displacement have been accompanied by an increase in teenage pregnancies as well as unsafe abortions. We spoke with the World Health Organization (WHO) representative in Liberia, who estimates that up to 80 per cent of displaced girls have had an induced abortion by the age of 15, and we met girls there as young as 11 who were pregnant. Such early pregnancy has serious implications for the health and well-being of young girls, whose bodies have simply not developed enough to deliver safely and who are not mature enough to be parents. Girls aged 10 to 14 are five times more likely to die in pregnancy and childbirth than women aged 20 to 24. Unsafe abortions also carry great risk for the approximately 2 million young women aged 15 to 19 who undergo them every year.[31]

Sexually Transmitted Infections (STIs): In a women's training centre outside Freetown, Sierra Leone, where many young women abducted by the rebels during the long war were receiving vocational training and learning how to read, we spoke to a nurse about the women's health. "Our most urgent need right now is antibiotics," she said. "Almost all the girls here have STIs and when we have enough drugs I treat them. But right now I can't." She noted that many of the women had had these STIs for many years, presumably since they were first abducted and sexually assaulted, but even after treatment they became re-infected: Either they were having relations with untreated partners or they were so desperate for money they were having unprotected sex with strangers. "Some of them have syphilis," the nurse told us, "which can eventually kill them and their unborn baby if they get pregnant. But even simpler infections can easily develop into pelvic inflammatory disease and cause infertility. It would be such a shame for these girls, who are trying so hard to get their lives back in order, to have to suffer the stigma that infertility carries in our society. It would ruin their marriage prospects altogether."

STIs are reaching epidemic proportions globally. Yet most are relatively easy to treat, using a simple diagnostic approach that does not require laboratory analysis. It is hard to understand why this health issue is so neglected in emergency situations, especially since STIs spread so quickly in displaced populations. A study of Rwandan women attending antenatal clinics in refugee camps in Tanzania found that over 50 per cent were infected with some form of STI.[32] STIs are notoriously prevalent among military populations around the world (who have two to five times the rate for civilians), so conflict situations that involve extensive contact between civilians and combatants are especially likely to show high levels of these infections.

Effects of Sexual Violence

The health impact of sexual violence can be disastrous. Injuries, unwanted pregnancies, sexual dysfunction and HIV/AIDS are among the physical consequences. The mental effects include anxiety, post-traumatic stress disorders, depression and suicide.[33] Although global attention has been focused for more than a decade on sexual violence as a strategy of war and as a human rights issue, the women who have suffered need direct support immediately, which they are still not getting. Rape often involves serious physical damage to a woman's body, requiring treatment for abrasions and tears; some women even need suturing. Antibiotic treatment is necessary. If provided within 72 hours, emergency contraception can prevent an unwanted pregnancy. With the widespread use of rape in war, health systems must be prepared to provide such treatment and ensure that staff are trained to deal sensitively with patients.

The burden can be enormous. In a six-month period in 1999, hospitals in Brazzaville treated 1,600 cases of rape.[34] A recent report by Physicians for Human Rights indicates that over 50 per cent of Sierra Leonean women experienced sexual violence of some type during the conflict there; many continue to suffer from serious gynaecological problems.[35]

Mental Health

In one camp for Sierra Leonean refugees, a social worker offered us her analysis of the differing ways men and women react to camp life. The men, she said, lose their identity and their dignity. They sit around all day and then take out their frustrations on the women and children at night. In her view, the women are different. "They cope because they have to. They bend with the situation."

But how far do women have to bend before they break? In Morina, a small village outside Skanderaj in the heart of Kosovo, about 40 ethnic Albanian women and girls met with us to talk about their lives. They invited us into a large communal room where we sat on carpets and cushions around the walls. The women were restless, burning with the desire to communicate their common experience, their common trauma. Apart from one seven-year-old boy in the room, this village

> "Many people have acquired their PhDs studying us, but no one helps us," one woman said bitterly. "We have no rights, and those who should help do not want to. No one who was not in Srebrenica can know what we have lived through – how difficult it was to watch people die of hunger, children going from house to house asking for bread, so exhausted that there was no light in their eyes. I had two beautiful sons and a husband; now I have nothing."

had lost all its men when Serbian forces attacked on 2 April 1999. As they told their stories many women wept, wiping their eyes with the corners of their headscarves.

"When the Serb forces came we were all gathered into a burned-out barn. They took the men out with their hands up, they put them against a wall and they were all killed."

"My husband and son are missing, my in-laws were all killed."

"My father-in-law was executed with his four brothers, my husband is missing along with nine other relatives."

One woman described the hard choices they

had to make: "We women started walking towards Skanderaj but we had to leave my mother-in-law behind as she was paralysed." We listened in stunned silence as they described the fear that drove them from place to place. Having received no psychological support, they remained lost inside their pain, as though April 1999 had been only yesterday.

Another group caught in the past by the unresolved question of missing husbands and sons is the Mothers of Srebrenica, whose anger over the events of a decade ago spilled out in the first moments of our meeting. "Many people have acquired their PhDs studying us, but no one helps us," one woman said bitterly. "We have no rights, and those who should help do not want to. We are slowly dying. No one who was not in Srebrenica can know what we have lived through - how difficult it was to watch people die of hunger, children going from house to house asking for bread, so exhausted that there was no light in their eyes. We have to go on with our lives, but how? I had two beautiful sons and a husband; now I have nothing."

In many other conflict zones women have received little help in dealing with the trauma they experienced, although a few NGOs, with support from groups like UNIFEM and the United Nations Population Fund (UNFPA), are trying to tackle the problem. In Rwanda, AVEGA, a self-help organization of widows offering both physical and psychological care, has estimated that four out of five women have continued to suffer psychological trauma since the 1994 genocide. The AVEGA counsellors — whom we met in their modest house where every wall has photographs of strong, smiling women survivors — told us that many girls still have nightmares, and insist that they do not want to get married or ever have a sexual relationship. The Bosnian women's group Medica Zenica also provides both medical care and psychosocial assistance to women victims of sexual violence. They run a mobile clinic to treat gynaecological and obstetric problems. Their psychosocial workshops link local populations with returnees and the internally displaced, recognizing that shattered communities cannot be put back together without psychological support. "During the war we were open to everyone, but now it is more difficult to get donor funding, so we have to prioritize war-traumatized women," a representative of Medica Zenica told us. Like a number of women's groups we met in the occupied Palestinian territories and in Belgrade, Medica Zenica also runs a telephone hotline for women who need to talk about memories of war trauma and the taboo subjects of rape and domestic violence.

The women in settings where mental health issues are discussed, or where there are self-help groups, are fortunate. In Somalia we heard estimates that nine out of ten women were traumatized in some way or another, but very few of the women we met mentioned the need for psychosocial support, partly because they did not know such a thing existed and partly because, they told us, it would be embarrassing to admit they needed help. A young woman, Sahir, described to us her feelings of desolation. She often thought of suicide, she said. Sahir saw her father and brother killed; she was then raped and had a gun thrust so deeply into her vagina that she will never be able to bear children. Like many other traumatized women we met, Sahir chose to speak to us, strangers whom she would never see again, as a way to find a brief release not available in her daily life.

What we know about the psychological impact of conflict on individuals is mixed. There are numerous studies on post-traumatic stress among combatants (mostly men) and on the effects of war on children. There is a whole body of literature on psychiatric treatment for torture victims (again, mainly men), and there are various schools of thought on rape counselling. But shockingly little attention has been paid to the effects of conflict on the psychosocial status of women or on how women process and cope with their experiences. One very recent study of trauma in non-conflict situations indicates that there may be gender differences in the response to trauma. The study found that, although the lifetime prevalence of traumatic events is slightly higher for men, women run twice the risk of developing post-traumatic stress disorders, suggesting that certain types of trauma may have a deeper and longer-term psychological impact on women.[36]

Of course, it is not only women's mental health

that is important. Healthy psychosocial adjustment of men and boys who have experienced violence and conflict is also important to their families and communities. There are numerous indications that combat exposure and post-traumatic stress in men lead to higher levels of substance abuse and domestic violence. There is also some evidence that post-traumatic symptoms can abate for years, but then return in later life, particularly in stressful situations.[37]

Burden of Care for Others

In every society women bear the brunt of the burden of caring for those who are ill. This does not change when women are in the midst of war; they still try to protect and care for their children and the elderly, and they still provide support for their husbands, their siblings and their parents. The responsibility of care for others is so embedded that even in the most desperate conditions, women still try to take care of everyone around them. In our travels, we heard about the despair women felt when they watched their loved ones suffer or die, when their children were abused or starved or when they had to leave elderly relatives behind as they ran for their own lives. The guilt and helplessness that the women felt in these situations, and still feel, is an almost unbearable burden.

At the same time, the social responsibility of caring for the ill or disabled adds heavily to the workload of women in conflict and post-conflict situations. One woman whose child had been severely disabled by a landmine told us that her whole day is taken up with feeding and washing the child and helping him learn how to read, which she sees as his only hope of relief from his disability. Other women spoke of trying to keep the peace in households where husbands are depressed and drink too much, lashing out at their children. Still others spend hours lining up to get food or offer sex to strangers for the money to buy medicine. Truly the time and the emotional energy these women spend on caring for others is incalculable.

WOMEN'S HEALTH NEEDS: WHAT MUST BE DONE?

Clearly, women in conflict situations need sufficient food, safe drinking water, protection from violence, basic primary and reproductive health care, and psychosocial support. These are extensions of what women need anywhere. Yet even though war-affected women have greater needs, they often end up with few, if any, services.

The knowledge and the tools exist to protect women's health, even in complex emergencies — but is the political will there? There are guidelines for psychosocial counselling, for providing reproductive health services, for ensuring safety in camp situations, for gender-aware food distribution. But these services and protection arrangements still remain the exception, not the norm.

In the area of reproductive health, for example, a large group of NGOs, UN agencies and bilateral donors have worked together to determine the standards which should be applied and have developed a Minimum Initial Service Package of supplies and interventions to be provided in emergency situations. WHO, UNHCR and UNFPA have produced a field manual that provides detailed guidelines for basic care during acute emergencies and for expanded services when the situation stabilizes. An accompanying set of pre-packaged supplies, stocked by UNFPA for immediate deployment, includes everything needed for various interventions, from safe home-birthing to family planning to STI treatment to hospital-based emergency obstetric care. Training health staff to attend to reproductive health is also an important part of the package.

There is also international policy support for these concerns. The Programme of Action of the International Conference on Population and Development (ICPD), endorsed by 179 nations in Cairo in 1994, recognized the need to ensure reproductive rights and provide reproductive health care in emergency situations, especially for women and adolescents.

Five years later, at a special session of the General Assembly, governments reaffirmed that:

"Adequate and sufficient international support should be extended to meet the basic needs of refugee populations, including the provision of access to adequate accommodation, education, protection from violence, health services including reproductive health and family planning, and other basic social services, including clean water, sanitation, and nutrition."[38]

Yet although attention to reproductive health in emergencies has increased dramatically in the past five years, it is still not institutionalized as a part of every humanitarian response, partly because the humanitarian community has had difficulty internalizing gender concerns and partly because funds have fallen short.

The same applies for psychosocial support. Although there is less consensus on the effectiveness of different types of intervention, there is a growing awareness of the need to provide basic counselling for victims of conflict, and particularly for women who have experienced sexual violence. A number of groups, such as the International Rescue Committee, have developed programmes of intervention, but again these are only in a few countries because of limited funding. An important area of work is that of supporting indigenous modes of healing, which can be more effective than Western-style counselling in many contexts. For instance, ritual purification ceremonies have been successful in West Africa. Faith-based support has also been critical for healing, yet is often neglected in the humanitarian response.

There are good examples of health support that can be built on. In a three-month period in 1999 Albania received, accommodated and cared for almost 500,000 refugees from Kosovo, yet there were no serious outbreaks of infectious disease. The Albanian Government coordinated with numerous UN agencies and NGOs to ensure that all the camp populations had food and water, basic primary health care and protection against infectious diseases. For the first time, reproductive health care was widely provided and psychosocial needs were anticipated, even if services were still very basic. As a result, most of the refugees were able to return to Kosovo a few months later with their physical health intact.

Even in the most difficult circumstances, programmes can be up and running quickly. A good example is the initiative from the DRC, when government and insurgent health personnel met together in Nairobi with NGOs, UN agencies and donors to map out a plan to reduce their nation's extraordinary rates of mortality. They developed a unique minimum package of services, designed for war conditions and aimed at immediately reducing avoidable deaths. The package set out 30 actions to be taken in health zones in crisis, directed at the seven leading causes of death and ill health: malaria, measles, diarrhoeal diseases, acute respiratory infections, malnutrition, pregnancy-related problems and HIV/tuberculosis. To be included, the actions had to satisfy a dual standard: They had to show proven cost-effectiveness in saving lives and be practical under local conditions.[39]

Another lesson to be learned is from Guinea where, instead of establishing separate services for refugees, the local health system was strengthened to allow it to support the additional population. The integration of Liberian and Sierra Leonean refugees with the local populations had a positive effect not only on the well-being of the refugees but also on the health of their Guinean host communities. The refugee assistance programme contributed to the improvement of the health system by strengthening its economic base — UNHCR paid fees for the refugee services — and by repairing roads and bridges for transporting food aid. The programme helped local and refugee women alike to obtain better antenatal care and childbirth assistance.[40] The number of health providers in the area increased from 3 to 28, and a new ambulance improved emergency care.

The presence of the refugees also transformed the economy in remote rural villages of Guinea. Farmers planted more crops to feed the growing numbers of people, trade increased and more money circulated, since even the most desperate refugee families managed to bring some resources with them. In this case, refugee assistance was able to support the refugees' own coping mechanisms instead of creating dependency in camps. No new health agencies arrived on the scene; instead, the Ministry of Health and Médecins Sans Frontières, long a partner in the area, simply intensified their work. They developed an integrated approach that was cost-effective and development-oriented. The overall yearly cost of medical assistance to the refugees was estimated at US$4 per person, much lower than the yearly cost of medical services in refugee camps which averages US$20 per refugee.

Many humanitarian agencies would do more for women's health, and for health in general, if they only had the staff and the resources. Yet health programmes are notoriously underfunded. Each year, when the annual UN Inter-Agency Consolidated Appeals are launched for countries in crisis, health programmes receive less than a quarter of the funds requested. For some countries, donors provide no emergency support for the health sector at all. Within the health sector, some issues appeal to donors more than others: Children's health gets more attention than women's health; immunization gets more attention than HIV prevention. Yet our examples show that with sufficient resources and will, and with women's participation in planning and providing services, there are ways to provide good, efficient and sensitive health care during and after conflicts. So what is the problem? It appears to be a matter of establishing that women in conflict zones have the same human rights as other women and that the international community bears some responsibility for helping them protect and rebuild their lives.

It is tragic that basic health care for women affected by war must compete with food, shelter and landmine clearing. All these interventions are required to ensure that people survive as healthy, contributing members of their societies. The needs of war-affected populations are all linked. Providing health services alone cannot save lives if other vital requirements — for security, food, water, shelter, sanitation and household goods — are not satisfied. Surely there is enough money to support all of these important interventions. Surely the physical and mental health of individuals and communities is critical for conflict resolution, for national rehabilitation and for recovery.

3

RECOMMENDATIONS

1. Psychosocial support and reproductive health services for women affected by conflict to be an integral part of emergency assistance and post-conflict reconstruction. Special attention should be provided to those who have experienced physical trauma, torture and sexual violence. All agencies providing health support and social services should include psychosocial counselling and referrals. The United Nations Population Fund (UNFPA) should take the lead in providing these services, working in close cooperation with the World Health Organization (WHO), UNHCR, and UNICEF.

2. Recognition of the special health needs of women who have experienced war-related injuries, including amputations, and for equal provision of physical rehabilitation and prosthesis support.

3. Special attention to providing adequate food supplies for displaced and war-affected women, girls and families in order to protect health and to prevent the sexual exploitation of women and girls. The World Food Programme (WFP) and other relief agencies should strengthen capacities to monitor the gender impact of food distribution practices.

4. Protection against HIV/AIDS and the provision of reproductive health through the implementation of the Minimum Initial Services Package (MISP) as defined by the Interagency Manual on Reproductive Health for Refugees (WHO, UNHCR, UNFPA, 1999). Special attention must be paid to the needs of particularly vulnerable groups affected by conflict, such as displaced women, adolescents, girl-headed households and sex workers.

5. Immediate provision of emergency contraception and STI treatment for rape survivors to prevent unwanted pregnancies and protect the health of women.

An orphan girl in Liberia.

hiv/aids

War is a strong ally of HIV. It means we say goodbye to our communities and prevention strategies and we say hello to HIV and AIDS.

— A Save the Children worker in Burundi

Marie, a tall and quiet woman of 24, lives with her two-year-old and her baby on the edge of a frontier town in the eastern part of the Democratic Republic of the Congo (DRC). The area has changed hands among rebel groups and foreign troops a number of times in the past few years, each time via armed attacks during which civilians were caught in the middle. It is not a town that many of its residents would choose to live in —

it is simply a place they have run to in order to escape worse fighting somewhere else. Some come to get access to food, which arrives irregularly from relief agencies. Others hope to find treatment for their illnesses or wounds, or to find work or missing family members.

The three-room health post is pockmarked from mortar fire and nearly empty of furniture and supplies. The one trained nurse can provide advice but little else. There are only occasional medicines and supplies, brought by charities when it is safe to visit. People coming to the clinic with injuries or wounds

— and there are many — can usually be treated only with soap and water. Many infections go untreated. Anyone who needs blood must be transfused from a friend or relative, using inadequate and sometimes unsterilized transfusion supplies. When Marie delivered her babies at home in her hut, she got help from a traditional birth attendant whose razor blade had already been used for many births.

The town is filled mostly with women and children. Many of the men from the region have fled or been killed or have gone to the bush with rebel groups. A recent Human Rights Watch report has documented frightening levels of violence in the town and the surrounding region.[1] Many of the women that Marie knows have been raped by soldiers from one group or another. Marie also was raped when she was 20 years old but she considers herself "one of the lucky ones — it wasn't gang rape, and I wasn't hurt badly and it was only once." Given the experiences of many women she knows, she is thankful for this.

There are no jobs for Marie or her friends and they have no family left to help them, so quite often they resort to selling sex for money, food or even to "buy" protection from rebel leaders. Marie is embarrassed about this, but feels she has no choice. "I am only thankful that my mother and father cannot see the way I am living now because they did not raise me to do these things. But what else can I do? There is no one to help. I must take care of my children."

Marie knows that sex with many partners can be unhealthy but she doesn't really know any details and she has no access to information about sexually transmitted infections or HIV. Nor does she have access to basic supplies such as condoms or contraceptives to prevent an unwanted pregnancy. She has no power to negotiate protection with the men who come to her hut.

There is much that Marie is unaware of — and it will probably cost her her life. She does not know that HIV is spread through sex or through contact with contaminated blood. She doesn't realize that many of the soldiers who are deployed in the region, some of whom come to her hut to buy sex,

are infected with HIV. She has no idea that women are physiologically more vulnerable to HIV infection than men and that violent sex such as rape makes women especially vulnerable. She would be shocked to learn that the odds of an infected woman passing the infection to her baby during delivery or breastfeeding are one in three and that her children are probably infected. And if she knew these things, there is little she could do about them.

The odds are very much against Marie. Almost 1.3 million adults and children are living with HIV in the DRC. In North Kivu, near where Marie

Marie will probably live long enough to watch her baby die of AIDS and maybe even to bury her two-year-old. She will almost surely suffer extended illness and pain and die alone, without any family to care for her. The immediate cause of the deaths in this fragile family may be AIDS, but the real causes would be poverty and neglect, war, ignorance, greed, discrimination and exploitation.

lives, a recent study showed infection rates of 54 per cent among adult women, 32 per cent among adult men and 26 per cent among children.[2] Marie will probably live long enough to watch her baby die of AIDS and maybe even to bury her two-year-old. She will almost surely suffer extended illness and pain and die alone, without any family to care for her. The immediate cause of the deaths in this young and fragile family may be AIDS, but the real causes would be poverty and neglect, war, ignorance, greed, discrimination and exploitation.

Who is to blame for Marie's plight? Is it the men who infected her, knowingly or unknowingly? The birth attendant who used a contaminated blade to cut the umbilical cord? The government that for decades neglected the region, leading to poverty and war — and also never trained the birth attendant? The neighbouring government that supports the rebels but does not support any health care or education in the town? The international community which looked the other way as the conflict got worse? The arms dealers who profit from it? The humanitarian community which doesn't protect or provide basic health care or food to the civilians? The donors who don't provide the resources for the humanitarian community to do so? Well-meaning but naive groups who believe that their support for HIV prevention should focus on abstinence? Marie's church which, even if she could get condoms and get men to use them, would tell her that condom use is a sin? The members of the Security Council who pass resolutions on HIV/AIDS and conflict but continue to sell small arms to anyone who can pay?

All are to blame. And even if peace could be brought about, in too many of the places we visited, HIV/AIDS will continue to kill.

THE LINK BETWEEN HIV/AIDS AND CONFLICT

HIV transmission occurs in a number of ways: through exposure to infected blood; exposure to body fluids during unprotected sexual relations; or from mother to child during pregnancy, delivery or breastfeeding. Over 40 million people were living with HIV/AIDS at the end of 2001, and more than 20 million have died since the virus was first identified.[3] Although 70 per cent of those infected right now are from sub-Saharan Africa, the epidemic continues to grow in other parts of the world. Transmission is influenced by a complex set of social, cultural and economic factors, including gender inequality, economies of labour migration which separate families, levels of commercial or "survival" sex, dangerous traditional practices, intravenous drug use and unsanitary medical procedures. Although many countries with high infection rates have not been in war, there is evidence that conflict conditions exacerbate the epidemic.

If the virus exists within any of the populations involved, the risks associated with all these modes of transmission can increase during wars and displacement. Women are at special risk since they are already physiologically more vulnerable to infection and their place in social structures increases this vulnerability. In most places where the main form of transmission is sexual, women are infected in greater numbers than men and at younger ages.

The surest way to contract HIV is to be exposed to infected blood. During armed conflicts, civilians and combatants suffer torture, wounds and injuries requiring medical treatment. If they are exposed to infected blood, or if they receive medical care with contaminated instruments or get transfusions of unscreened blood, then their risks are magnified. In many war zones the damage to health systems results in the inability to maintain even basic "universal precautions" of sterilizing instruments or cleaning hospital linen. Equipment and supplies for screening blood may be destroyed or unavailable at the same time that the need for transfusions increases dramatically. An International Committee of the Red Cross (ICRC) study has documented that the farther they are from health centres, the longer individuals bleed before getting treatment and the more blood they will need to survive. Those who are injured by antipersonnel mines require very large amounts; burn patients require even more.[4]

In Sierra Leone, a country with one of the highest maternal mortality rates in the world, a woman from the north who haemorrhages at delivery will face a terrible gamble — the blood she needs to survive cannot be screened in any of the regional hospitals and it will take too long to get to Freetown. One maternal health worker told us, "We can train the staff to do emergency deliveries, we can supply the hospital with the obstetrical equipment, we can even provide an ambulance to get a woman in difficulties to the hospital quickly enough to save her life — but without a blood banking system, without the ability to test blood for HIV, we may be sentencing her to death."

Sexual violence and exploitation, all too common in conflict and post-conflict settings, contribute to transmission as well, both directly and indirectly. Rape by an infected man directly exposes women to the virus, and the abrasions or tearing of vaginal tissues which may result increase the risk of infection dramatically. Indirect effects are also insidious. Sexual violence often has lasting psychosocial consequences, including depression, stigma and discrimination, which can lead women into further cycles of exploitation and also contribute to other high risk activities such as drug use or sex work. Tragically and most cruelly, in some conflicts (such as Rwanda), the planned HIV infection of women has been a tool of ethnic warfare.

The mixing of civilians and combatants (either regular military forces or rebel forces) can increase the chances of infection since military forces almost always have much greater rates of sexually transmitted infections (STIs) and HIV than civilian populations.[5] In many conflict settings combatants are involved in sexual exploitation of women, regular relations with sex workers and, in some places, high levels of sexual violence.

STIs, which often go untreated due to ignorance and lack of adequate health care facilities, spread quickly in situations of poverty, powerlessness and social instability — and all of these epitomize conflict situations. The disintegration of communities and family life can lead to the break-up of stable relationships as well as the disruption of social norms governing men's and women's sexual behaviour. Forced migration mixes groups with varying HIV infection rates and can increase risks of infection in groups less aware of HIV/AIDS and of means of prevention. A clear example is that of Rwanda, where 1992 infection patterns were high in urban areas (27 per cent of pregnant women infected) and low in rural areas (just over 1 per cent) but where urban and rural rates became nearly identical by 1997 due to the huge population movements during and after the years of ethnic conflict. Since rates of infection in most countries are higher in urban areas, rural people who flee to cities are especially vulnerable.

The economic destitution and the psychological trauma of war-affected populations also increase their risk behaviours, while at the same time access to information and modes of prevention are diminished. In Angola there are fears that current relatively low infection rates (8.6 per cent of the population) will rise dramatically in the near future. After 30 years of civil war and approximately 4 million displaced people, many women have no way to support themselves and their families except through selling their bodies.

In Sierra Leone, the Women in Crisis Movement has established support for young women driven into the sex trade in Freetown. The women are provided with literacy and vocational training, HIV prevention skills and treatment for STIs in participating clinics. However, despite the sense of belonging that the group has provided, and the new skills that the women are learning, until the local economy can provide more jobs, or the women can establish sustainable businesses, they will remain at risk of exploitation and of HIV/AIDS. As one member stated, " We are trying to rebuild our lives after so many bad experiences and this project is helping us do that. But so much depends on being able to get food, transport and housing — most of us don't even have the basic things so many still do sex just to survive."

Normal medical procedures, such as childbirth, become more dangerous during conflict, as do unsafe abortions or treatment for abortion complications. Some traditional practices, such as female genital mutilation (FGM), also contribute to HIV vulnerability among women, especially when women are subject to violent sex. In Somalia, where the culture places a high value on chastity for women, there was very little STI transmission among women before the civil war. However, the disruption of communities and families and the decline of traditional protections for women have changed patterns of relations among women and men.

Dire poverty has driven many women to have sex for survival and, as we learned from many Somali women we met, sexual violence has increased dramatically. Since most Somali women have experienced genital mutilation, including infibulation, rape is very likely to damage their genital tissues, increasing their risk of STIs, including HIV/AIDS. Since the HIV/AIDS epidemic is growing so rapidly in the neighbouring countries where many Somalis are living as refugees, there is widespread concern that the epidemic will reach crisis proportions in Somalia as well. The low rates reported for the country may have more to do with lack of good data than with the actual disease patterns.

Conflict also often disrupts food production and markets, and leaves poor people unable to meet basic food requirements. Poor nutrition hastens the onset of AIDS among HIV positive people, thereby weakening families and communities in a never-ending downward spiral.

In many countries, refugee camp situations are not secure for women. Men who have lost their status in their communities or families may resort to drinking or abuse and engage in unprotected sex with multiple partners. Young people who have lost role models engage in sex early. Some refugees bring STIs with them; others contract them in the camp or in nearby towns. If camps do not have active STI treatment services and HIV prevention programmes, they can become dangerous places for residents. A study in Rwandan refugee camps in Tanzania showed that women and men reported frequent experience with STIs. Over half of women receiving prenatal care were infected, with 3 per cent having gonorrhea and 4 per cent syphilis. Six per cent of males had syphilis. Since STIs greatly increase the risk of HIV infection, and given that the HIV prevalence in Rwanda and Tanzania is already high, these refugees are in great danger.

All of these factors contribute to increased exposure to HIV among women in war zones. They are exacerbated by the already low status of women and girls in most regions of the world that are experiencing armed conflict. Women in the places we visited are powerless to control their sexual relationships or to negotiate safe sex. They were at the mercy of their partners or of strangers even in peacetime; they become even more vulnerable during conflict.

Even in settings where HIV prevention programmes have been well established and where women have reached a level of equality, the onset of war can severely disrupt such programmes, causing a breakdown in access to health information, damage to health infrastructure, lack of access to services and shortages of supplies such as STI treatment drugs or condoms. This lack of services, combined with poverty, can severely limit women's abilities to control their exposure to HIV. As one refugee told us, " I know all about AIDS because we had a prevention programme back home. All of us here know how you get it and how to keep from getting it. Lots of people started using condoms back home. But here in this camp, they aren't always available and in the city they are expensive — so what should we do? Sometimes my husband and I are together without protection even when we know better."

Even as conflicts subside, extremely difficult economic and social conditions often leave many people unemployed and unable to resume their normal community or family lives. Where AIDS and opportunistic infections are already a problem, women bear the largest burden of care for family members.[6] This responsibility can keep girls from going to school and prevent women's involvement in the work force, thus amplifying

Very few of the militaries in the countries we visited have the resources to establish strong prevention and care programmes. As one general told us, "The war now is with AIDS — but it was easier to get guns than it is to get the tools to fight AIDS."

their low status. In this regard, HIV is a direct threat to both human and national security since the epidemic undermines the economic and social participation of the population during a critical time of national rehabilitation and recovery. As a senior Congolese official told us, "We have the beginnings of peace in our country now and we have so much to do to recover. We need everyone to participate and we need them to be healthy to do that. If we let this epidemic go on, then we will jeopardize everything. We have to stop it now."

As reported in Bosnia and Herzegovina and Guatemala, as well as other settings, levels of sexual violence and exploitation may actually increase after war is over. It is common for traumatized individuals in many post-conflict situations to turn to drugs or alcohol, which are strongly associated with gender violence and increased exposure to HIV. The socioeconomic collapse in Tajikistan has led to heavy drug trafficking from Afghanistan, and it is estimated that 30 per cent of the national economy depends on the drug trade.[7]

These drugs permeate the society, and school children as young as 12 have begun to inject drugs, leaving a wide-open door for HIV.[8]

SEXUAL VIOLENCE AND EXPLOITATION

In February 1994 at my parents' house, seven men raped a widow who was staying with the family. The men said, "At least one of us must be HIV positive." The widow contracted AIDS and she has already died.

— A survivor of the Rwandan genocide

Sexual violence and exploitation are inexcusable under any circumstances, but in the face of HIV/AIDS and conflict they take on new menace. Of all the things we saw or learned about during our visits, one of the most cruel occurred in Rwanda during the genocide there, when Hutu men who knew that they were infected with HIV purposely attempted to infect Tutsi women as a strategy of war. The Interahamwe leaders directly encouraged their militias to rape Tutsi women in order to dilute Tutsi ethnicity; infecting the women with a virus that would eventually kill them seemed an even more effective means of genocide. AVEGA, a support group for Rwandan women, has documented that many rape survivors were infected with HIV. Veronica, an AVEGA member, told us, "The genocide was planned for a long time. Arms were brought in from outside the country for that purpose. They started killing everyone including unborn babies. They would kill a mother after killing her own children in front of her. Men in groups of between 30 and 50 would rape a woman. They would all wait their turn. This was the beginning of the spread of HIV/AIDS. Today many of us are infected because of rape."

Even in the relatively wealthier places we visited, war had taken such a toll on the local economy that women were selling sex to men who had resources of some kind — money, housing or food. From East Timor to Bosnia, Colombia to Liberia, girls and women were forced into such work to survive. In none of these places did women have adequate access to HIV protection. East Timor, for example, had very low HIV prevalence for many years, but there is increasing infection today. The high incidence of sexual violence during the war and the new patterns of relations between East Timorese women and foreigners, including peacekeepers, businesspeople and aid workers, seem to be factors. When sex is used as a commodity, women and girls have little negotiating power over the use of condoms — and an offer of more money from men who don't want to use protection is all too difficult to refuse. In Bosnia, Myanmar, the Ukraine and other sites, economic and social disarray have fed a burgeoning sex industry, including trafficking. In the Ukraine, in a ten-year period, rates of syphilis infection increased by a factor of twenty, and will undoubtedly lead to an increase in HIV infection rates.

Many countries are on the brink of more severe epidemics. Now is the time to take action, but the resources are rarely available. Sierra Leone is one such country and has a fighting chance to stop the epidemic if action is taken now — yet few donors seem interested in funding HIV prevention activities. "It seems strange," said one UN agency representative, "that donors only seem to want to fund governance projects here — courts, elections, tribunals, civil service training, police training — and no one wants to support HIV prevention. If we don't work on stopping HIV now, there won't be people left to govern. Already, the military is very concerned about preventing infection among soldiers in the new army and they see it as a serious security issue. But there is only one UN agency that brings condoms into the country (UNFPA) and they don't have the resources to meet the national demand."[9]

MILITARY-CIVILIAN INTERACTION

The Joint UN Programme on HIV/AIDS (UNAIDS) has noted that "Military personnel are a population group at special risk of exposure to sexually transmitted diseases (STDs) including HIV. In peacetime, STD infection rates among armed forces are generally 2 to 5 times higher than in civilian populations; in time of conflict the difference can be 50 times higher or more."[10] The circumstances of military service make soldiers both more vulnerable to HIV infection and more likely to pass it on. Troops are usually young, sexually active and separated from their normal partners. They often have greater access to resources than the civilian population and may frequent commercial sex workers. The military ethos of risk-taking can undermine HIV prevention even when soldiers are aware of risks. The "macho" attitudes that are part of military socialization may also lead to carelessness about protection and even to exploitative abuse of power, including sexual violence. Military camps also attract sex workers and other risk-prone "camp followers."

In Eritrea and Ethiopia the deployment of national armies to the borders during the war was reputed to have been followed closely by the movement of sex workers to the area. The months of inactivity between battles left plenty of time for troops to take leave and spend their time drinking and visiting local brothels. In Eritrea women made up a significant proportion of the armed forces and many young people, who might not have become sexually active at home, became involved in relationships at the front. The National Union of Eritrean Youth and Students, concerned about these young people, quickly mobilized an HIV awareness and prevention programme in camps.

For young soldiers (men and women) who are in the midst of a war and have seen their fellow soldiers die in combat, fatalism becomes a risk factor. As one young Eritrean soldier stated, "I have seen so many of my friends die at the front and I know that I might die. Why should I worry about a disease that would take years to kill me when I might die tomorrow?"[11] Combatants who return to their homes and communities may bring back whatever behaviours they have adopted as well as any STIs, including HIV, that they may have contracted. This is another way in which HIV spreads back into civilian society. The Director of an HIV/AIDS programme in the Ethiopian military has observed that HIV issues were neglected during the 1991 demobilization after the government was overthrown and that it may have been one of the major transmission factors for the epidemic there. He noted in 2000 that, "if HIV awareness is not paid attention to this time, uncontrolled demobilization will be catastrophic."[12]

The risks of infection are even higher among non-state combatants (rebels and insurgents) who often have very little military discipline and no access to health information or services. Such groups have been responsible for very high levels of rape and sexual abuse in many conflicts, including many of the places we visited. The levels of STI/HIV infection in some of these groups have been estimated at up to 50 per cent; one can imagine the impact on transmission to women within the civilian population.

Multiple troop movements and population displacements in the DRC, and to and from neighbouring countries with high HIV prevalence rates, have left the DRC well set for "an explosion of HIV/AIDS," according to a WHO official in a report on HIV in the region. "I can hardly think of a better vector than tens of thousands of young men with hard currency roaming around the country," noted another relief worker.[13] HIV prevalence among the uniformed services is high in places where the epidemic is most serious. Although the data is not very reliable, it is believed that rates range up to 30 per cent in Tanzania and 40-60 per cent in Angola and the DRC. Zimbabwe, which has troops deployed in the DRC, may have up to 70 per cent infected.[14]

Although military services present exceptional opportunities to prevent HIV through awareness and training of troops in organized hierarchical settings, and even through use of uniformed services to raise awareness in civilian populations, very few of the militaries in the countries we visited have the resources to establish strong prevention and care programmes. As one general told us, "The war now is with AIDS — but it was easier to get guns than it is to get the tools to fight AIDS."

Peacekeeping Troops: Vectors or Victims?
Peacekeeping forces can also have an impact on HIV transmission. These forces are composed of a variety of national troop contingents who have widely varying levels of knowledge about HIV as well as different patterns of interaction with the local population. Such forces can become a part of the problem or part of the solution, depending on their training and their behaviours.

When the recent war between Eritrea and

Ethiopia came to an end, the two countries agreed to receive peacekeeping forces to monitor the border areas until they were demarcated. As the negotiations for the UN Mission in Eritrea and Ethiopia (UNMEE) proceeded, the Eritrean Government expressed serious concern about the possibility that there might be HIV-infected soldiers among the peacekeeping troops and asked that all troops be tested. The Eritrean military screens for HIV, the government noted, and so should any other military force on its territory. This point has remained in contention for over a year, and Eritrea has yet to sign the agreement.[15]

The Department of Peacekeeping Operations (DPKO), however, cannot require testing of military personnel contributed for service with the United Nations, as this is determined by the national policies of each contributing country. A UNAIDS panel of experts has unanimously agreed that HIV/AIDS testing should be voluntary. The UN has decided to accept this policy recommendation and does not require testing for civilian staff going to serve in a peacekeeping mission. While the testing policies of contingents may vary, it is increasingly becoming a national requirement for troops contributed for service with the UN. In addition to testing prior to deployment, some troop contributors also test their troops upon their return home.

The Eritrean Government was responding to concerns expressed in Cambodia when the presence of international forces was associated with a dramatic growth in the sex industry.[16] Although this has not been empirically proven, there is very good evidence that no matter how the virus gets introduced, situations conducive to unprotected sex with multiple partners — including commercial sex workers — increase vulnerability to HIV infection. A 1998 UNAIDS report, "AIDS and the Military," indicated that 45 per cent of a contingent of foreign troops who had been in Cambodia had had sex with a sex worker or another local woman.

Many troops deployed internationally have mixed with host populations in intimate ways. In Liberia and Sierra Leone, ECOMOG troops are known to have left thousands of children behind,

born to local women.[17] Many of these women were also exposed to STIs and HIV. Over one third of countries which provide troops for peacekeeping missions have medium or high HIV prevalence levels in their own populations and may not screen troops who are deployed. As early as 1995, the U.S. State Department noted that "Worldwide peacekeeping operations may pose a danger of spreading HIV … Peacekeepers could be both a source of HIV infection to local populations and be infected by them, thus becoming a source of infection when they return home."[18] Increasing concerns about this issue led to an unprecedented discussion in the Security Council in 2000 when U.S. Ambassador Richard Holbrooke introduced discussions on the relationship between HIV, conflict and security.[19] It was the first time that the Security Council had ever discussed a health issue.

Resolution 1308, adopted by the UN Security Council in 2000, recognized the spread of HIV/AIDS and STIs as potential threats to international peace and security and also recommended that HIV prevention be incorporated into all peacekeeping initiatives.[20] The Security Council reinforced this resolution later in the year with the adoption of Resolution 1325, which addressed the issues of women and armed conflict. The Security Council specifically called for "training guidelines and materials on the protection, rights, and particular needs of women, as well as on the importance of involving women in all peacekeeping and peace building measures, (inviting) Member States to incorporate these elements as well as HIV/AIDS awareness training into national training programmes for military and civilian police personnel in preparation for deployment." Some months later, the UN General Assembly Special Session (UNGASS) on HIV/AIDS unanimously adopted the Declaration of Commitment on HIV/AIDS, which also presented specific objectives related to HIV/AIDS awareness and training among personnel involved in international peacekeeping operations (see box, p. 58).

Recent studies done in Sierra Leone showed that although most of the 17,000 troops in the United Nations Mission in Sierra Leone (UNAMSIL) were engaged in constructive initiatives in the country, including building schools and roads, rehabilitating services and providing health care in rural areas near their camps, there were reports that some could be involved in commercial sexual activities, or in the sexual exploitation of minors. The absence of viable employment opportunities has forced many Sierra Leoneans to resort to commercial sex activities as a means of survival. Thousands of young women walk the streets at night looking for someone who will pay them. In a wide set of interviews with health workers, local officials and women's groups in the country, 73 per cent of those interviewed saw indiscriminate sexual activity as a contributing risk factor for HIV.[21]

UNAMSIL has taken a series of measures to further prevent misconduct and to discipline personnel when misconduct has been documented. The UNAMSIL Personnel Conduct Committee has created a dedicated phone line to handle complaints by civilians. There is also an inter-agency Coordination Committee for Prevention of Sexual Exploitation, of which UNAMSIL is part. All cases of misconduct by military personnel are brought to the attention of a Provost Marshal for investigation.

During UN missions in Kosovo (UNMIK) and in the DRC (MONUC), as well as in UNMEE, there have also been well-publicized cases of sexual misconduct by peacekeepers with local women or girls. Clearly sexual relations occur in conflict and post-conflict environments; these can be either consensual or forced. Whenever the HIV virus enters this system, no matter who brings it in, it can flourish.

Our discussions with peacekeeping mission personnel and others we consulted were heated — especially on the issue of mandatory testing. To us, it seemed logical that peacekeepers should be screened before they were deployed, that UN personnel should never bring such a risk with them to a place they were there to protect. Yet we also realize that peacekeeping missions are made up of individual national contingents, many of which may not have the resources for strong testing and counselling programmes. When we considered a number of issues, such as the fact that detection of

the virus takes some time, that pre-deployment screening would not help in cases where peacekeepers contracted the virus after deployment, and that voluntary counselling and testing programmes for prevention are most effective, we determined that we should recommend massive strengthening of such programmes in all militaries of countries that deploy peacekeeping forces.

WHAT CAN BE DONE TO PROTECT WOMEN AND STOP THE EPIDEMIC?

The issues of HIV and conflict have gained considerable public attention in the past few years. UN agencies, international non-governmental organizations (NGOs) and research and action groups, national organizations and advocacy groups, and academics have all begun to document the dynamics of the relationship, and a number of guidelines for action have been produced. However, attention to the gender aspects of this relationship have lagged behind, both in terms of documentation and in terms of operational programmes to ameliorate the tragic situations we have reviewed.

Despite the lack of systematic programmes of HIV prevention, care and support in conflict situations and the dismal lack of attention to gender issues in the humanitarian response, there are a number of lessons learned:

• Making sure that women have adequate access to food, basic health services and protection from exploitation and abuse would reduce their vulnerability to HIV infection.

• Protection from sexual violence in all its forms — during war, in camps for refugees and internally displaced persons (IDPs) and in post-conflict situations — can help reduce direct exposure and later risky behaviours.

• Provision of basic HIV prevention information and services reduces the risks of infection. Information can be shared in many ways — through media, religious institutions, community groups and health and social services. To effect changes in behaviours, information must be culturally appropriate and relevant and targeted to specific population groups.

• Utilizing gender analysis while designing prevention and care programmes makes them more effective. HIV requires a continuum of care; gender aspects vary according to the position along the continuum.

• Educating men and boys about HIV and gender issues is very important for the prevention of HIV in women and girls and can be done even in conflict situations.

• Empowering girls with knowledge and awareness of HIV prevention and with the skills to negotiate their relationships is critical to ensuring their later health.

• Preventing unwanted pregnancies can reduce the risks of HIV transmission during deliveries as well as during unsafe abortions, which are prevalent in conflict situations. Preventing unwanted pregnancy in HIV positive women will also prevent many cases of mother-to-child transmission.

• Reinforcing community support systems can alleviate the burden of AIDS care on women, allowing them to carry on with other productive activities.

• Voluntary counselling and testing (VCT) reinforces prevention, can help infected women to get the information and services they need and can lessen the stigma of infection. VCT requires skilled counsellors in order to be effective.

• Uniformed services can be excellent contexts for gender and HIV-awareness building, since they have organized structures of communication. In many places, the military is respected and influential and can set the tone for thinking about HIV prevention and care.

The international community has recognized the urgency of the AIDS epidemic and the necessity of HIV programming in humanitarian response and post-conflict programming, as reflected in the UNGASS on AIDS. Security Council Resolutions 1308 and 1325 both specifically cite the special concerns of women. The UN

Consolidated Appeals process has begun to include projects on HIV prevention and care. Guidelines have been developed and proposals written. But, as we saw so graphically, none of these conferences, resolutions or guidelines have yet been able to help Marie, or the young women on the streets in Freetown, or those taking up 80 per cent of the hospital beds in Burundi or those lost souls injecting drugs in Tajikistan.

Good initiatives are happening: Counselling and training is provided in refugee camps in Tanzania, gender and HIV training is being provided for UNAMSIL troops, youth are being trained as peer educators in the DRC and women are getting vocational training and health education in Rwanda. But this is not nearly enough. All of these programmes should be expanded a hundred-fold. This will depend on political will and on resources — and, despite all the global talk about AIDS, both are in short supply. One example: During the past two years, of the HIV-related projects included in the UN Consolidated Appeals for 19 complex conflict countries, less than 10 per cent have been funded.

The Global Fund to Fight AIDS, Tuberculosis and Malaria was created as a public-private partnership in 2001 to combat these diseases in heavily affected poor nations. A trust fund that provides grants for prevention, treatment and care, it has so far only attracted about $2 billion of the estimated $7 billion required to cover needs. It was designed to promote multisectoral planning and to provide flexible and quick support for projects proposed by governments, and has already disbursed a first tranche of funds of almost $400 million for dozens of projects.[22] However, the process shows preference for developed health systems and only two "conflict" countries received support for programmes in the first tranche: Rwanda and Burundi.

We are concerned that the Global Fund may not be very well suited for supporting HIV programmes in conflict for a number of reasons. First, countries in conflict (or without governments at all) are likely to lack the institutions, human resources and skills to develop proposals and submit applications to the Fund. According to requirements, propos-als must be submitted based on government and civil society collaboration on a coherent national plan of action to address the three diseases, and on established mechanisms for the management and monitoring of funds and activities.

Our experience in conflict areas such as Somalia and Liberia make us question whether these countries can possibly receive support from the Fund, since they would be unable to meet the basic requirements for application. Further, some of the factors which the Fund uses to assess applications are also problematic in conflict situations. These include: "ability to demonstrate measurable results," which would presumably require better health information and data bases than exist in many war zones; political commitment at the "highest" level, which may be hard to come by in countries where the leadership is more focused on security or on ethnic conflict than on health; and prevalence of disease, which may bias the funding to high prevalence countries and neglect those with current low prevalence but where conflict has created conditions suited to rapid transmission. Although the Fund is a very important global initiative we believe that, as currently configured, it cannot take the place of funding for HIV in humanitarian programmes.

With sufficient resources, basic HIV prevention can be provided in emergency situations and expanded as conflicts are settled and access to populations increases. Basic prevention includes protection against sexual violence, provision of HIV/AIDS information, ensuring universal precautions and a safe blood supply, and providing female and male condoms. Expanded programmes require treatment of STIs, targeted education and communication initiatives, VCT, treatment of opportunistic infections and prevention of mother-to-child transmission through prophylaxis. Care and support of those with AIDS is also important, including provision of good nutrition. All of these are doable with current knowledge, as long as there is strong political will. In regards to antiretroviral treatment, resources must be made available so that the world's poor can be treated equally and that their rights to health can be affirmed by the international community.

RECOMMENDATIONS

1. All HIV/AIDS programmes and funding in conflict situations to address the disproportionate disease burden carried by women. Mandatory gender analysis and specific strategies for meeting the needs of women and girls should seek to prevent infection and increase access to treatment, care and support.

2. HIV/AIDS awareness and prevention programmes to be implemented during conflict and in post-conflict situations, with care and support provided whenever there is access to affected populations. National governments, national and international NGOs and UN agencies should incorporate HIV/AIDS prevention into all humanitarian assistance. Donors should strongly support these interventions.

3. Vulnerability assessments to be carried out in each humanitarian situation to determine links between conflict, displacement and gender. Information and data collection should be strengthened in order to document this relationship and to guide appropriate responses. Governments and agencies should work together to document vulnerabilities.

4. Clear guidelines for HIV/AIDS prevention in peacekeeping operations. All troop-contributing countries should make available voluntary and confidential HIV/AIDS testing for their peacekeeping personnel. Counselling and testing should be provided for all contingent forces and civilian personnel participating in emergency and peace operations before and during deployment on a regular basis. HIV prevention as well as gender training should be provided in all missions to all personnel.

5. The Inter-Agency Standing Committee (IASC) Reference Group on HIV/AIDS in Emergency Settings to develop clear policy guidelines for HIV prevention and care in humanitarian situations and application of these guidelines to be supported by national authorities, humanitarian agencies and donors.

6. The Global Fund to Fight AIDS, TB and Malaria to make special provisions for support of HIV/AIDS programmes in conflict situations, including in countries without the government capacity to manage the application process. In such cases NGOs and UN agencies should be eligible to submit proposals. Further, we encourage the systematic consideration of gender issues in all programme funding.

7. Institutions and organizations to address HIV prevention in conflict situations. In particular, the New Partnership for Africa's Development (NEPAD) should take a leadership role in that region.

8. The development and enforcement of codes of conduct for all UN and international NGO staff to protect against abuse and exploitation of women and girls. All such staff should received training in prevention of sexual and gender-based violence, as well as reproductive health information, including STI and HIV/AIDS prevention.

Japanese peacekeepers arrive in Dili, East Timor, April 2002.

women & peace operations

I was against the creation of a Gender Affairs Unit for the UN's Transitional Authority in East Timor. I did not think a Gender Unit would help rebuild institutions from the ashes of what the militia left. I was wrong. The first regulation I passed guaranteed human rights standards, including CEDAW as a foundation of all new government institutions we created. The Unit brought this to life, reaching out to East Timorese women and, together with UNIFEM, provided support that resulted in a higher percentage of women in the Constituent Assembly than in many other countries. The Unit worked with East Timorese women to create what is now the East Timorese Government Office for the Advancement of Women.
—Sergio Vieira de Mello
Special Representative of the
UN Secretary-General, East Timor[1]

Of the 14 war-torn areas we visited, international peacekeepers were present in nearly half of them.[2] Women in the local communities we visited were deeply affected by what is usually referred to as a "peacekeeping environment." The vast majority of them had awaited the UN peacekeeping mission with hope. They wanted to see the end of war, and once the peacekeepers arrived, many women saw direct benefits from the UN presence. In Kosovo we met Tatania, who was able to support her family with her earnings as a translator in the peacekeeping mission. In the Former Yugoslav Republic of Macedonia (FYROM), we met Vezna, who had been rescued by peacekeepers from traffickers who had kept her locked up in Kosovo as a sexual slave. In the Democratic Republic of the Congo (DRC) and Sierra Leone, we met humanitarian personnel who had been able to assist women in dangerous areas because of the protective presence of peacekeepers. We met inspired and dedicated mission leaders and force commanders who understood that protecting women from violence was an important part of their work. We saw how the UN mission in Sierra Leone had made efforts to strengthen the monitoring and documenting of abuses of women's human rights. And we met women whose participation in political negotiations had been facilitated by the nation-building missions present in Afghanistan, East Timor and Kosovo.

Yet sometimes opportunities to promote gender equality were squandered by inaction: not consulting women in the host community about the peace operation or not employing them in professional positions. We also heard the frustrations of the few senior women working in missions — they complained of limited opportunities for advancement, insufficient authority and resources to carry out their responsibilities, lack of support from headquarters and even sexual harassment.

Perhaps most disturbing of everything we saw and learned was the association, in the vast majority of peacekeeping environments, between the arrival of peacekeeping personnel and increased prostitution, sexual exploitation and HIV/AIDS infection. We are acutely aware that it is not UN peacekeepers alone who contribute to creating these conditions. The collapse of a normal economy, accompanied by the collapse of law and order, contribute to this environment of exploitation. Anyone can be an exploiter: members of armed groups, the government, regional organizations and the private sector. We have no wish to see our criticism of these activities and crimes — which we would condemn no matter who perpetrated them — be used to undermine the UN, an institution in which we believe very deeply and which we have served in peacekeeping environ-

ments. We also respect the fact that the UN itself is working hard to investigate and correct these abuses. In proposing new ways to strengthen the gender responsiveness of peace operations, we are joining these efforts, mindful of the challenge issued by Lakhdar Brahimi, former Chairman of the Panel on UN Peace Operations, to tell the Security Council and the United Nations Secretariat what they need to know, not simply what they want to hear. It is with the intent of strengthening the organization's ability to fulfill its mission that we describe the negative as well as the positive experiences of women that we met.

The UN Security Council has deployed 53 peacekeeping operations in conflict and post-conflict situations since 1948.[3] Countries contribute troops known as "blue helmets" or "blue berets" to serve under the UN flag and, depending on their mandate, these troops may patrol borders, monitor ceasefires and assist local communities in their search for durable peace. In recent years the scope of peacekeeping has widened to include civilian police officers, electoral experts and observers, mine action experts, human rights officers and humanitarian, political and public information specialists. Their responsibilities range from assisting in the implementation of peace agreements to protecting and delivering humanitarian assistance; from assisting with the demobilization of former fighters and their return to civilian life to supervising and conducting elections; from training and restructuring local police forces to monitoring respect of human rights and investigating alleged violations.

The size of recent peacekeeping missions ranges from 113 peacekeepers in the Military Observer Group in India and Pakistan to 17,275 in the UN Mission in Sierra Leone (UNAMSIL). In addition to the activities related to the implementation of their mandates, peacekeeping operations provide an injection of resources, foreign currency and business opportunities for conflict-affected countries. These can sometimes be short-lived, limited to the duration of a peacekeeping mission.[4] The mission in India and Pakistan has an annual budget of US$6.2 million, while UNAMSIL, the largest UN operation at present, costs about US$2 million per day or approximately US$717.6 million annually.

United Nations peacekeeping operations are supported by the Department of Peacekeeping Operations (DPKO) of the UN Secretariat. In addition individual countries as well as regional and sub-regional organizations and arrangements, such as the Economic Community of West African States (ECOWAS), the Organization of African Unity, now replaced by the African Union (AU), the Organisation for Security and Cooperation in Europe (OSCE) and the North Atlantic Treaty Organization (NATO), deploy their own peacekeeping operations.

A large influx of foreign, comparatively well-paid international peacekeeping personnel — military and non-military — inevitably has an economic, social and cultural impact on the local population, including women. Young women are likely to become involved in and affected by what are known as "peacekeeping economies": industries and services such as bars and hotels that spring up near military bases. Many women also find work in support positions for the mission, as secretaries and language assistants; very few women or men are hired locally as professionals. When the UN is responsible for nation building, as it was in East Timor, it takes on a wide range of responsibilities that determine everything from a population's access to water, energy and sanitation, among other resources, to defining legal status, constitutional guarantees and creating an electoral framework — all of which have a direct effect on women.

The "light footprint" strategy of the United Nations Assistance Mission in Afghanistan (UNAMA) has given increased recognition to the role of national professional staff in a UN peace operation. Such arrangements offer the opportunity not only to build, and build on, national capacities, but also allow women to play a more active role in re-building their nation.

Three fleeting references were made to women and peacekeeping in the 1995 Beijing Platform for Action, and it was not until 2000 that the UN thoroughly mapped the issues and elements needed to include gender in all aspects of multidimensional peace operations, in the Windhoek Declaration and Namibia Plan of Action.[5] Soon after, in Resolution 1325, and again in an open session devoted to the subject in July 2002, the Security Council confirmed the relevance of routinely including gender perspectives when executing peacekeeping missions.

As gender issues have moved onto the peacekeeping agenda, the UN has deployed gender specialists, first in the UN Mission in Kosovo (UNMIK), the UN Transitional Administration in East Timor (UNTAET) and in Sierra Leone (UNAMSIL) in 1999, and then in the Democratic Republic of the Congo (MONUC) in 2000. We visited each of these and offer here some preliminary views about their achievements and the obstacles they face. Without question, a more thorough analysis is needed to determine how these initiatives can better serve women in a peacekeeping environment. As Jean-Marie Guéhenno, Under-Secretary-General for the UN Department of Peacekeeping Operations (DPKO), said last July in an assessment of gender mainstreaming in peace operations, "Far more remains to be done, both in the field and at Headquarters."[6]

BRINGING A GENDER PERSPECTIVE INTO PEACE OPERATIONS

The concept of gender mainstreaming has been defined by the United Nations as "the process of assessing the implications for women and men of any planned action, including legislation, policies or programmes, in any area and at all levels. It is a strategy for making the concerns and experiences of women as well as of men an integral part of the design, implementation, monitoring and evaluation of policies and programmes in all political, economic and societal spheres, so that women and men benefit equally, and inequality is not perpetuated. The ultimate goal of mainstreaming is to achieve gender equality."[7]

In peace operations, the fruits of gender mainstreaming can be seen in political statements of good will, training and the appointment of a few women to senior positions. But it cannot be seen in concrete strategies and procedures, from planning and assessment through to the withdrawal phase. Gender mainstreaming requires specialized expertise and training in all aspects of mission operation. It requires programmatic integration of gender into all elements of activity, throughout the various "pillars" of governance and humanitarian efforts. It requires regular monitoring, reporting and evaluation of progress made and obstacles encountered, as well as systems for holding the operation accountable to achieving its goals. Finally, it requires resources to put all of these measures in place.

Gender mainstreaming needs to start from the very beginning of a mission to ensure that structures and programmes are designed to address the different needs of women and men for protection, assistance, justice and reconstruction. To the best of our knowledge, gender expertise has not been utilized during assessment missions or technical surveys conducted prior to the design or establishment of UN peacekeeping operations nor, most importantly, in the blueprint for action, the concept of operation or the budget.

Even after the initial planning phases, where appropriate, a mission should monitor and report on progress made in mainstreaming gender issues throughout the peace operation. In this way, the Secretary-General can respond more effectively to the Security Council's call to include "information about gender mainstreaming throughout peacekeeping missions and all other aspects relating to women" in his reports to the Council.

Despite the importance of these strategies, procedures and resources, most are not in place. Instead efforts are focused mainly in three areas: (1) increasing the number of women leading and serving in peace operations, often referred to as "gender balance"; (2) dedicating experts within peace operations to focus exclusively on gender; and (3) gender training. The first has not been achieved, the second has occurred in five operations, and the third is being standardized, and will be ready for delivery to Troop Contributors in 2003. It should be made compulsory.

Improving Gender Balance in the Staffing of Peace Operations

In 2000 DPKO stated that, "Women's presence [in peacekeeping missions] improves access and

support for local women; it makes male peacekeepers more reflective and responsible; and it broadens the repertoire of skills and styles available within the mission, often with the effect of reducing conflict and confrontation."[8] In addition, the necessity of women's equal participation in peace processes is asserted again and again, directly and indirectly, in the UN Charter, the Beijing Platform for Action, by ECOSOC, the Security Council, the General Assembly, the Hague Agenda for Peace and the Namibia Plan of Action, among others. Yet women's participation in peace processes, and in peace operations in particular, has been anything but equal or fair.

In the 32 years between 1957 and 1989, only 0.1 per cent of the field-based military personnel in UN peacekeeping missions were female.[9] And despite the fact that in 1996 the Secretary-General recommended that by the year 2000 women constitute 50 per cent of staff in the UN system, including field missions,[10] women made up only 4 per cent of police and 3 per cent of military in UN operations in 2000.[11] At UN Headquarters between 1994 and 2000, women represented only 18 per cent of those employed at the director level and none at the senior director level. By 2002 the gender balance at the UN Headquarters had improved to the extent that women and men were "nearly evenly balanced," according to a report by the Secretary-General. But the report acknowledged that the perception of parity "disguises differences in gender representation by category, department or office." In fact, the number of women in the most senior positions — under-secretary-general and assistant secretary-general — actually fell 1.6 per cent from 2001 to 2002, while the number of women in director positions increased by only 1.3 per cent.[12]

The UN Charter states that it will "place no restrictions on the eligibility of men and women to participate in any capacity and under conditions of equality in its principal and subsidiary organs."[13] Yet up to 2000, when Resolution 1325 was passed, only four women had ever served as Special Representatives of the Secretary-General (SRSG) — in-theatre heads of mission — in peacekeeping operations. With Resolution 1325 the Security

Council urged the Secretary-General to appoint more women as his Special Representatives and Envoys in peace-related functions. At the time, there were no women holding the position. Two years later, only Heidi Tagliavini of Switzerland served as SRSG in Georgia, and three women served as Deputy SRSGs.

The main obstacle, in our view, is not the alleged dearth of qualified women but a misperception about what is required to serve in a position of leadership in a peacekeeping force. As former Ministers of Defence and Finance, we know that the ideal criteria for leading and participating in peace operations are not, as many believe, strictly military or even political in nature. Contemporary peacekeeping requires skills that can lead a war-torn society through a process of nation building, economic development and reconstruction. By broadening the qualifications, we can broaden the pool of candidates.

However, discrimination also limits women's participation in UN peace operations. Women attribute their inability to enter or to move up the ranks to the fact that many posts are not advertised, and people are picked from an "old boys" network instead. We believe there must be more transparency and accountability, and reiterate the call for the establishment of an advisory group to facilitate the search and appointment of senior staff. However, although the United Nations can request female peacekeeping personnel, the onus is on contributing countries to recruit, train and deploy more women as military, civilian and police personnel. They must be encouraged and provided with incentives to do so.

Discrimination against women extends to the host community as well. Peace operations rarely take affirmative measures to create and fill "national officer posts." An increase in the number of professional employment opportunities for the host population would ensure less international domination of UN missions, and help to harmonize the priorities of the host community and the mission. At the same time it would strengthen the national skill base and provide continuity when the mission withdraws. In most cases, however, peace operations employ women from the host community in support functions, and opportunities to work in other missions are limited, given that the ratio of locally recruited to internationally recruited staff is almost 2:1. Apart from the fact that such staff have empathy with and understanding of populations emerging from conflict, increasing the selection of qualified national staff would be an excellent way to develop national capacity and foster cross-regional learning.

We are pleased to learn that the Secretary-General has indeed taken action to that end. The implementation of the Brahimi panel recommendations and the implementation of another recommendation to establish a roster of pre-vetted candidates, including at the most senior levels, is also underway.

Gender mainstreaming needs to start from the very beginning of a mission to ensure that structures and programmes are designed to address the different needs of women and men for protection, assistance, justice and reconstruction.

East Timor is one of the few operations where the host community has played an important role in the peacekeeping mission. Although it was a struggle, women in East Timor managed to negotiate their own participation within UNTAET by lobbying at the Lisbon donor conference to ensure that East Timorese counterparts to the international staff were employed in the Gender Unit.

Gender Advisers and Units: Delivering the Mandate to Women

Over the past two years, four out of 15 peace operations have had dedicated staff working on gender issues: These staff are usually referred to as gender units or offices even though they may have only one staff person. UNTAET in East Timor, UNMIK in Kosovo and MONUC in the DRC have gender units/offices, while UNAMSIL in Sierra Leone has a gender specialist within the Human Rights Section of the mission.

Although their mandates may vary across missions, in general gender advisers and units are expected to: ensure that gender concerns are integrated into all of the mission's programmes and activities; raise gender awareness among international staff at all levels of authority; conduct gender training for peacekeepers, military observers and civilian police; and, in some cases, build the capacity of organizations to include women in the peace process and help form a national machinery for women.

So far, the range of responsibilities given to gender advisers appears to exceed both their authority and their limited resources. One or two people, no matter how dedicated and energetic, cannot fulfill or even coordinate these tasks, particularly if they do not have appropriate seniority. Aside from needing adequate staff, gender units need a strategy and plan of action that comes from the highest level, indicating a serious commitment to integrating gender issues in all activities of the mission. Although the units' effectiveness relies almost entirely on the commitment of the operational management team, particularly the SRSG, the few gender advisers in office have not had consistent access to the Head of Mission. In addition, they occupy lower positions in the hierarchy than those they are expected to coordinate with or even oversee. In a bureaucracy, this can be debilitating.

At present, gender advisers have no official channel through which to communicate or receive support from UN Headquarters or from UN agencies in the mission area. As a result, these advisers told us they lack clarity about whom to turn to for support and guidance and often feel isolated. Although the Best Practices Unit in DPKO is the focal point for gender mainstreaming in peacekeeping missions, it has no dedicated post to deal with gender issues on a full time basis. An institutional response is long overdue. We fully support the Secretary-General's 2000 call for the establishment of a Gender Unit in the Office of the Under-Secretary-General of DPKO,[14] and echo similar affirmations made by many members of both the General Assembly[15] and the Security Council.[16]

The Secretary-General explained the wide range of activities this unit would need to undertake to effectively address gender concerns, which we reproduce to show the breadth and range of the tasks that would be assigned "beginning with needs assessment missions through post-conflict peacebuilding. Gender perspectives should be considered in analyses, policy and strategy development and planning of peace support operations, as well as training programmes and instruments developed to support effective implementation of those operations, such as guidelines, handbooks and codes of conduct. All aspects and all levels of peace support operations require attention to gender perspectives, including political analysis, military operations, civilian police activities, electoral assistance, human rights support, humanitarian assistance, including for refugees and displaced persons, development and reconstruction activities and public information. Training of troops and civilian police on gender issues is critical. In the context of complex missions where interim governments will be established, gender balance in interim bodies and development of capacity within those important bodies to work with gender perspectives need to be considered. Experience has shown that it is important to ensure attention to gender perspectives from the very outset of peacebuilding and peacekeeping missions, including through incorporation in the initial mandates. All reports of the individual mission to the Security Council should include explicit routine reporting on progress in integrating gender perspectives as well as information on the number and levels of women involved in all aspects of the mission." [17]

The Secretary-General called for a Gender Unit in the Department of Peacekeeping Operations that would include a gender adviser at the director level and a general adviser at the senior staff level, supported by an administrative assistant. After months of negotiation and discussion, this proposal has been reduced to one post. Again, one person cannot hope to fulfill or coordinate these activities and provide adequate support to field-based personnel. Limiting this function to one person is setting them up to fail.

Despite enormous constraints, gender units have been able to strengthen peace operations' responsiveness to women, often by drawing upon the operational strength of the UN system at country level. By leveraging the technical, financial and programme resources of operational bodies on the ground such as UNIFEM and the UN Population Fund (UNFPA), the units are able to provide support far beyond their own limited means. In East Timor UNTAET's Gender Affairs Unit cooperated with UNIFEM to provide technical support for programmes reaching East Timorese women. In Sierra Leone, UNFPA, UNAIDS and UNIFEM are working with the peacekeeping mission on issues of HIV/AIDS and gender.

Gender Training in the Peacekeeping Environment

Protecting refugees is vastly different from guarding prisoners of war. Prosecuting criminal traffickers in war is vastly different from protecting women victims of trafficking. Establishing the rule of law is different than simply enforcing it. All staff of peace support operations need training, including gender training, so they can carry out the wider range of tasks required of them in today's post-conflict situations, and to help them adjust and be responsive to the cultural milieu in which they will function. Training peacekeeping personnel on gender issues can also promote gender mainstreaming within an operation, irrespective of the number and level of women an operation may employ. When the Gender Unit in East Timor helped to ensure gender training in the induction sessions for mid- and high-level management as well as for international and national civilian police and other mission personnel, this resulted in better planning and delivery of services for women and men in the host population.[18]

Although training is the primary responsibility of individual governments, the United Nations and regional organizations should ensure consistent approaches and encourage collaboration. Achieving this, in our view, would require a full-fledged review of content as well as strategy: analysing who provides training, who receives it, when it takes place, for how long and with which resources. Ideally, training should take place prior to deployment, but once a mission is assembled, in-service training initiatives can be

extremely useful. The inclusion of gender training in the induction courses for peacekeeping personnel in UNAMSIL, MONUC, UNTAET and UNMEE is encouraging, particularly since the courses involved UN agencies, humanitarian organizations, and local women's groups in the host country.

Some excellent materials have already been developed on gender and peace support operations, including those from the Canadian Department of Foreign Affairs and International Trade and the United Kingdom's Department for International Development.[19] DPKO's Training and Evaluation Service has adapted materials for use in UN field operations and for military personnel and civilian police at the national level. These materials will be complementary to the training programme for civilian peacekeeping personnel on the special needs of women and children, developed by the United Nations Institute for Training and Research. The UN Inter-Agency Standing Committee (IASC) is currently exploring the relevant training activities where sexual abuse and exploitation issues could be integrated and is encouraging the sharing of experiences in an effort to prevent these abuses from happening.

MAKING A DIFFERENCE FOR WOMEN
Protection and assistance

Peace operations protect people at risk by making sure that humanitarian assistance reaches them and by separating armed elements from civilians in camp settings. In many situations peacekeepers are the only ones with access to those in need, whether they are in rebel-controlled territories, in landmine-infested regions or in flight from one conflict area to another. In these circumstances military personnel may be called on to protect the delivery of humanitarian assistance — to protect relief workers and supplies — or even to assess humanitarian conditions.

The systematic targeting of civilians — who now constitute more than 75 per cent of all casualties related to war — led the Security Council to give peacekeepers explicit authority to protect civilians in cases where it is considered appropriate and feasible.[20] As currently constituted, however, UN missions do not have the capacity to protect more than a small fraction of the hundreds of thousands of civilians who are in danger. And without increased resources for international peace operations, this is not likely to change. This is why mandates authorizing the protection of civilians in conflict are often the source of heated debate within the Security Council. "We fought long and hard to include protection in MONUC's mandate," a former Council member told us. "Some members' reluctance was based on the impossibility of doing so with limited resources. Raising expectations without delivery sets the UN back even further." Nevertheless, a mission can enhance its protection capabilities by working with local women's groups and the resident humanitarian community to assess the situation and to better protect and assist women in need.

Gender Responsive Civilian Police and Rule of Law Teams

The potential for rule of law experts to help guarantee women's rights in the process of nation building remains untested, but if they utilize the unique opportunity presented by the peace process to influence the design and reform of the constitution, judiciary, legislation and the policy and electoral process, they can have a profound impact. The Panel on UN Peace Operations recommended that a revolving on-call list of about 100 police officers and related experts should be created by that system to be available on seven days' notice to be sent to conflict areas.

Parallel arrangements with a minimum quota of 30 per cent women should be established for judicial, penal, human rights and other relevant specialists, who will make up rule of law teams with the police. In response to the Panel's recommendation, the UN Executive Committee on Peace and Security has set up a task force for rule of law issues that involves eleven UN agencies and departments collaborating together. This task force will: (1) establish guidelines based on lessons learned by others; (2) develop, improve and maintain a rapid deployment capacity on rule of law; and (3) look for ways in which the UN can better draw on the expertise and resources of other institutions (civil society organizations, universi-

ties, etc.) when carrying out peace operations.

During the first four decades of the UN's existence only three of its peacekeeping missions included civilian police units (CIVPOL). But since the end of the Cold War, civilian police have been part of more than 20 UN peace missions and are second in number only to military personnel. The numbers of female CIVPOL have been extremely low throughout UN peacekeeping history, yet women are an important presence during many criminal investigations, including those involving rape, sexual assault, domestic violence and other crimes against women.

"In my culture, it is not common to talk about sex with men, let alone strange men," a woman in the DRC confided to us. "Many of the women who were raped like I was can identify their attackers, but find it difficult to report them to the police. We can talk to you because you are women like us. But we can't talk about these things with men. If only we had female police in MONUC to whom we can report these horrible things that happened to us."

In East Timor the value of female police also became apparent during the peace process. More than one-third of all criminal complaints received by the UN mission concerned violence against women by family members. Together with the local women's movement, UNTAET's Gender Unit launched an awareness campaign on domestic violence that culminated in the establishment of a special civilian police unit staffed by women to handle cases of rape, domestic violence and other gender related crimes. This created an environment where women felt safer to report cases, especially when — despite limited funds and the shortage of female CIVPOL, female interpreters and female specialists with expertise in this area — a CIVPOL officer was designated as a focal point for gender related crimes in each district.[21]

CIVPOL can do a great deal to combat the increase in trafficking of women that occurs in conflict by establishing better border control. Ironically, however, this is an area where CIVPOL have been accused of complicity and in some cases active involvement. Some positive measures have been taken in recent years. In September 2000 UNMIK established a Trafficking and Prostitution

Investigation Unit which had a presence in all five regions of Kosovo by the end of 2001.[22]

Human rights monitoring is one of the most important but under-utilized ways of improving women's protection. Although human rights components are now systematically included in peacekeeping operations, they often lack necessary resources, human and financial, including gender expertise. If appropriately staffed and resourced, human rights components have the potential to engage in monitoring gender-specific violations and to build capacity through training and other projects that enhance national and local capacity for women's protection.

In Bosnia and Herzegovina and Cambodia we saw new models of community policing that hold promise for increasing women's security in a peacekeeping environment. With support from UNIFEM, women's groups sensitized police forces and community leaders about violence against women. As a result, police now work to prevent domestic violence and trafficking in Cambodia, where one in every six women is a victim of violence by family members.[23] In Bosnia, women could only file complaints against their perpetrators through a public interview procedure. Women's organizations launched a protest campaign, which led the local police to assign a special team that would guarantee the privacy and protection of victims to receive complaints.

Ending Exploitation

The main perpetrators of sexual violence and exploitation in conflict situations are typically the armed forces of parties to a conflict. Although peacekeeping troops have been associated with sexual exploitation and violations, the vast majority of peacekeepers carry out their duties with professionalism and a duty to care. Nevertheless, violations have been documented in Angola, Bosnia and Herzegovina, Cambodia, the DRC, East Timor, Kosovo, Liberia, Mozambique, Sierra Leone and Somalia.

International human rights lawyer Barbara Bedont attributes this exploitation to a convergence of factors. "Peacekeepers are often stationed in post-conflict situations where the state has col-lapsed, the justice system is not operational, crime is rampant, and women are impoverished and vulnerable to abuse. These societies develop into prime routes for trafficking in both drugs and persons. Meanwhile, foreign troops stationed as part of a peacekeeping mission feed a demand for prostitution. As a result, rape, trafficking in women and children, sexual enslavement, and child abuse often co-exist alongside peacekeeping missions."[24]

UN policies are extremely ambiguous in regulating interaction between UN peacekeeping personnel and the local female population, in particular with respect to:

- Sexual relations with women in the host community
- Marriage with local women during the term of duty
- Cohabitation with local women in premises, including live-in employees (e.g. maids)
- Financial and legal responsibility for children parented by peacekeepers
- Prostitution off and on duty
- Minimum age of sexual consent

The most commonly reported abuses involving peacekeepers and local women are those associated with sex work. In Bosnia, it is estimated that internationals — including police monitors, soldiers, mechanics, social workers and aid workers — account for about 30 per cent of brothel revenues.[25] According to Madeleine Rees, head of the Sarajevo office for the UN Office of the High Commissioner for Human Rights (OHCHR), the increased demand for sex workers has led to an increase in trafficking. "Foreigners are charged more than locals and generate disproportionately high profits in the estimated 900-plus brothels across Bosnia," she pointed out. "Stopping the internationals from patronizing brothels is the only thing that will make the trafficking of women less lucrative."[26]

We learned of starving Kosovar Albanian families who, as the demand for young girls increased with the arrival of peacekeepers, sold their daughters into prostitution. More than 1000 girls not yet 15 or 16 years old are reportedly working in Macedonian brothels. In Sierra Leone, the estimates of young girls involved in the sex trade are even higher. "I am the only person who has an income in my family," a 19-year-old commercial sex worker told us in Freetown. "Since UNAMSIL's arrival, I have been able to make enough money to support my family. My clients are mainly peacekeepers. Of course I do not like to trade my body for money, but what choice do I have?"

Often international staff in peace operations employ live-in domestic workers, many of whom are expected to do more than clean house. "They expected much more. And if we didn't have sexual relations, there were many other girls who would," Marija, a young Bosnian, told us. Although some peacekeepers have established more permanent intimate connections with local women, such relationships can rarely be considered purely voluntary, tinged as they are by the necessities of hunger and the need for housing or jobs.

The peace operation's leadership rarely gives much thought to the impact on women, both those who are sex workers and those who have personal relationships with peacekeepers, after the mission leaves. In the UN Transitional Authority in Cambodia in the early 1990s, many international personnel took "wives" whom they lived with while they were in the country, a practice that has been common in other areas with UN peacekeepers. Once the personnel left, the women were ostracized by a society which had "strict ideals … about women's virtue."[27] A decade later, we met women in Cambodia who still spoke about the shame heaped on women who had lived with peacekeepers.

Nor has peacekeeping leadership developed a comprehensive policy to deal with the rising numbers of children born of peacekeeping personnel. In Liberia 6,600 children have been registered as being fathered by peacekeepers between 1990 and 1998.[28] In Kosovo popular songs played on the radio warn young girls against having children by peacekeepers.[29] Children of peacekeeping personnel may never see their fathers and are often stigmatized. They usually grow up in poverty and face rejection from their family and community. Many end up living and working on the streets. In some countries, they may not even be granted citizenship.

Meanwhile some reports indicate that up to 46,000 military and police working as UN peacekeepers around the world are more likely to contract HIV than be killed in action.[30] Security Council Resolution 1308 (2000) recognized the need to incorporate HIV/AIDS prevention awareness skills and advice in aspects of DPKO's training for peacekeeping personnel.

Codes of Conduct, Accountability and Justice

When UN personnel commit actual crimes such as rape or trafficking, it is often difficult to bring them to justice. Under the 1946 Convention on the Privileges and Rights of the United Nations, UN personnel and experts have immunity from legal processes.[31] The contributing country retains exclusive criminal jurisdiction over military personnel. As Barbara Bedont indicates, "History has shown that contributing states are remiss in prosecuting their soldiers."[32] In fact, even though the only recourse is to send personnel home when violations occur, this rarely happens for fear of adverse political consequences and because missions are typically understaffed. The UN Head of Mission does not have any authority to discipline troops, but only general responsibility for conduct,[33] which includes setting standards, training troops and investigating but not punishing misconduct.[34]

The United Nations does not keep systematic records of accusations against peacekeepers, and while there is a provision for immunity in the Status of Force Agreements (SOFA), there is also an obligation on the part of DPKO to demand and for Member States to supply the information about those soldiers repatriated due to misbehaviour.

Prosecutions carried out by the soldier's home country are generally not made public because they take place in military courts, which are closed procedures. As a result, much of the information on crimes committed by peacekeepers must be drawn from press accounts and reports of human rights organizations, or generalized from the few countries that have dealt with the actions of their peacekeepers.

In issuing the Bulletin on Observance by United Nations Forces of International

Humanitarian Law, the Secretary-General took an important step towards holding peacekeeping personnel accountable under international law.[35] But the full impact of this Bulletin is limited by the fact that, while it must be advocated through the Secretary-General's Special Representative to all staff in the peacekeeping operation, enforcement is still left up to troop-contributing states.

Short of legal action, peacekeepers are held accountable to the UN Code of Personal Conduct for Blue Helmets[36] which, according to Radhika Coomaraswamy, the UN Special Rapporteur on Violence against Women, does not sufficiently protect women from sexual exploitation and trafficking.[37] Although codes of conduct can be useful tools for deterring peacekeeping violations, this code is a skeletal outline of basic human rights principles and trivializes violations against women, referring to "immoral acts of sexual, physical or psychological abuse."

Other codes aiming to regulate the conduct of peacekeeping personnel, particularly in field operations, are also inadequate. For example, the Peacekeeping Handbook for Junior Ranks gives no information on the legal repercussions of becoming involved with locals, and instead offers only the most general advice: "Be forewarned of facing long sexual abstinence. Do not involve yourself in any sexual relationship, which may create long-lasting complications for you and others. Do not involve yourself with a sexual affair with any member of the local population."

With mixed results, some peace operations have tried to enforce these codes. The UN missions in Bosnia and Herzegovina (UNMIBH) and in Kosovo (UNMIK) adopted a "zero tolerance" policy for staff members involved in trafficking or prostitution. According to the missions, this means that allegations of misconduct are investigated and disciplinary action is taken for those found guilty. We have yet to learn of any prosecutions, but a former U.S. policewoman with UNMIBH was dismissed after she reported the "extensive use" of brothels by UN police and other peacekeepers in Bosnia.[38] Though the police offi-cer was later vindicated, only eight of the alleged perpetrators were sent home and none has been prosecuted.[39]

In response to allegations made about its peacekeeping personnel, UNAMSIL established a Coordination Committee for the Prevention of Sexual Exploitation and Abuse. This Committee includes representatives of UN agencies, NGOs and the government who will look into allegations of sexual abuse. UNAMSIL now requires all newly arrived peacekeepers to participate in a sensitization programme dealing with appropriate sexual

> "In my culture, it is not common to talk about sex with men, let alone strange men," a woman in the DRC confided. "Many of the women who were raped like I was can identify their attackers, but find it difficult to report them to the police. If only we had female police in MONUC to whom we can report these horrible things that happened to us."

conduct. While these are clearly important steps, they do not in any way substitute for a full-fledged disciplinary mechanism.

To increase the protection of women in peacekeeping environments, we support the Secretary-General's call to establish an Ombudsperson in every peace operation who would handle reports of abuse by peacekeeping personnel. Together with an Inspector General or an office set up specifically for this purpose, she or he could carry out investigations and impose disciplinary measures in cooperation with the SRSG, the Force Commander and the Office of Internal Oversight Services. In all instances, a community relations office with national staff, similar to the model established in the Cambodia mission, should act as liaison with the host community and facilitate the complaints process.

The International Criminal Court offers one means of ensuring the accountability of peacekeepers. In a Relationship Agreement between the

ICC and the United Nations, the latter has promised to cooperate with and assist the work of the Court. Specifically, Article 19 of the Agreement states that:

" ... the Court exercises its jurisdiction over a natural person who is alleged to be criminally responsible for a crime or crimes within the jurisdiction of the Court and who, pursuant to the provisions of the Charter of the United Nations, the Convention on the Privileges and Immunities of the United Nations or other agreements concluded by the Organization, enjoys privileges and immunities in connection with his or her work for the Organization, the United Nations undertakes to cooperate with the Court in such a case or cases and, if necessary, will waive the privileges and immunities of the person or persons concerned in accordance with the provisions of the relevant instruments."

The Statute offers ample safeguards against politically motivated prosecutions and is relevant only when national authorities fail to act. But on 12 July 2002, the possibility of ensuring accountability was postponed for one year when the U.S. government tied immunity for its peacekeepers to the renewal of the mandate of the UN Mission in Bosnia and Herzegovina. By agreeing to delay the implementation of this article, the Security Council is sending the wrong message: that those who commit crimes against women can do so without fear of punishment. For as long as the Statute's authorization to prosecute peacekeepers is delayed, so too is justice for women.

5

RECOMMENDATIONS

ON WOMEN AND PEACE OPERATIONS THE EXPERTS CALL FOR:

1. Gender experts and expertise to be included at all levels and in all aspects of peace operations, including technical surveys and the design of concepts of operation, training, staffing and programmes. To this end, a Memorandum of Understanding should set out the roles and responsibilities among the Department of Peacekeeping Operations (DPKO), the Department of Political Affairs (DPA), the United Nations Development Fund for Women (UNIFEM) and the Division for the Advancement of Women (DAW).

2. A review of training programmes on and approaches to the gender dimensions of conflict resolution and peace-building for humanitarian, military and civilian personnel. United Nations entities active in this area should lead this process with support provided by the Special Advisor on Gender Issues and Advancement of Women and the Task Force on Women, Peace and Security with a view to developing guidance on training policy and standards.

3. All UN peace operations to include a human rights monitoring component, with an explicit mandate and sufficient resources to investigate, document and report human rights violations against women.

4. The improvement and strengthening of codes of conduct for international and local humanitarian and peacekeeping personnel and for these codes to be consistent with international humanitarian and human rights law and made compulsory. An office of oversight for crimes against women should be established in all peace operations. The office should regularly monitor and report on compliance with the principles set forth in the Inter-Agency Standing Committee (IASC) Task Force on the Protection from Sexual Exploitation and Abuse in Humanitarian Crises.

5. No exemptions for peacekeepers from prosecution by international tribunals, the International Criminal Court and national courts in the host country for all crimes committed, including those against women. All states maintaining peacekeeping forces should take necessary measures to bring to justice their own nationals responsible for such crimes, as called for by the Security Council (S/RES/1400 (2002).

6. UN peace operations to improve opportunities for collaboration with women's groups to address gender issues in a peacekeeping environment.

7. Member states and DPKO to increase women's representation in peace operations, including through the recruitment of police, military and civilian personnel.

THE
INDEPENDENT
EXPERTS'
ASSESSMENT
ON

organizing for peace

History will acknowledge the crucial role of women human rights defenders in building up sane and safe societies . . . Which values are we betraying when exposing crimes committed in our name by our own governments? Certainly not the values that are enshrined in each and every one of our constitutions – values that our governments and armies so often trample. Rather than "traitors," we are the very guardians of these values.

— Marieme Helie-Lucas
Founder, Women Living Under Muslim Laws [1]

In April of 1915, World War I had been raging across Europe for nine months. According to some estimates, more than 5,500 soldiers died every day in a war that would ultimately leave 8.5 million dead.[2] Many people were numbed by the devastation, but a group of women activists decided they could not sit and wait for the end of war. Instead — for the first time in history — women crossed borders in wartime to talk about how to end the carnage. They gathered in The Hague, over 1,000 women from 12 warring and neutral countries, and convened the first International Congress of Women (ICW). Their plan of action did not simply call for universal disarmament and an end to the war. It demanded equality between women and men and

PHOTO BY CHARLES DHARAPAK–AP/WIDE WORLD

PROGRESS OF THE WORLD'S WOMEN 2002 • **77**

among nations, and the creation of a non-partisan international organization to mediate disputes between countries.[3]

The ICW sent 30 delegates on the first women's peace mission to bring the plan of action to the heads of European states. Meanwhile, ICW president Jane Addams, who later won the Nobel Peace Prize for her efforts,[4] met with US President Woodrow Wilson, providing him with many of the "14 points" that he took to the Versailles talks that ended the war.[5] ICW participants went on to form the Women's International League for Peace and Freedom (WILPF), which is still active today.[6]

Contemporary women's peace missions are rarely greeted with the deference that heads of state accorded the delegates from the International Congress of Women. But this indifference has not stopped women from organizing for peace. They are still active, and their work is still just as vital. Throughout our journey — in the Mano River countries of Guinea, Liberia and Sierra Leone; in the Middle East and Latin America; in the Balkans, Cambodia, East Timor, and the Great Lakes region of Africa (Burundi, the eastern Democratic Republic of the Congo and Rwanda) — we met brave and tireless women who had much in common with the women of the ICW. They shared the ability to see beyond national boundaries, even while their governments maintained isolationist or pro-war positions. They shared a vision of peace based on respect for the dignity of the individual, regardless of nationality, ethnicity or economic background. And they shared the understanding that peace is linked inextricably with equality between women and men, a concept introduced by the ICW and recognized some 85 years later in a statement made by Security Council President Anwarul Karim Chowdhury of Bangladesh on International Women's Day, 8 March 2000: "Members of the Security Council … affirm that the equal access and full participation of women in power structures and their full involvement in all efforts for the prevention and resolution of conflicts are essential for the maintenance and promotion of peace and security."[7] We were inspired by the women peace activists we met, who were working steadfastly in the midst of deadly conflict, undeterred by threats to their safety, limited resources or their marginalization by decision makers.

Women have sacrificed their lives for peace. They have challenged militarism and urged reconciliation over retribution. They have opposed the development, testing and proliferation of nuclear weapons, other weapons of mass destruction and the small arms trade. They have contributed to peacebuilding as activists, as community leaders, as survivors of the most cataclysmic horrors of war. They have transformed peace processes on every continent by organizing across political, religious and ethnic affiliations. But their efforts are rarely supported or rewarded.

"Women are half of every community … Are they, therefore, not also half of every solution?" asked Dr. Theo-Ben Gurirab, Namibia's Minister of Foreign Affairs, who acted as President of the Security Council during October 2000 when Resolution 1325 was unanimously passed. It is a question that needs answering, for despite their peace-building efforts, women are rarely present at the peace table. It takes fierce determination and intense lobbying for them to be included as participants in transitional governments. Political parties that are building democracy rarely turn to them.

WOMEN'S PEACE WORK
Grass-Roots Organizing

Women's leadership role is most visible in their communities; it is here that they organize to end conflict and build the skills necessary for peace-building and reconstruction. "The role of women in the overthrow of the regime was extremely important," said Stasa Zajovic from the Serbian peace group Women in Black, which is also part of an international network. For years, Women in Black members stood in silence outside government offices, holding placards calling for peace and denouncing the government of Slobodan Milosevic. Stones were thrown at them, they were spat upon, beaten, and arrested, yet every week they returned and stood in silent witness. "By turning our discontent into public demonstrations and acts of civil disobedience, we transformed ethical principles into concrete acts of disloyalty towards the regime," stated Zajovic. "Along with many other women's organizations operating in war zones, we built networks of solidarity combining feminism and anti-militarism. We created alternative women's policy on the local, regional and global level, entering women's resistance to war and militarism into alternative history."

The government did everything it could to isolate the group. "They demonized us so much that the people were afraid of us," said Zajovic. A turning point came when Women in Black was awarded the Millennium Peace Prize by International Alert and UNIFEM: "After the Prize, women from inside the country, in small towns and villages, were proud of us for the first time."

Efforts like those of Women in Black as well as many other civil society groups created and run by women provide a visible alternative to violence and hatred. Women create campaigns and demonstrations, institute human rights reporting, lobby for ceasefires and build networks to care for victims of war. For Ruth building peace in her village outside of Freetown, Sierra Leone, meant taking in the children of neighbours, friends or family members who were killed in the war. For Tatiana in Kosovo peace work meant rebuilding damaged houses as well as friendships with former neighbours who had turned against her during the conflict. In Bosnia women have established mobile health clinics to provide gynaecological and psychosocial care to women survivors of rape and assault, most of whom had never seen a doctor or a counsellor. In Colombia, we joined some 20,000 women organized by the new National Movement of Women Against the War in a march to demand an end to a conflict that kills approximately 3,500 each year. Their protest, "We won't give birth to more sons to send to war," rang through the streets of Medellín. Mercedes Vargas, a teacher and union leader, travelled eight hours by bus from the provincial capital of Manizales to join the demonstration. "The women have something in common," she told us. "We want peace. We are here demanding a negotiated end to this conflict."

In some conflicts, women's social status becomes a basis for organizing. In Kosovo we met Sonia, who was part of a group of widows that met regularly. "As widows, we share a lot in common," she told us. "We struggle to claim our inheritance from our late husbands' families and, sometimes, even the custody of our children. We want to know where our husbands are buried so we pressure the authorities to investigate their disappearances. And we turn to each other to help raise our children and the orphans who lost both parents to the war."

AVEGA, the association of Rwandan widows, originally met under a tree in Kigali. Within a week of their first gathering, more than 50 women had joined. Like so many other self-help and humanitarian organizations created by women, the association provides psychological and social support and health services to its members. As one member told us, "We've always faced uncertainty, but had to carry on with our lives and care for Rwanda's children. Otherwise, what would happen to the next generation? But widows of the genocide in Rwanda are discriminated against and blamed for the HIV epidemic. With little help from the government or local authorities, we have little choice but to rebuild our nation and try to heal the wounds ourselves."[8]

Many women believe it is a mistake to use social categories when offering support. "It's not only widows who are raising children by themselves, caring for the sick and elderly, or struggling to claim their lost property," said Elsie, the leader of a non-governmental organization (NGO) in Rwanda, who is raising a child born of rape. "Many women in this village have come together to support each other. They all have special needs and different fears. They don't want to be divided or privileged differently because of their social status — because one lost her husband to war, and another never married. What about Sophie, who is supporting her family and her husband who is sick with HIV/AIDS, and Cenina, whose husband fled the village in fear of retaliation by other village members?"

Organizing Across Borders

Women's organizing at the grass-roots level often lays the groundwork for organizing across borders — in sub-regions and internationally. The Mano River Union Women's Network for Peace, which has members from Guinea, Liberia and Sierra Leone, brings together high-level women from established political networks as well as grass-roots women, all searching for a way to end the fighting that has debilitated their three countries. "Women's networks have been pivotal in the resolution of the conflict in Sierra Leone, and in getting negotiations started between the Mano River countries," said Isha Dyfan, an activist from Sierra Leone.

Dyfan is a former member of the Women's Forum, which was created long before the war started in Sierra Leone in 1991. Because the Forum had already brought women together, "we were able to raise our voices and opinions to the highest level. Our national network helped us to reach out regionally and internationally," said Dyfan. Eventually the Sierra Leonean women became involved in the regional Mano River Union Women's Network for Peace, the continent-wide Federation of African Women's Peace Networks (FERFAP), which was created with support from UNIFEM, and with WILPF on the international level.

Women in Black, founded in Israel in 1988, has become a model for a different kind of cross-border organizing. Women in Black groups, like the one Zajovic is part of in Serbia, exist around the world, creating an international network of women with a shared vision of peace and demilitarization. Support from the network provides a measure of solidarity for members in many countries who confront regimes bent on aggression.

International conferences can provide a similar sense of solidarity. Luz Mendez, one of the few women to participate in Guatemala's official peace negotiations, told us how important it was for her to meet other activists at the 1995 Fourth World Conference on Women in Beijing: "I had felt so isolated during the negotiations in Guatemala. In Beijing, I found many other women sharing the same struggles. I returned invigorated, with new ideas and strategies. And I had an international platform to support my arguments."

GETTING TO THE PEACE TABLE

On 2 May 2000 92 Somali women stood outside a huge military tent in the town of Arta, Djibouti. The Somali National Peace Conference was about to begin, the fourteenth attempt since 1991 to find a peaceful solution to the civil war. The women had been chosen to be part of delegations representing traditional clans, but their ultimate goal was to break out of clan-based allegiances. "We knew that peace in our country would come from cross-clan reconciliation, not official negotiations among warlords and faction leaders," one delegate told us during our visit to the country a year later. "So we cared for the wounded and built schools in communities regardless of clan, ethnic and political affiliations."

At the Conference, the women presented themselves as a 'sixth clan' (delegations came from four major clans and a coalition of minor ones) that reached beyond ethnicity to a "vision of gender equality," said Asha Hagi Elmi, a leader of the Sixth Clan Coalition. "In Arta, we presented 'buranbur' — a special poetic verse sung by women — to show the suffering of women and children during 10 years of civil war. We lobbied for a quota for women in the future legislature, the Transitional National Assembly (TNA). But we faced opposition from the male delegates, who told us that no man would agree to be represented by women."

But the women did not give up easily and ultimately helped create a National Charter that guaranteed women 25 seats in the 245-member TNA, and protected the human rights of women, children and minorities as well. Although the Charter has yet to be implemented, as a document it "ranks among the top in the region and the best in the Muslim world," said Hagi Elmi.[9]

As the Somali women's experience shows, it is not easy to translate women's activism into a presence at the peace table. Certainly not all women's groups want to be at the table if it involves negotiating with the warlords or tyrants who helped create the conflict, but most peace activists feel that women's presence is essential. Yet women are rarely included in formal negotiations, whether as members of political parties, civil society or special interest groups. Their organizing efforts are ignored, as are their roles as combatants and political leaders in national liberation movements. In Colombia, despite the fact that as many as 30 per cent of the fighters of the Revolutionary Armed Forces of Colombia (FARC) are women, FARC included only one woman, Mariana Paez, among its representatives to official negotiations with the government.[10] Women were absent from the Dayton peace talks that ended the war in Bosnia and Herzegovina.[11]

According to Inonge Mbikusita Lewanika, President of FERFAP, "Women establish their credibility as peacemakers at the grass-roots level but they are marginalized from official negotiations. Making it from the grass mat to the peace table has nothing to do with their qualifications as peacemakers. Once the foreign mediators come and the official negotiations start, you have to be able to sit at the table and speak their language. Often women are not trained or given the chance."

When women are present, the nature of the dialogue changes. Women's concerns come not merely out of their own experiences but out of their rootedness in their communities. They represent different constituencies: those in need of education, of health care, of jobs and of land. They have a different experience of war from male fighters and politicians.

Former U.S. Senator George Mitchell, who mediated the Northern Ireland peace talks, credits women with helping to achieve an agreement in those negotiations: "The emergence of women as a political force was a significant factor in achieving the agreement. Women were among the first to express their weariness of the conflict.... The two women that made it to the [negotiating] table had a tough time at first. They were treated quite rudely by some of the male politicians ... Through their own perseverance and talent, by the end of the process they were valued contributors. When the agreement included the creation of a new Northern Ireland Assembly, women got elected there too. Overall, in achieving the level of stability now enjoyed, women's involvement at all levels was a very important factor."[12]

Training and Facilitating

Throughout our visits, when we did meet women who had made it to the peace table and beyond, it was through a combination of women's organizing and support from the international community. International organizations that support women's activism have seen that, as FERFAP president Inonge Mbikusita Lewanika indicates, women need training and preparation to open the doors that are consistently shut in their faces. Organizations such as Search for Common Ground, International Alert, the U.S. Institute for Peace and many other groups have been providing training for women to develop negotiation skills and leadership.

International groups have also become facilitators, helping to bring together groups of women so they can plan strategy as well as learn new leadership skills. UNIFEM is one of the pioneers of this approach, particularly in Burundi where it forged a partnership with the NGOs International Alert and Search for Common Ground. This type of capacity-building work led to the All-Party Burundi Women's Peace Conference, convened by UNIFEM and the Mwalimu Julius Nyerere Foundation in July 2000 in Arusha, Tanzania. Despite restrictions on Burundians leaving the country, the delegates found ways to get there, because it would be one of the last chances for women to affect the peace accords, which all-male delegations had been hammering out for four years. Winnie Byanyima, a Ugandan Member of Parliament, who served as a facilitator at the Women's Conference, described the importance of the meeting:

"The men who had been negotiating didn't feel that women had any right to be there. These men felt they had a right to be there because they were fighters, or had been elected to some parliament before the war escalated. Burundi women who had suffered so much didn't have any legitimacy in their eyes. But by bringing in women the documents have more legitimacy now. People from the grass roots have made their input to the future. The conference created a space that was necessary but lacking, not only between women in political parties and women working for peace and reconciliation at the grass-roots level, but also between international facilitators and women."

Since that meeting, the process has been replicated in other parts of the Great Lakes region. In 2001 UNIFEM was asked by Sir Ketumile Masire, the former President of Botswana, and the facilitator of the Inter-Congolese Dialogue to help develop methods for promoting women's participation in the Dialogue. Two sessions were convened, providing training to women on the gender dimensions of constitutional, electoral and judicial reform. Ultimately, 40 women from government, opposition parties and civil society participated in the Sun City talks in March 2002.

International organizations can also be facilitators, bringing different groups together for working sessions. A particularly successful partnership enabled Afghan women in the diaspora to meet with women from inside the country to develop an agenda on how to contribute to national reconstruction. With the fall of the Taliban, it was essential that women meet quickly. They had to get to know international donors who were supporting reconstruction and they had to get to know each other so they could present their demands for women's participation as a united front.

In December 2001 Equality Now, the European Women's Lobby, V-Day, the Center for Strategic Initiatives of Women and The Feminist Majority Foundation all hosted the Afghan Women's Summit for Democracy in Brussels, in collaboration with the Gender Advisor to the Secretary-General of the United Nations and UNIFEM. At its conclusion, 40 women participated in a two-day Women's Roundtable, hosted by UNIFEM and the Belgian Government, which brought the women together with donors and heads of UN agencies. The Brussels Action Plan — which included recommendations on education, media and culture, health, refugees and internally displaced persons and human rights and the constitution — was adopted, and informed the UN Transitional Assistance Programme for Afghanistan in 2002.

Quotas: Tradition and cultural practices can present formidable obstacles to the inclusion of women in peace processes or post-war governance unless a formal mechanism is in place to support this. To date, the use of quotas has been one of the most successful methods for guaranteeing a minimum percentage of women in official negotiations as well as in government positions. We visited many countries where the use of quotas had brought women into the political process. As noted above, quotas ensured Somali women's participation at the Arta peace conference.[13] In Mozambique the Organizacáo da Mulher Mocambicana, created in 1973, still recruits women for decision-making positions, and women now make up 30 per cent of Mozambique's legislative bodies. Similarly, in South Africa, the African National Congress's commitment to a party quota resulted in 29 per cent representation of women in the nation's first parliamentary elections in 1994.

The Beijing Platform for Action (PFA) calls for a 30 per cent minimum representation of women in decision-making bodies, and Security Council Resolution 1325 urges the appointment of women in decision-making bodies and peace processes. Some NGOs have expressed dissatisfaction at the 30 per cent minimum, especially when considering the lack of progress since Beijing. Instead, they call for parity, with a range of 45 to 55 per cent as acceptable in a democracy.

But the international community has been equivocal at best about honouring the calls for either formal or informal quotas. The United Nations has not always supported quotas in countries with UN mandated transitional governments. Within the organization itself, only one woman currently serves as a Special Representative of the Secretary-General. In East Timor women's groups overwhelmingly supported quotas for the national election when they met at the National Congress of Women, held prior to the elections.[14] But we were informed by several women that the UN's Department of Political Affairs (DPA) told the transitional government that the UN did not support quotas.[15]

"At one stage we were told that they would pull out and would not run the elections in East Timor if we insisted on quotas," Milena Pires, Deputy

Speaker of the East Timor National Council, told us. "We had comments from two missions that I know of that considered that gender was a luxury in East Timor. In the end we offered training, with UNIFEM's support, to more than 160 potential women candidates for the constituent assembly, and 24 women were elected out of 88 members. However, now there have been replacements. One political party decided that the woman they had placed first on their list wasn't able to represent their interests, so they replaced her with a man who came after her on the list."

Quotas alone cannot guarantee the emergence of a "gender perspective" in the political process—although one is more likely to develop when a critical mass of women are in decision-making positions. We recognize that, especially when numbers are small and cultural barriers enormous, quotas can only put women in power; they cannot guarantee that grass-roots concerns will be addressed. In Bosnia several women parliamentarians told us they did not support action to legislate parental leave because they believed in women's traditional role in the family. The Minister of Foreign Trade agreed with them: "Just because I am a woman," she told us, "I will not fight for women's rights."

These disconnects may occur for many reasons. They may be the result of a lack of communication, outreach and advocacy. Sometimes they are due to continued violence, or a lack of financial and operational support from donors and national governments that should be promoting gender issues at all levels. Quotas must be seen as a temporary solution to increase gender balance. They are a first step on the path to gender equality, both a practical and a symbolic measure to support women's leadership. But they cannot replace long-term strategies that address the socio-economic constraints that keep women from participating in the political process.

RESTORING THE RULE OF LAW AND WOMEN'S ACCESS TO JUSTICE

Peace negotiations and post-conflict reconstruction must do more than focus on ending warfare.

The nation-building process that is mandated by the peace agreement should include the revision of key laws in order to recognize women's contributions, to build gender equality and to protect women. Failing to establish a firm foundation built on law increases the danger of chronic instability and collapse into violent confrontation all over again. Support for the rule of law, multi-party systems and elections have become the benchmarks of peace-building. Without these women cannot live in safety.

For Ruth building peace in her village outside of Freetown, Sierra Leone, meant taking in the children of neighbours, friends or family members killed in the war. For Tatiana in Kosovo peace work meant rebuilding damaged houses as well as friendships with former neighbours who had turned against her during the conflict. In Bosnia women have established mobile health clinics to provide gynaecological and psychosocial care to women survivors of rape and assault, most of whom had never seen a doctor or a counsellor.

In many places we visited, threats from armed groups, including the national military, have drastically reduced women's ability to work for peace. In Colombia, we met with the daughter of a murdered political activist; her mother had ignored warnings from paramilitaries to drop out of a local city council race. In August 2000 paramilitaries burst into their house and forcibly removed the woman and her husband. When their children went to the police to report the disappearance, they were beaten and told to go home. The bodies of the parents were later found in the town dump.

Constitutional Reform

No matter how many women are included in peace negotiations or the reforms that may ensue, it is up to all participants, women and men, to ensure that gender issues are addressed at all levels. Gender equality should be enshrined in a nation's constitution and bill of rights and be specified in all relevant clauses, including those setting up the parliament, the executive and the judiciary branches. The Convention on the Elimination of All Forms of Discrimination against Women (CEDAW) is the core international document for women's rights, but a full range of guarantees are set out in other treaties and consensus documents. These include the International Covenant on Economic, Social and Cultural Rights, the Convention on the Elimination of All Forms of Racial Discrimination and the International Covenant on Civil and Political Rights, as well as the Convention on the Rights of the Child and the Beijing Platform for Action. Women have a right to expect that all of these will be reflected in post-conflict constitutions that embody the needs of the local population. In Guatemala the peace accords spelled out the government's responsibility to revise national legislation to eliminate discrimination against women using CEDAW as a guide, although, as with other aspects of the peace accords, this has not been carried out.[16]

The constitution should contain simple and clear language so it is accessible to all, not just legal scholars. It should be written with gender-sensitive rather than neutral language to avoid ambiguity and to ensure fairness and equality. Translating the document into local languages ensures that all the different ethnicities within a country are aware of their rights.

Typically, producing a gender-sensitive constitution is a hard-fought effort. Women's networks, supported by international organizations that can supply the knowledge and the funds, have been central in the fight. In Rwanda a Legal and Constitutional Commission is responsible for reforming the old constitution. Three of the twelve commissioners are women, and women make up more than 50 per cent of the Commission's employees. Both the United Nations Development Programme (UNDP) and UNIFEM have provided support, including training on CEDAW which, the women told us, provided a focus for their efforts.

In Cambodia UNIFEM-supported consultations among women have led to constitutional protections for rural women, equal pay for domestic workers and paid maternity leave. Like Cambodia, East Timor was a nation with almost nothing left when the fighting ended. Women's groups got together to make their needs clear and a coalition of national and international organizations, such as Oxfam and the Asia Foundation, helped establish a Gender and Constitution Working Group that developed a ten-article Charter of Women's Rights. Nine of the ten articles were adopted into the Constitution, which guarantees, among other things, social, health and educational rights, equal access to traditional law and protection from domestic violence. It also provides citizenship protections for children born of rape.

Electoral Issues

Constitutional and political reform must ensure women's citizenship and their right to vote and stand for public office. Quotas and proportional representation on ballots can help elect women into office. Proportional representation encourages voters to focus on parties and their policies, rather than on particular individuals, so women candidates are less likely to be defeated by bias and negative stereotypes.

In East Timor when the UN Transitional Administration (UNTAET) informed women's groups that they would not be able to use quotas in the national election, activists looked for other ways to get women elected. UNIFEM and the UNTAET gender adviser put together a training workshop for women who would consider running for office. "We planned for about 50 women and one workshop," Lorraine Corner, the UNIFEM regional advisor in Bangkok told us. "But we were afraid no one would come. In fact, we had 180 applications and had to expand the number of workshops."

Along with helping to support the workshops, the then UN Special Representative, Sergio Vieira de Mello, used incentives to get women on the ballot. He promised transportation and media access — space in newspapers, ads on radio and television — to those parties that not only ran women candidates but put them near the top of their lists. "Only a few of the women we trained got into office," said Sherrill Whittington, the UNTAET gender adviser, "but that turned out not to be the point. They went back to their towns and ran voter education workshops for women. They are preparing a new generation of women to vote and to run for office."

Judicial Reforms

Women seeking post-war justice and a new national standard for their legal protection can draw upon the precedents set by international courts, as well as on international customary law and even on non-binding tribunals. War crimes trials in national courts can play an important role in judicial reform by helping to rebuild the judiciary and the criminal justice system: Lawyers and judges may be put in place who know and respect international humanitarian law, and open court proceedings become a model for the future. It is also essential to monitor human rights in the immediate post-war phase so that the highest possible standard of law is enforced.

However, national judicial systems in post-conflict societies have rarely delivered for women. Most investigations at the national level do not focus on violations against women. When they do, they lack both the systems and the capacity to carry out forensic investigations. The judiciary often do not protect female witnesses from reprisal, enforce sentences or offer compensation. And too often, judicial systems discriminate against women by discounting the violence they experience, indulging in sexual innuendo and humiliating them in the courtroom.

In Cambodia, Croatia and Kosovo, UNIFEM-supported women's groups have worked with the judiciary to sensitize judges and lawyers. But much more can be done. Legal literacy programmes can help raise women's awareness about the operation of the courts and the judicial system. Police units trained to recognize and investigate crimes against women can enhance legal access. Counselling programmes can advance the process of healing and reconstruction.

IMPLEMENTATION

It has become clear to us during our visits to conflict areas that peace agreements, electoral and judicial reform and government restructuring are only as good as their implementation. Time and again women described the wonderful documents that had been created and signed — and the failure to implement most of what had been promised. Asha Hagi Elmi of Somalia correctly calls the National Charter of Somalia "one of the best in the Muslim world" in terms of women's rights. Yet Somalia today is one of the most dangerous places on earth, still ruled by warring factions that have no commitment to honouring the Charter.

In spite of the ground-breaking contributions made by women's groups in Burundi, Liberia and many other areas, the gender equity mechanisms created during peace negotiations often remain weak.

> **In conflict situations, political activists and their organizations frequently face security threats; many have been killed and many more abducted, beaten and tortured. Women are particularly vulnerable, first because they are subject to sexual attacks in addition to the other dangers, and second because they are often seen as stepping outside their traditional role – which can lend cultural justification to the idea that they need to be 'taught a lesson.'**

Renewed violence can stop implementation in its tracks. In Guatemala, according to Luz Mendez, the coordinator of the National Union of Guatemalan Women, "almost five years after the signing of the peace accords, the majority of the commitments referring to women have not been implemented." Many women's groups believe the government is unwilling to honour its promises to women, as well as other aspects of the peace agreement.

In the peace accords the Guatemalan Government committed to promoting legal reform that included the classification of sexual harassment as a criminal offense. "If the offense is committed against an indigenous woman, it is considered an aggravation in determining the penalty," Mendez told us, because indigenous women "confront higher levels of gender-based violence as a result of their double discrimination, both as women and as indigenous people."

Indigenous women's groups have been lobbying unsuccessfully since the accords were first signed to have this reform approved. "This experience erodes people's trust in the peace process. It is extremely important to support the strengthening of women's organizations both during the armed conflict and the peace-building so that they will be better prepared to impact the implementation of the peace agreements," Mendez said.

While it is ultimately a state responsibility to honour the agreements that have been signed, and to create an environment in which they can be implemented, the international community also has a role to play. Whether international donors are in a country as advisers, as peace-keepers or as educators, they must keep gender issues at the forefront of their work. They must focus more effort on supporting the implementation process through training, support of women's organizations and capacity-building. Specific mechanisms must be put in place to guarantee women's continued presence through constitutional, judicial, legislative and electoral reforms. And, of course, they must work to guarantee the peace that will allow reforms to be implemented.

WHAT DO WOMEN NEED?

Women's participation in peace processes and new governments, and their efforts to rebuild judicial and civil infrastructure, cannot be achieved unless their organizing is supported. The women organizers we met needed four things to contribute to peace processes and decision-making about security: safety, resources, political space and access to decision makers.

Safety: In conflict situations, political activists and their organizations frequently face security threats; many have been killed and many more abducted, beaten and tortured. Women are particularly vulnerable, first because they are subject to sexual attacks in addition to the other dangers, and second because they are often seen as stepping outside their traditional role — which can lend cultural justification to the idea that they need to be "taught a lesson." Without adequate protection, women are frequently compelled to abandon activism. We suspect this persecution has drastically reduced the number of women's organizations in many places we visited. An enabling environment, that allows organizations and individuals to express their opinions in safety and security, would sustain current activities and encourage more women to become active.

Resources: Almost all the groups we visited, whether they are coping with a country in conflict, in transition or in post-conflict reconstruction, have significant unmet needs. A much larger pool of funds is needed to maximize the potential of women's organizing efforts. In many places we visited, the financial outlay necessary to keep an organization going or enhance its effectiveness would be minimal and the benefits enormous. Women told us that just a computer or a cell phone, or even some paper and books, would make a major difference in their work. There is often fierce competition for humanitarian and development resources, which does not enhance collaboration between groups. Longer-term investments in human resources would be more expensive, but no less crucial. Often, foundations and donors will only fund projects and not the ongoing costs of maintaining staff and institutions, making it nearly impossible for long-term endeavours to develop properly. However, support should not be thought of as only material aid. Frequently, even activists with very limited resources emphasized that international political solidarity and messages of support are priceless.

While UNIFEM has been able to provide funds to "innovative and catalytic" programmes, it cannot begin to meet all the challenges it confronts on its current budget. It is operational in only a handful of countries. We returned from our journey more convinced than ever that women's peace work reinforces the broader effort to extend and protect human rights and expands the political space that allows women to address gender issues. We believe that ensuring the support this work needs and deserves will require a dedicated pool of funds, such as a United Nations Trust Fund. This fund would be able to leverage the political, financial and technical support women's civil society organizations and women leaders need so they can have a significant impact on peace efforts nationally, regionally and internationally.

Political Space: Sometimes ensuring that women play an important role in building peace requires carving out space and time for a women-only gathering. Recent initiatives show what can be accomplished with foresight and funding. To enhance the participation of women in the Inter-Congolese Dialogue (ICD), Femme Afrique Solidarite and WOPPA-DRC (Women As Partners for Peace in Africa — Democratic Republic of the Congo) created space for women to find common ground. These cross-party meetings gave women an opportunity to develop a joint declaration and plan of action that offered a gender perspective to the Dialogue. Thanks to the political space provided by UNIFEM, a similar consensus was achieved by women observers of the Burundi peace process, many of whose recommendations were included in the final document.

Access to decision makers: While activists and NGOs are often viewed as a source of innovative ideas and information, governments and international organizations sometimes regard them as a nuisance or even a threat to their interests. Activists who have won an opportunity to meet with decision makers at the national or international level often told us how crucial it was to share information and to build relationships. NGOs have a formal relationship with the United Nations Economic and Social Council (ECOSOC) through Article 71 of the UN Charter. However, the doors to the General Assembly and the Security Council, where peace and security matters are discussed, remain officially closed.

Secretary-General Kofi Annan has called NGOs "the conscience of humanity." To truly become this conscience, the voices of women's organizations must be heard and heeded by governance structures in which they are fully and consistently represented. Kofi Annan understood this when he said at the 2000 meeting to evaluate progress made in implementing the Beijing Platform for Action, "Five years ago, you went to Beijing with a simple statement: 'We are not guests on this planet. We belong here.' Five years on, I would venture that we all know this is an understatement … not only do women belong on this planet … the future of this planet depends on women."

6

RECOMMENDATIONS

ON ORGANIZING FOR PEACE THE EXPERTS CALL FOR:

1. The Secretary-General, in keeping with his personal commitment, to increase the number of women in senior positions in peace-related functions. Priority should be given to achieving gender parity in his appointment of women as Special Representatives and Envoys, beginning with a minimum of 30 per cent in the next three years, with a view to gender parity by 2015.

2. Gender equality to be recognized in all peace processes, agreements and transitional governance structures. International and regional organizations and all participating parties involved in peace processes should advocate for gender parity, maintaining a minimum 30 per cent representation of women in peace negotiations, and ensure that women's needs are taken into consideration and specifically addressed in all such agreements.

3. A United Nations Trust Fund for Women's Peace-building. This Trust Fund would leverage the political, financial and technical support needed for women's civil society organizations and women leaders to have an impact on peace efforts nationally, regionally and internationally. The Fund should be managed by UNIFEM, in consultation with other UN bodies and women's civil society organizations.

4. UNIFEM to work closely with the Department of Political Affairs (DPA) to ensure that gender issues are incorporated in peace-building and post-conflict reconstruction in order to integrate gender perspectives in peace-building and to support women's full and equal participation in decision-making; and for UNFPA to strengthen its work in emergency situations in order to build women's capacity in conflict situations. UNIFEM and UNFPA should be represented in all relevant inter-agency bodies.

5. Peace negotiations and agreements to have a gender perspective through the full integration of women's concerns and participation in peace processes. Women's peace tables should be established and enabled through financial, political and technical assistance.

6. The UN and donors to invest in women's organizations as a strategy for conflict prevention, resolution and peace-building. Donors should exercise flexibility in responding to urgent needs and time-sensitive opportunities, and foster partnerships and networks between international, regional and local peace initiatives.

7. National electoral laws and international electoral assistance to establish quotas to achieve gender parity in decision-making positions, beginning with a minimum of 30 per cent, to ensure voter registration and education for women, to increase the ratio of women in electoral commissions and observer missions and to provide training for women candidates.

This woman, a survivor of genocide, can now own land in Rwanda.

justice

Chantal was living in a UN refugee centre in Goma in the eastern part of the Democratic Republic of the Congo (DRC) when we met her. She was anxious to return to her native Rwanda. At first sight, Chantal could have been any strong young village woman, a farmer from Rwanda's high, steep hills, who brought her produce to market and carried water and wood for miles. But her face was absolutely blank and her eyes stared ahead as she described her last five years deep in the forests of the DRC with a group of Interahamwe militia. The militia used thousands of women like Chantal, kidnapped from Rwanda or local towns and villages in the DRC, as human

shields, as porters, as sex slaves. "We ate when we went to villages," Chantal told us. "We walked and walked in the forest. We carried very heavy loads of what we took from their places. Often there was fighting. Every man raped me."

Most survivors of sexual violence do not talk about it. Chantal was able to tell her story because she felt no risk of stigma or rejection from her husband, family or community; she had already lost everybody. We doubt very much that Chantal will ever see justice done. She is not likely to receive reparations for the violations she suffered, or to see her perpetrators prosecuted. She probably won't receive adequate medical or psychosocial support. Chantal may have contracted HIV/AIDS from the multiple rapes, but it is unlikely that she will ever be tested. Even if she is tested, and is HIV-positive, she will probably not have access to treatment or care. If Chantal has children some day, they may have the chance to go to school, but Chantal herself is not likely to receive any form of education or training. If she makes it back home, she will have to struggle to claim the property she lived on, the inheritance due to her and the possessions she left behind. The chances are very high that Chantal will be raped again.

Our visits to conflict situations confirmed the stark reality that women are being denied justice. With few exceptions, those who commit heinous crimes against women in war are not punished, nor are women granted redress. Worse yet, little is being done to prevent new abuses.

Throughout history soldiers have abducted, raped, tortured and enslaved women in wartime. But attacks against women and girls in contemporary conflicts occur on a greater scale and have reached an even higher level of depravity. They spread terror, destroy families and shatter community cohesiveness. Violence does not happen randomly — it is planned and deliberate. We spoke with women who survived rape, torture, mutilation and assault, and women who lost their families, their homes and their livelihoods. One of the advisers to this report, Isha Dyfan, is a survivor of Sierra Leone's civil war. Dyfan was a public figure in Freetown in the early 1990s, a lawyer and an activist for peace and women's issues. When she received death threats, she sent her daughter to Guinea for safety. One morning Dyfan arrived on the main street in Freetown to find the area around her office in flames. She fled to Guinea, leaving all her possessions behind.

Dyfan is passionate in her support for legal redress for Sierra Leoneans. "No one can put a price tag on what we've lost," she told us. "Our homes, our children's future, the feet and hands cut by diamond-hungry rebels. We cannot be compensated. But now we must begin to rebuild,

and truth and reconciliation are necessary for this. In some ways, justice is an intangible thing. But it is also very concrete and mundane. We hope the Special Court and the Truth and Reconciliation Commission will provide a safe place where the truth can be spoken without fear.

"We need to hear that these atrocities are condemned to at least relieve some of the shame and the grief. It is not just a legal issue. It is about people's lives. Something must be done so the society that was affected by the conflict can invest in peace. That is why we need both a Special Court, to deal with the planners of the war, and a Truth Commission, so that people can speak about what happened."

Increased levels of violence against women continue during the post-conflict period. Criminal activity often thrives in such situations, where law enforcement is weak and there is rarely an effective judicial system. Women are exposed to physical and sexual violence in camps, on the street or in their homes. They may be attacked by returning combatants, neighbours or family members. Women have nowhere to turn: Law enforcement agents, military officials, peacekeeping forces or civilian police may be complicit or themselves guilty of these acts. The failure to prevent and punish such crimes is a betrayal of women on a massive scale.

THE NEED FOR ACCOUNTABILITY

Accountability on the part of states and societies for crimes against women means more than punishing perpetrators. It means establishing the rule of law and a just social and political order. Without this, there can be no lasting peace. Impunity weakens the foundation of societies emerging from conflict by legitimizing violence and inequality. It prolongs instability and injustice and exposes women to the threat of renewed conflict.

Despite the fact that international humanitarian, human rights and refugee law protects women against war-time atrocities, [1] Dr. Kelly D. Askin, Director of the International Criminal Justice Institute, points to the limitations of these laws: "Treaties have been drafted outlawing, in excruciating detail, everything from particular kinds of bullets to the destruction of historical buildings, while maintaining enormous silence or providing only vague provisions on crimes against women." Ultimately, she argues, "provisions are needed in international humanitarian law that take women's experiences of sexual violence as a starting point rather than just a by-product of war."[2]

Rarely have women been consulted about the form, scope and modalities for seeking accountability. Women's stake in these processes has been minimized or denied and, in most cases, crimes against them go unrecorded. In Rwanda, for example, thousands of women were raped and tortured during the genocide. Only a few of the survivors have testified to the sufferings they endured or have seen any attempt to hold the perpetrators accountable.

Historically, women have been underrepresented in judicial processes. Only one woman has served as a judge on the International Court of Justice since it was established more than 80 years ago. The 34-member International Law Commission had no women throughout its 55-year history until 2001, when two women were elected. No more than three women have served at any one time among the 14 permanent judges of the International Criminal Tribunals for the former Yugoslavia (ICTY) and for Rwanda (ICTR). [3]

Impunity for violations against women exposes the weak link in all legal frameworks: accountability is subject to political will. In the DRC women described their frustrations. One activist told us: "Large numbers of atrocities have been committed during the war here, but even now there is no justice. We cannot go to local authorities, as they have no power. We call for the establishment of a truth and reconciliation commission and an international criminal tribunal for the DRC. We know those who have committed war crimes and their accomplices. We will testify to ensure that they are brought to justice. But the Security Council must accelerate its decisions on the situation in our country."

The failure throughout history to deal with crimes committed against women in war has only recently begun to be addressed. The jurisprudence of the ICTY and ICTR are examples of this.

However, change is slow and in many cases non-existent. Those responsible for the enslavement of at least 200,000 girls and women by the Japanese Army during World War II as so-called "comfort women" have never been tried by any local or international court. This glaring injustice led a coalition of grass-roots non-governmental organizations (NGOs) to convene a People's Tribunal in December 2000, a half century after the atrocities were committed. Seventy-five survivors came to testify before the Women's International War Crimes Tribunal on Japan's Military Sexual Slavery. What drove the women to appear before the Tribunal was the wish to tell their story before it was lost to history.

Suhanah, an elderly survivor from Indonesia, was one of those who testified. "I was a virgin. Ten men raped me," she told the Tribunal. "One got off and another replaced him. They treated us like animals." Maxima Regala Dela Cruz from the Philippines also bore witness, after more than 50 years of silence: "We went back home and we were crying. We couldn't tell anyone or we would be executed. It was so shameful so we dug a deep hole and covered it." The outcome of the Tribunal was not legally binding but the goal, as expressed by the organizers, was "not vengeance but justice ... not only for the survivors, but for those who have perished and for generations to come." [4] Trials such as this one can give victims of atrocities the satisfaction of knowing that their grievances are being heard and documented, and that future crimes can be prevented, sanctioned and punished.

Reparations are also important for achieving justice and accountability for women. They may take the form of restitution, compensation, rehabilitation or guarantees that similar crimes will not be committed in the future. State-to-state reparations for violations of humanitarian law are owed to the injured state rather than individual victims, according the International Law Commission, but "the individuals concerned should be regarded as the ultimate beneficiaries and in that sense as the holders of the relevant rights." In other words, if a nation receives reparations for intrusions by an army whose soldiers attacked and exploited women, that nation must ensure that women will be among the beneficiaries of such reparations. Increasingly there are international norms that recognize reparations due to an individual. The UN Commission on Human Rights has appointed a Special Rapporteur on the right to reparations, and principles relating to the right to a remedy have been drafted. In addition, individuals have the right to reparations under Article 75 of the Rome Statute of the International Criminal Court (ICC).

Many obstacles prevent women from seeking justice. They may not have enough money to travel to a trial or the ability to take time off from work or to leave their families; they may be intimidated or disillusioned by the justice system. Support services and legal aid are rarely provided to women, and gender bias within the judicial process — the very process that regulates how equality is achieved in society — prevents women from receiving fair treatment as witnesses, as complainants and in investigations. Women are often blamed for the crimes committed against them and risk retribution for pursuing justice. According to Dr. Askin, "There should be no shame or stigma whatsoever attached to survivors of rape crimes — the shame and dishonour belongs on the physical perpetrator(s) and others responsible for the crimes, and to some extent on the legal, protective, and enforcement systems and global society which have ignored, silenced or otherwise failed to respond appropriately to gender-based crimes."[5]

The social and political instability of judicial systems during conflict and in post-conflict situations further impedes women's access to justice. As structures of power and authority shift, conflicting legal standards and judicial methods may be applied, ranging from international, military and customary laws, to national and traditional approaches to justice. Women confronted with this barrage of contradictory systems may be frustrated in their efforts to seek redress.

Women's rights advocates worldwide have slowly and steadily constructed an international legal framework to address these grievances and concerns. The campaign to end violence against women took root and gained momentum throughout the 1990s on the agendas of UN World Conferences, from Vienna in 1993 to Cairo in 1994 to Beijing in 1995, where the principles for codifying international law on violence against women began to be recognized. Those principles were later tested and articulated in landmark decisions by the International Criminal Tribunals for the Former Yugoslavia and Rwanda and ultimately informed the definition of crimes of sexual violence included in the Rome Statute of the ICC.

Ensuring accountability within the justice system for crimes against women will require a range of strategies. These could be carried out at national, regional or international levels, and through a variety of judicial methods: the ICC, ad hoc tribunals, special courts and tribunals and national justice systems. Non-judicial methods, such as truth and reconciliation commissions and traditional mechanisms, can also play an important role in establishing accountability for crimes against women in war. A combination of methods may be appropriate in order to ensure that all victims secure redress.

THE INTERNATIONAL CRIMINAL COURT

The establishment of the International Criminal Court marks a new era of international justice and accountability for women. The Rome Statute of the ICC includes forms of sexual violence, including rape, sexual slavery, enforced prostitution, forced pregnancy and enforced sterilization, in the definition of crimes against humanity and war crimes. Persecution with gender as a basis, and the crime of enslavement, including the trafficking of women and children, are also listed as crimes against humanity. A statement in the commentary of the Statute explains further that rape and other sexual violence can constitute acts of genocide.[6]

Formed in 1997 the Women's Caucus for Gender Justice in the ICC galvanized hundreds of groups and individuals to bring a gender perspective into the substance and procedure of the new Court. The Statute's rules of procedure guarantee witness protection for women who testify. This reduces the risk of retaliation against women who give evidence. A Victim and Witnesses Unit (VWU) within the ICC will provide protection,

INTERNATIONAL CUSTOMARY LAW: Unlike treaty law, international customary law is not adopted formally by governments. It is created by the common practice of states developed over a period of time and the belief of states that they are legally bound to follow that practice. That belief can be evidenced in a variety of ways, including on the basis of resolutions and declarations — on women's rights, for example — adopted by the United Nations and other intergovernmental bodies, as well as from patterns of national practice, including legislation and national court decisions. International customary law is binding on all states once the norms have been accepted or acquiesced to by the international community as a whole. The Statute of the ICC illustrates this process. According to Justice Theodor Meron of the ICTY, the crimes recognized by the ICC Statute, including the gender-specific offences, may well "take on a life of their own as an authoritative and largely customary statement of international humanitarian and criminal law, and ... become a model for national laws to be enforced under the principle of universality of jurisdiction."[7]

Universal jurisdiction covers grave breaches of the Geneva Conventions, certain very serious human rights violations (like torture) and genocide. All states have a duty to prosecute the perpetrators, regardless of their nationality, the nationality of the victims or where the crimes took place.

CRIMES AGAINST HUMANITY are acts of violence committed as part of a widespread or systematic attack directed against any civilian population, with knowledge of the attack. According to the ICTY, crimes against humanity, which can occur in war or peace time, are "serious acts of violence which harm human beings by striking what is most essential to them: their life, liberty, physical welfare, health and/or dignity. They are inhumane acts that by their extent and gravity go beyond the limits tolerable to the international community, which must perforce demand their punishment."[8] Rape is explicitly listed among the crimes against humanity within the jurisdictions of both ad hoc tribunals (ICTY/ICTR). In the cases of Akayesu and Kunarac, the Tribunals convicted the accused of rape as a crime against humanity when the crimes were committed during the course of a widespread or systematic attack against civilians.

GENOCIDE was first defined in the Convention on the Prevention and Punishment of the Crime of Genocide of 1948, which has since passed into international customary law. Acts of genocide are committed with the intent to destroy, in whole or in part, a national, ethnic, racial or religious group, by killing or causing serious bodily or mental harm to members of the group, deliberately inflicting conditions calculated to bring about destruction of the group in whole or in part, imposing measures intended to prevent births or forcibly transferring children of the group to another group. In the Akayesu case, the ICTR found the defendant guilty of genocide, based in part on evidence that he had witnessed and encouraged rapes and forced nudity of women during the genocidal campaign against Rwanda's Tutsi population.

counselling and other security measures. The VWU calls explicitly for staff "with expertise in trauma, including trauma related to crimes of sexual violence." The Court will also establish reparations through compensation, restitution and rehabilitation, which may take the form of communal reconstruction and healing programmes. In a notable innovation, the ICC will create a Trust Fund for victims. The ICC Statute requires that its judges, both male and female, have legal expertise on specific issues, including violence against women. It also calls for "fair representation of women and men" among judges.[9]

Perhaps the most significant effects of the ICC for women will be at the national level, as the Statute is intended to set in motion a process of national law reform. States that ratify the Statute will need to amend their national law and adopt new legislation, if necessary, to ensure conformity with the Statute's provisions. If this does not happen, the state runs the risk of being deemed unwilling or unable to investigate or prosecute certain crimes. Since the Court operates on the principle of 'complementarity' — proceeding with investigation and prosecution only when national governments are unwilling or unable to do so — the ratification process acts as a driving force for national and local judicial systems to improve monitoring and reporting and to address crimes of sexual violence against women.

AD HOC TRIBUNALS

The International Criminal Tribunals for the Former Yugoslavia and Rwanda have raised the standards of accountability for crimes of sexual violence against women. Even though the judgements handed down by these courts constitute a tiny fraction of cases, they set historic precedents in prosecuting war crimes, crimes against humanity and genocide.[10] In so doing, the judgements of the ad hoc Tribunals have clarified definitions of sexual violence, recognizing rape as a means of torture and a form of persecution. Sexual slavery, forced nudity and sexual mutilation are included within the scope of the judgements, and the Tribunals have noted explicitly that forced impregnation, forced marriage,

forced abortion and sexual humiliation are serious violations of international law, and within their jurisdiction.

The Tribunals have also recognized that sexual violence is a weapon of war, used as a tool of terror and destruction, as is clear from the description of the testimony of Witness A:

"Witness A explained that she testified before the ICTR in order to see the perpetrators brought to justice. She told how for three months, until the genocide was stopped, she did not leave her bedroom. There were constantly men in her house, raping her. One group of men would sit in the living room, while another group was waiting in the bedroom. While one perpetrator was raping her, another one would get ready to take over. The mother-in-law and the children of Witness A were in the same house during all this time. Until today witness A is still suffering from the sexual violence she experienced during 1994. Her stomach is still very swollen. Some days she is not in touch with her surroundings as she sees in her mind the militiamen coming into her bedroom and undressing, over and over again. But she emphasized the fact that the men who raped her are not the only ones who are guilty. More important are the men and women who planned the genocide and gave the orders. 'They were killing the men and raping the women,' she said, 'that was the plan.'"[11]

Despite the achievements of the ad hoc Tribunals, they have been hampered by serious lapses and inconsistencies. The actual process of prosecuting crimes of sexual and gender violence in the proceedings of both Tribunals has been slow, as well as painful for victims and witnesses. According to the Honourable Elizabeth Odio-Benito, a former judge of the ICTY, the Tribunal was not at first prepared to consider crimes of sexual violence against women: "About one year after the Tribunal was set up, we faced the first public appearance of the Court. I was one of the three judges in this trial. I noticed that rape and sexual violence were absent in the indictment. This being my first experience as a judge, I did not always behave in the traditional way. I pointed out the necessity to examine crimes of rape and sexual violence. Everybody was very shocked by this. But soon they learned that this would be very successful. Sexual violence started to appear among the charges."[12]

The Honourable Navanethem Pillay, President of the ICTR, has emphasized the importance of how and by whom the law is applied: "Who interprets the law is at least as important as who makes the law, if not more so . . . I cannot stress how critical I consider it to be that women are represented and a gender perspective integrated at all levels of the investigation, prosecution, defence, witness protection and judiciary."[13] Women judges and prosecutors have played a key role in advancing the interpretation of the law with respect to crimes against women in both ad hoc Tribunals. However, to be fully effective, both female and male judges should be experienced in gender issues.

Over the past eight years, the ad hoc Tribunals have established numerous measures to ensure that victims and witnesses are protected. The process has been difficult and has, at times, failed the women involved. Noeleen Heyzer, Executive Director of UNIFEM, has been one of the international women leaders to bring these lapses to the attention of the Security Council. Reflecting the needs of Rwandan women, she has called for better witness protection, counselling and security, as well as sanctions against Tribunal staff who do not respect the rights of witnesses, and a separate chamber with female judges to hear cases of women survivors of sexual violence. If gender-based crimes are to be prosecuted, they need to be investigated and indicted according to international standards, and the investigators and prosecutors need to be trained in gender crimes and sensitive to the needs of the victims.

When we visited Rwanda, we met with women who were still struggling, after eight years, to come to terms with what they had experienced. "We feel great pain to know that our attackers, the people who killed our husbands and male relatives, who tortured, raped and mutilated us, have not been punished," a young woman told us. "Many of these people are in exile. It is as if they are being reward-

ed for the crimes that they committed. They deserve to be punished. And what is happening to us here? We have been reduced to suffering, begging and misery. It is as if we are the guilty ones. We would like you to be a voice for us, by asking the United Nations and the international community for justice. Then we can rebuild our lives."

The determination of women survivors has been the driving force behind the successful prosecutions of both Tribunals despite the psychological duress, intimidation, indignities and physical threats that women who testify have endured. When a doctor assigned to victims testifying before the ICTY proposed that they be provided with psychological support during testimony, the initial response was that the Tribunal was "not engaged in 'social work,' but important legal proceedings."[14]

> **"We feel great pain to know that our attackers, the people who killed our husbands and male relatives, who tortured, raped and mutilated us, have not been punished," a young Rwandan woman told us. "Many of these people are in exile. It is as if they are being rewarded for the crimes that they committed. And what is happening to us here? We have been reduced to suffering, begging and misery. It is as if we are the guilty ones."**

In some cases, women have withdrawn because the Tribunals have failed to provide adequate support and protection. The ICTR in particular has come under criticism for failing to protect women witnesses. In one fact-finding mission, defence lawyers were found to have degraded and discredited women by demanding that they name, unnecessarily and in extreme detail, sexual organs and how they were used during violations. A number of women have reported that lawyers for the accused and judges have mocked and humiliated them by joining in the general laughter at their embarrassed responses.

Women have not received witness protection as required by the Rules of the Tribunal. In one case when a woman was called to testify, she told investigators that anonymity was essential because the accused knew her and she was concerned about retaliation against her family. But when she arrived at the Tribunal and toured the Trial Chamber she realized that she could not remain anonymous from the accused. Fearing for her safety and the safety of her family, she refused to testify.[15]

Although Tribunal rules require confidentiality, judges have taken little or no action to prevent and punish the copying of confidential court transcripts, which in some cases have been sent back to the communities where witnesses are living among the killers. A number of women seeking justice at the ICTR paid with their lives. Partly in response to this, the UN Security Council resolved that 18 *ad litem* judges are to be appointed to the ICTR, to expedite the hundreds of pending cases.

Given the risks, why do so many women consider it their responsibility to testify? A support officer of the ICTY Victims and Witnesses Unit provided several reasons:

"Frequently I wonder, and frequently I am asked, why do witnesses come to testify?… I have learned that witnesses come for reasons that seem to fit into four main areas: To speak for the dead; to look for justice in the present; to help the truth be known by the world; in the hope that such crimes can be prevented in the future."[16]

SPECIAL COURTS AND TRIBUNALS

Viet Nguyen-Gillham, a counsellor for the Centre for Victims of Torture in Sierra Leone, has described the difficulties involved in assisting survivors who are still traumatized by the war. Some were forced by rebel forces to witness atrocities: "They would place bets on whether the baby in the womb was male or female," she said, "then they would slit the woman's belly open." Nguyen-Gillham is struggling to find ways to help people recover and return to a meaningful community life. "There's only so much sensitization you can do," she explained. "If there's no more assistance forthcoming, and no legal system to punish the offenders, the violence will perpetuate itself."

Since judicial systems in the country had virtually collapsed by the end of the conflict, the Special Court for Sierra Leone was created by an international treaty between the United Nations and the Government of Sierra Leone to provide justice for crimes committed during the war.[17] The innovative court structure will involve both national and international judges and lawyers and will draw upon international and national legal systems. The Statute of the Special Court refers explicitly to crimes of sexual violence and stipulates that "due consideration should be given in the appointment of staff, to the employment of prosecutors and investigators experienced in gender-related crimes and juvenile justice."

Unlike the ICTY and ICTR, the Special Court is funded on a voluntary basis by donor countries. Although the Court's independence is guaranteed by its Statute, some NGOs have raised concerns as to whether the Court can function independently from the government and ensure that the interests of all victims are properly served.[18] Despite the potential difficulties, many hope that the hybrid character of the Court and its location in Sierra Leone will provide an opportunity to rebuild the domestic judicial system and make it easier for women affected by the conflict to participate in and attend trials.

In East Timor a combination of methods are being used to attempt to bring perpetrators to account for war crimes and crimes against humanity committed at the time of the August 1999 referendum on independence. But the women of East Timor are not yet convinced these methods will work. We met Maria, who fled her village as everything she owned burned to the ground in fires set by Indonesian-supported militia. Like many of the women we spoke to, she knew the people who had committed crimes against her community, but had never had the satisfaction of seeing them tried. "We know who these people are," she told us, "We know them by name, by face and we know that many are still hiding in West Timor. We will not agree to live side-by-side with them in East Timor unless justice is done."

Despite efforts to try those who committed serious crimes, public confidence in systems of justice-seeking has weakened in East Timor. The UN Transitional Administration in East Timor (UNTAET) established a Serious Crimes Investigation Unit to investigate hundreds of human rights violations that took place in 1999, including sexual violence and rape. Although the Unit secured the conviction of a former militia leader for crimes against humanity in November 2001, additional progress has been slow, due in part to the lack of resources. Most of the top militia commanders believed to have been responsible for the worst violations during the 1999 massacres have not been indicted.[19]

In August 2002 the Indonesian Ad Hoc Human Rights Tribunal convicted the former Governor of East Timor of war crimes, but he received only a 3-year sentence. A general and five other officers charged with allowing subordinates to take part in the massacres were acquitted. Mary Robinson, the High Commissioner for Human Rights at the time, criticized the verdict and called for broader jurisdiction and more thorough investigations. During her visit to Dili in August 2002, the High Commissioner met with the East Timorese Women's Communications Forum (Fokupers) and other women who are continuing the quest for justice. The women sent a formal letter to the High Commissioner, stating that they rejected the authority of the Indonesian Ad Hoc Tribunal. They called for the establishment of an international tribunal for East Timor instead: "Women have been interrogated, abused, raped, forced to be sexual slaves ... East Timorese women and all victims and families of victims are still waiting for justice. Many of the women we work with ask us, 'when will this justice come?'"

NATIONAL APPROACHES

Getting indictments for crimes against women has proven to be most difficult at the national level. In the countries we visited, we found that national judicial systems have not delivered for women. After a peace agreement is signed and the fighting stops, governments emerging from conflict face enormous challenges in rebuilding the judicial system. Judges, lawyers and other legal experts may have fled or been killed. In some cases, broad amnesties may be granted to specific individuals or groups of individuals, which invariably result in impunity for crimes against women.[20] Investigations at the national level rarely focus on violations against women. When they do, the lack of technical capacities and the absence of systematic procedures for forensic investigations hamper effective prosecution. Too often, national courts discriminate against women, detaining them without due process, dismissing their testimony and subjecting them to public humiliation. When a judge presiding over a case in Bosnia ridiculed a victim of trafficking by asking her if she was a virgin, other women were discouraged from testifying against traffickers.

> "Frequently I wonder, and frequently I am asked, why do witnesses come to testify?...I have learned that witnesses come for reasons that seem to fit into four main areas: To speak for the dead; to look for justice in the present; to help the truth be known by the world; in the hope that such crimes can be prevented in the future."

An effective national justice system is vital for women. Without it, and without laws that adequately protect them from domestic violence, rape and other gender-based violence, women cannot seek justice or compensation. They may lose confidence and hope in the possibility of justice. A Congolese lawyer we met in the DRC told us, "You can't have justice in a context like this. Magistrates are not paid. They can't refuse gifts. It's the same with the security services ... women don't see the point in complaining. Even if they say something, what will change?"

In attempting to set new national standards for their protection, women can look to international conventions and customary laws, the jurisprudence of the ICTY and ICTR, and the ICC Statute, and demand that these precedents be used during national trials. Despite the difficulty inherent in this, such trials may have several advantages over international tribunals. National courts generally have better access to evidence and can involve witnesses who might be unable to travel outside the country; they engage the local population, enabling them to claim ownership; and they help build a collective historical memory. Some legal experts argue that war crimes trials in national courts can also play an important role in re-establishing the national judiciary by building court infrastructure and training local judges and lawyers.

In the process of rebuilding their societies, women in conflict situations may have the opportunity to reform laws and traditions that restricted their human rights even before the conflict began. They may be able to put an end to patterns of discrimination that have gone on for centuries. In Kampala, in 2000, a coalition of Sudanese and international human rights and women's groups created a shared vision for a future transitional government in the Sudan which would "cancel any laws and policies that are incompatible with the rights of women as enshrined in international human rights conventions." They also called on political parties to "ensure adequate representation of women at all levels, including the highest."[21]

However, the co-existence of multiple legal systems at the national level can limit women's access to justice. In many post-conflict situations, family law codified under colonial regimes may continue to be applied, perpetuating some of the most egregious forms of gender inequality. In Mozambique, despite a comprehensive process of constitutional reform, men continue to maintain the head-of-household status granted to them by a Civil Code based on Portuguese colonial law. In the DRC, the 1987 Family Code is based on Belgian colonial law that requires married women to obtain their husbands' permission before taking any kind of judicial action. In Somalia and Sudan, traditional leaders have introduced militant, conservative and highly politicized interpretations of *Sharia* in local-level Islamic courts. Rulings typically include harsh punishments and stringent restrictions on women's participation in public life.

"First, there is the colonial law, and then the customary law, and also Muslim law in our system," said Isha Dyfan, the Sierra Leonean lawyer and women's advocate. "For women, and even for lawyers, this proliferation of law is like a minefield, and really discourages them from facing the legal system. There has to be a consolidation of national and international law, so that women can apply the Convention on the Elimination of All Forms of Discrimination against Women (CEDAW) and the Convention on the Rights of the Child (CRC) and other international standards."[22]

"The best way to ensure that the highest standards of protection for women are enforced," she says, "is to use legal experts on women's rights as advisers to local and national systems of transitional justice."

TRUTH AND RECONCILIATION COMMISSIONS
"Maybe I can learn to forgive, but I will never forget."
— Rose, a survivor of the genocide in Rwanda

Truth commissions provide a public forum for victims to express their grievances and seek reconciliation. Testimony and other evidence gathered from survivors establishes an official public record of crimes committed. Whereas the truth-telling functions of criminal trials are restricted by law and procedure to deal only with facts that are legally relevant to the case at hand, truth commissions are able to develop a more comprehensive record and understanding of the full scale of violations.

More than 20 countries have established truth commissions or similar processes.[23] Generally, these have been created, vested with authority, sponsored and/or funded by governments, international organizations or both. Some non-governmental human rights investigations have also adopted truth commission-like roles, as was the case with the Women's International War Crimes Tribunal on Japan's Military Sexual Slavery.

The work of truth commissions — in which people describe what happened to them in their own words — can answer the need for a cathartic public recounting of suffering. When truth commissions have gender-sensitive mandates and procedures, they can legitimize women's experiences, making them part of the official public record. Like prosecutions, truth commissions are most effective when the affected populations feel a degree of ownership in the process. For women, this usually requires special measures to inform them about the commission's structure, functions and procedures.

Truth and reconciliation commissions do not fulfil the requirement under international law to prosecute grave crimes. Nevertheless, "If you look at the experience of countries in the past, and the impact that information from truth commissions has had in feeding into prosecutions that followed, I think we can argue very strongly that truth commissions are complementary and even strengthen prosecutions," argues Priscilla Hayner, Program Director of the International Center for Transitional Justice, based in New York City.[24]

For truth commissions to serve women, their mandates must reflect the nature of the violence and human rights violations against women. Crimes that are not explicitly mentioned in mandates are at risk of being ignored or underemphasized. This is especially true for crimes of sexual violence, since crimes against women traditionally have been given less importance and less credibility by public institutions, and victims have often been treated as if they were criminals themselves. When compared to the actual frequency of violations committed against women during armed conflict, testimony about these violations, including rape and sexual violence, is given to truth commissions far less often than testimony about other abuses.[25] This is due in part to the stigma associated with reporting these crimes, in part to the lack of protection and support for women survivors and in part to women's lack of familiarity with the processes.

Women often downplay their own experiences and focus on crimes committed against their husbands, sons and families. In some cases they may speak more easily about crimes committed against other women, saying, for example, "Oh yes there were rapes, I saw it, but it never happened to me." One consequence of underreporting is that commissioners may perceive crimes against women as

non-political, or unrelated to the type of violence that they are investigating. This was the case in South Africa where some members of the South African Amnesty Committee are said to have believed that rape was a non-political crime, outside the reach of their investigation.[26]

Reportedly, most truth commissions have not been proactive in seeking out, encouraging or facilitating testimony from women.[27] Commissioners, like judges in criminal tribunals, may not be sensitive to the violations women experience in conflict or the long-term effects of those violations. Gender-sensitive policies and procedures would allow women to appear before panels of women commissioners and to give testimony *in camera* (in closed sessions). The act establishing a truth and reconciliation commission in Sierra Leone, for example, directs it to pay "special attention to the subject of sexual abuses" and refers to the importance of confidentiality and witness-sensitive procedures when investigating gender-based crimes.

Like trials, truth commissions require investigation and fact-finding. Yet monitoring and reporting violations during conflict is one of the most neglected and under-resourced activities. Human rights organizations, women's groups and United Nations Special Rapporteurs all have key roles to play in gathering the necessary evidence.

TRADITIONAL JUSTICE

In post-conflict situations where widespread atrocities have been committed, national judicial systems may lack adequate financial and human resources to handle the large number of cases. In addition, national judicial systems may be subject to ethnic or religious bias arising from the conflict. Given the limited number of cases that international and national courts can handle, traditional and community-based approaches are being viewed in some cases as a complementary, if not alternative, system of justice

Traditional approaches to justice often involve religious leaders, village elders and local officials in resolving domestic or communal conflicts, including rape and domestic violence. However, it is essential that traditional justice mechanisms are consistent with international human rights standards and protect the rights of witnesses, victims and defendants.

In a unique use of traditional courts, the Government of Rwanda shifted approximately 115,000 defendants accused of atrocities during the country's genocide into a traditional justice system known as *gacaca* courts. Many of the accused have remained in overpopulated prisons for years without trials. The *gacaca* courts will relieve the burden on the national court system that, by some estimates, would have required hundreds of years to try all of the accused. The *gacaca* system will not consider "first category offenses," which include charges brought against those believed to be responsible for the genocide, or those accused of rape. It will focus instead primarily on those who caused physical injury and who destroyed property. Women parliamentarians were instrumental in advocating that the crime of rape during genocide be changed from category four — or on a par with common theft — to the most serious category one offense. But since the national courts are so overwhelmed with cases, some fear that by excluding crimes of rape from the *gacaca* process, many perpetrators may never be tried.

While the *gacaca* courts are less costly and faster than the international war crimes tribunal taking place in Arusha, concerns have also been raised that these courts will not be able to maintain international human rights standards. Some observers worry that the courts may institutionalize patterns of discrimination against women that have historically been part of traditional approaches to justice, especially since in the first nominations women were not elected to the courts. In addition, many Rwandans are worried about safety. "Women stayed behind [in their communities] and saw more. We will have to say where our husbands were at the time. We are afraid for our families," one woman told us. We heard similar fears from many others. A worker from Catholic Relief Services added, "If there is any danger to their families, the women will not speak out." Yet numerous Rwandans remain anxious to see justice done, and to see it done in their own country where they can observe the process. Many agree with the woman who told us that the *gacaca* system "reflects the collective identity of Rwandans and is in touch with the culture."

In times of war and societal breakdown, crimes against women reach new levels of brutality and frequency. These assaults on individuals and basic decency must be identified, and those responsible must be held to account. Each conflict runs its own brutal course and demands a unique approach to seeking accountability. Recognizing the tragedies of history is one way to protect against their recurrence. Without accountability for crimes against women, the legal foundations of new governments will be weakened, the credibility of governing institutions will be undermined and women will continue to suffer discrimination.

7

RECOMMENDATIONS

1. The Secretary-General to appoint a panel of experts to assess the gaps in international and national laws and standards pertaining to the protection of women in conflict and post-conflict situations and women's role in peace-building.

2. States parties to the Statute of the International Criminal Court to undertake national law reform to ensure compatibility with the Statute as a matter of priority, with particular attention given to the substantive and procedural provisions regarding crimes against women.

3. National legal systems to penalize and remedy all forms of violence against women in conflict and post-conflict situations. Specially trained police units should be established to investigate crimes against women and law enforcement officials, including judges, police and armed forces, should be sensitized about such crimes. Women's access to justice should be ensured through legal literacy programmes, support services and legal aid.

4. Gender equality in constitutional, legislative and policy reforms. The principle of gender should be integrated into all relevant constitutional clauses, reaffirming the principles of non-discrimination, equality, affirmative action, freedom and security. Special attention should be given to family, civil and labour laws and land reforms.

5. Rapid establishment by the UN of interim judicial systems capable of dealing effectively with violations against women by family members and society at large. Rape and sexual violence should be addressed by post-conflict truth- and justice-seeking mechanisms at national and local levels. The treatment of crimes against women in traditional mechanisms should be consistent with international standards.

A Kosovo Serb woman holds up photos of her missing family members.

media power

In retrospect, I realize how much of my perception about women in war was influenced by the media. The incessant images of desperation and victimization tell only part of the story. The other part, the strength, courage and resilience, is rarely captured.

— Rafeeuddin Ahmed
Chef de Cabinet to UN Secretary-General
Kurt Waldheim

L ike millions of people around the world, we stared riveted at the television screen on September 11, 2001. Calling family and friends from our Kinshasa hotel, we sometimes heard in the background the same news story we were listening to thousands of miles away. For days we were consumed by the tragedy of lost lives in New York, Washington DC and Pennsylvania. Tragedies cannot be compared — there is no competition — but as we watched the Twin Towers fall over and over again, we wished that the ongoing tragedy in the Democratic Republic of the Congo (DRC), which has become a slaughterhouse claiming 2.5 million lives since 1998,[1] would get the same international news coverage and arouse similar sympathy.

The visit to the DRC was one of the hardest parts of our journey, due to the carnage and brutality of the war and the desperate poverty in this rich country the size of western Europe. To be in such a broken place on September 11 added to our grief and despair, allowing us to see firsthand how terror is a daily experience for so many around the world. But we also saw that people survive, exhibiting a kind of strength, hope and resilience that defies the imagination. We wondered why the media rarely presented this part of the story.

The power of the media in warfare is formidable. It can be a mediator or an interpreter or even a facilitator of conflict, if only by editing away facts that do not fit the demands of air time or print space. Hardly a soul on earth is beyond the reach of some form of modern media, be it television, movies, radio, newspapers, posters, audio and videotapes or the World Wide Web. Almost no one, therefore, is free from the reach of those who control the media — whether government, opposition or private sector groups who own, manage or otherwise influence its operation.

Because these political and commercial influences have such a powerful impact, Women and Media was identified as one of 12 critical areas of concern in the Beijing Platform for Action (PFA).[2] In ascribing to the PFA, 189 nations made a commitment to increase women's participation in and access to media, and to promote balanced and non-stereotyped images of women. However, we have seen little change in the mainstream media; the perspectives on women are rarely nuanced, especially in conflict situations. When women appear, they are often portrayed as victims rather than as activists or analysts.[3] They are shown huddling pathetically in doorways, crying and cradling their injured children in their arms. Ironically these images, designed to evoke sympathy, make it easier to objectify the women who survive and the horrors they have lived through. In addition an insensitive interview can cause secondary trauma, which is compounded if a woman's story is misrepresented or sensationalized. During the war in Bosnia and Herzegovina journalists swarmed around rape victims, sometimes requesting interviews only with those who had been gang-raped.[4] Apart from sexual violence and victimization, the mainstream media rarely consider women newsworthy in their varied roles in the peacekeeping and conflict resolution processes.

The dearth of women's voices and perspectives has disturbing policy implications. The so-called CNN Effect — the way in which CNN's coverage can define a story — has become so pervasive that former UN Secretary-General Boutros Boutros-Ghali called CNN the "16th member of the Security Council."[5] Richard Holbrooke, former US Ambassador to the UN, also acknowledged the network's role at a 1999 conference:

"Bosnia had a story line, a very clear story line, and as a result of that story line the press, led by the *New York Times* and CNN, had an amazing impact on policy in the United States. ... the reason the West finally, belatedly intervened was heavily related to media coverage. The reason Rwanda did not get the same kind of attention was heavily related to media coverage — or the lack thereof. Just a week ago, I was on a panel at the Museum of Broadcasting in New York where Christiane Amanpour was challenged by a panelist who said, 'You did a great job in Bosnia, why didn't you go to Rwanda where far more people died?' Her answer was astonishing: politely, but firmly, 'I was in Rwanda. I did cover it. I knew what was happening but the O.J. Simpson trial was on and I couldn't get on the air for CNN.'"[6]

In recent years media ownership has become centralized in the hands of just 10 multinational media companies, whose power extends far beyond their countries of origin.[7] Although they cover the news, their business is primarily entertainment, and they influence the world through movies, TV and radio shows, comic strips and music videos, most of which portray women in stereotypical ways.

According to a 1995 UNESCO study, women constitute only 3 per cent of the staff of media organizations worldwide.[8] The Annenberg Public Policy Center reported in 2002 that women made up only 14 per cent of top U.S. media, telecom and e-company executives, and 13 per cent of their boards of directors.[9] This is part of the reason why women worldwide are the subject of only 7 per cent of stories on politics and government, and in the US are only 18 per cent of those interviewed for such stories.[10]

The relative shortage of women at all levels in journalism, but especially in war coverage, can have a profound effect on the type of news that is produced and disseminated. Fairness and Accuracy in Reporting (FAIR), a U.S.-based organization that monitors the media, conducted a survey of *New York Times* and *Washington Post* op-ed pages for the three weeks after the September 11 attacks, and found a striking gender imbalance. At the *Post* only seven of 107 op-ed pieces were written by women, while at the *Times* eight out of 79 were written by women.[11]

A conference sponsored by the International Women's Media Foundation (IWMF) illuminated the ways in which women's presence can alter the news: "The change in the reports from the field was instantly noticeable," observed a Russian participant at the conference. After women emerged as war correspondents in the era of perestroika and glasnost, "it had a remarkable impact on politicians, editors and the public. Women showed not only the quantity of people killed, but the impact on civilians caught in the battlegrounds." Another participant in the conference, from the Philippines, said that in her experience, "Men tend to concentrate on quotes from government officials and focus on conflicts, while women tend to look at the impact on the greatest number of people or sectors."[12] According to the Institute for Media Policy and Civil Society (IMPACS), "Media in the hands of women often produces a different kind of intervention."[13]

PROPAGANDA AND CENSORSHIP

When hate is spread along airwaves, across television screens and on the Internet, calls for violence against women become part of war propaganda. In 1994 prior to the genocide in Rwanda, journalists at government-owned Radio Television Libre des Mille Collines broadcast messages inciting genocide and encouraging Hutus to rape Tutsi women and then either to kill them or leave some alive to bear so-called Hutu children. In the massacre that enveloped the country, "almost all females who survived the genocide were direct victims of rape or other sexual violence, or were profoundly affected by it."[14] Estimates of the number of women raped range from at least 250,000 to 500,000. Afterwards the UN commander in Rwanda in 1994, General Romeo Dallaire, was quoted as saying that "Simply jamming Hutu broadcasts and replacing them with messages of peace and reconciliation would have had a significant impact on the course of events in Rwanda."[15] Article 3 of the Genocide Convention states that direct and public incitement to commit genocide is a punishable offense. This article was the basis upon which the International Criminal Tribunal for Rwanda (ICTR) sentenced Georges Ruggiu, a Belgian citi-

> **The UN commander in Rwanda in 1994, General Romeo Dallaire, was quoted as saying that "Simply jamming Hutu broadcasts and replacing them with messages of peace and reconciliation would have had a significant impact on the course of events in Rwanda."**

zen, to two concurrent 12-year prison sentences after he pled guilty to broadcasting hate messages over the government-owned radio station.

In the former Yugoslavia neighbours raped and killed neighbours "with the help of the state media, national radio and TV and the newspapers with the largest circulation and the greatest privileges, which convinced people they could no longer live together, that they were threatened by their neighbours with whom they had had perfect relations for decades," said Sasa Mirkovic, the general manager of Radio B92 in Belgrade.[16] In Bosnia, Serb soldiers reportedly used sophisticated modern methods, props and dubbed dialogue to videotape women being raped and then sold the material as pornography.[17]

Although the right of freedom of expression is enshrined in the Universal Declaration of Human Rights, the problem of hate speech has led human rights advocates to re-examine whether limits need to be established. South Africa became one of the first countries in the world to constitutionally ban hate speech when its post-apartheid constitution forbade speech that incites hatred of a person because of race, religion, gender or sexual preference.

Truth is often considered the first casualty of war, whether owing to propaganda and hate speech or to censorship. According to IMPACS, when governments impose overt media censorship, it is often a sign of potentially violent conflict. The crackdown on the independent press and journalists in Liberia, Myanmar and Zimbabwe are just a few examples. Practices have evolved since the 1970s to exclude media from war coverage altogether, as the U.S. military did during the invasion of Grenada; to make them totally dependent upon the military for their safety, transport and communications, as the U.K. did in the Falklands; or to use both of these tactics, as the U.S. did in Desert Storm/Desert Shield.[18] Speaking of the war on terrorism in Afghanistan, Bill Kovach and Tom Rosenstiel of the Project on Excellence in Journalism said, "As the war moved abroad, the Pentagon made access to soldiers and the battlefield more difficult than it has ever been."[19]

In the aftermath of the September 11 attacks, Feminist International Radio Endeavour (FIRE) organized a women's "peacecast" to make up for the absence of women's voices in the mainstream media. Peggy Antrobus, a feminist economist from the Caribbean, told the audience, "Since most mainstream media presented a partial focus on news about the attacks, censoring other analysis, it was only on the Internet where I was able to find other interpretations."[20] According to the Project for Excellence in Journalism, four months into the war on terrorism, fact-based reporting in the U.S. media had dropped from 75 per cent to 63 per cent, as coverage shifted to opinion, analysis and speculation.[21] In May 2002 U.S. news anchor Dan Rather told a BBC interviewer that fear of being branded unpatriotic had constrained journalists: "What we are talking about here — whether one wants to recognize it or not, or call its by its proper name or not — is a form of self-censorship."[22]

When reporters go into situations where governments will not or cannot protect them, they face grave risks. Women correspondents face the same dangers as men — abduction, robbery, murder — but, in addition, they are in danger of gender-based violence. As Kathleen Currie, deputy director of the IWMF, has noted, "the threat of rape and sexual assault is always looming in these dangerous locales."[23] Those journalists who do try to tell the story despite censorship face retribution. On World Press Day in May 2002 UN Deputy-Secretary-General Louise Fréchette reported that 118 journalists were in jail. Numerous others have lost their lives.

Maria Cristina Caballero, a prize-winning journalist from Colombia, was almost one of them. In 1999 fearing for her life, she fled Colombia where she had been covering the war for several years. "I published pieces about abuses from all the factions, about the guerrillas and the forced recruitment of peasants. I had been exposing the massacres of peasants, such as the one committed in Mapiripan, where the paramilitaries tortured and killed people over the course of five days," she said. Eventually she realized that all sides were looking for her. "I was in a small jungle town, where I had gone to cover a story related to a guerrilla kidnapping. The guerrillas were all over the road and they were looking for me. I had to lie on the floor of a cart and some people of the town covered me with potatoes so that I could get out. I escaped by a miracle."

A number of statements, resolutions and sections of treaties already exist on the media's role in peace and security. Equally important, journalists and media organizations are reflecting more on their roles and responsibilities, establishing voluntary guidelines, conducting workshops on eliminating bias from reporting and taking other steps to enhance media professionalism. Tools such as "Reporting the World: A Practical Checklist for the Ethical Reporting of Conflicts in the 21st Century"[24] are useful for journalists reporting from war zones. Media Action International, a non-governmental organization (NGO), bridges the gap between journalism and humanitarian, post-conflict and development activities, and is helping to develop strategies to utilize mass media as a tool in fighting illiteracy, poverty and disease.[25]

INTERNATIONAL STATEMENTS, RESOLUTIONS AND SECTIONS OF TREATIES ON THE MEDIA

• Resolution 110 of the General Assembly (GA), adopted in 1947, condemned "all forms of propaganda, in whatsoever country conducted, which is either designated or likely to provoke or encourage any threat to the peace, breach of the peace, or act of aggression."

• Resolution 127 of the GA, adopted in 1947, invites Member States to "take measures within the limits of constitutional procedures, to combat the diffusion of false and distorted reports likely to injure friendly relations between States, as well as the other resolutions of the General Assembly concerning the mass media and their contribution to the strengthening of peace, trust and friendly relations among States."

• Article 19 of the Universal Declaration of Human Rights states that "everyone has the right to freedom of opinion and expression: this right includes freedom to hold opinions without interference and to seek, receive and impart information and ideas through any media and regardless of frontiers."

• Article 20 of the International Covenant on Civil and Political Rights of 1976 states that "any propaganda for war shall be prohibited by law."

• In 1978 the General Conference of the UN Educational, Scientific and Cultural Organization (UNESCO) issued a Declaration of Fundamental Principles, the Contribution of the Mass Media to Strengthening Peace and International Understanding, to the Promotion of Human Rights and to Countering Racialism, Apartheid and Incitement to War.

• The Committee of Ministers of the Council of Europe adopted a recommendation on equality between women and men in the media in 1984. Many other regional organizations have addressed a broad range of issues on the media.

• Article 4 of the Convention on the Elimination of All Forms of Racial Discrimination declares that "all dissemination of ideas based on racial superiority or hatred, incitement to racial discrimination ... and all other propaganda activities, which promote and incite racial discrimination ... [are] punishable by law."

A DIFFERENT STORY

Women are increasingly learning to use the media to tell their own story, to document human rights violations and to report on peace-building. Everywhere we went we saw women using media in creative ways to build peace. Everything from comic books to call-in radio shows, from street theatre to videos to traditional story telling is being utilized. Barely one month after the fall of the Taliban, five women pooled their own money to create *Seerat*, Afghanistan's first independent weekly newspaper run by and for women. They printed 500 copies of their handwritten publication, which included articles that urged the government to provide day care for its female employees, encouraged women to refuse to sit at

One of Ijambo's most successful programmes is a radio drama, 'Umubanyi Niwe Muryango' (Our Neighbours, Ourselves), about the friendship between a Hutu and a Tutsi family. In a survey conducted in 2002, an estimated 87 per cent of Burundians said they listened to the drama, and 82 per cent of those surveyed believed that Ijambo's programmes greatly helped reconciliation.

the back of buses and depicted the miserable conditions for returning refugee women. For an upcoming issue, *Seerat*'s editor, Aeen, said she planned to "expose the new government's refusal to play the music of female singers and musicians on state-run television and radio." [26]

Of the different types of media – government-owned, privately-owned, independent and community-based – women's media and information networks have tended to focus on the community level, where they can communicate in a local language about issues of local importance. Mirna

Cunningham, an indigenous woman from Nicaragua and director of the University of the Atlantic there, notes the importance of community media during conflict: "It is precisely when some media begins using language of intolerance that community media becomes even more crucial. It gives a voice to the marginalized people who are being targeted. It contributes to building bridges of understanding through the use of simple language where we all have a voice. It also provides for a more informed and critical audience that will not so easily fall prey to the hate messages."[27]

In the Middle East women's groups in Israel and the occupied Palestinian territories have initiated a public media correspondence. Each month, one organization publishes a letter in the sister organization's newspaper. The Jerusalem Centre for Women, a Palestinian group, wrote in its first letter, "It is a good start ... we should give credit to those women who dare to speak out loudly duirng these times of abyss. The [Israeli women's] letter addresses Palestinian people on the day that marks 35 years of Israeli military occupation of 22 per cent of historical Palestine on which we, Palestinians, strive to build our independent viable state beside Israel." Terri Greenblatt of Bat Shalom, an Israeli women's peace group participating in the dialogue, has described the process as "our joint attempt to provide an alternative voice in the media that allows women on each side to publicly claim that only mutual recognition and respect for each other's individual and collective rights will pave the way for peace making, as well as to challenge the notion that political partnerships are impossible at this time."[28]

Many activists are calling for community media to be considered as a vital part of post-conflict infrastructure alongside housing and water. The Kampala Declaration from the Know How Conference in Uganda in 2002 noted the importance of media, "especially early warning systems, so that women in conflict zones can reach out and get the support needed quickly."[29]

The Women's Caucus of the World Summit on the Information Society will be holding meetings in 2003 in Geneva and 2005 in Tunis, and will endeavour to take proposals about women's access to information and communications technology to the World Summit.

The majority of the world's 960 million illiterate people are women. They turn to radio – not print – to receive and create information. Radio is a perfect medium for reaching large numbers of people, especially during conflict when small transistors may be the only source of information for uprooted populations. According to FIRE, radio in Latin America is the most democratic medium and has a greater diversity of voices and ownership than other media. Since the cost of purchasing time on radio is relatively inexpensive, social groups can use even commercial radio to get their message out.[30]

In Tanzania in May 1999 more than 300 women from 50 countries met at the first Pan-African Women's Conference for a Culture of Peace and Non-Violence and called for a pan-African radio programme on gender and peace. National and regional initiatives are now building towards this vision. In the Great Lakes region of Africa, the NGO Search for Common Ground uses radio to educate children about prejudice and conflict resolution. It has established Burundi's first independent radio station, Ijambo, which reaches an estimated 12 million people throughout the region. One of Ijambo's most successful programmes is a radio drama, 'Umubanyi Niwe Muryango' (Our Neighbours, Ourselves), about the friendship between a Hutu and a Tutsi family. In a survey conducted in 2002, an estimated 87 per cent of Burundians said they listened to the drama, and 82 per cent of those surveyed believed that Ijambo's programmes greatly helped reconciliation.[31]

Bosnian women are using talk shows on Resolution Radio to teach conflict resolution skills. "The wounds are deep, and we need lots of time to heal," said Edita Pecenkovic, one of the hosts of the new women's network, Radio Jednostavno Zena (Simply Women). In Somalia, where over 85 per cent of the population listens to the BBC, the station's World Service Trust and the Africa Educational Trust have developed radio literacy programmes for the extremely high numbers

— some estimates cite nearly 98 per cent — of girls who do not go to school. The programmes are transmitted all over Somalia and in the neighbouring countries of Djibouti, Ethiopia, Kenya and Yemen, where many displaced Somalis live.

Radio has been used in several ways in the East Timor peace process. Radio programmes used various methods to encourage people to vote and to get women to participate as candidates, voters and election monitors. A song, "Please Decide," was composed for the 1999 elections and broadcast nationwide. The East Timorese Women's Communications Forum (Fokupers), an NGO that promotes women's human rights, currently runs two radio programmes that address issues like violence against women and women's leadership.

At the opposite end of the technology spectrum, women are finding that digital communication offers another kind of grass roots access. Although its reach is not nearly as broad as that of radio, the impact of the Internet in peace-building has been powerful, thanks to the "personal" interaction that takes place. In the occupied Palestinian territories at least 15 Internet cafes operated in Ramallah before the second Intifada. Many managed to remain open until 2002 when buildings and the electrical infrastructure were destroyed. The Love and Peace Station Internet Cafe, which is for women only, was the first of its kind. In 2001 the 106 women members, who were free to take off their headscarves in the cafe, were mostly young college-educated professionals who had been isolated by the Intifada and found the Internet a relatively cheap way to communicate with friends and family in other villages and countries. "I write my feelings. I feel better when I talk with another person about the people killed," said Ehaf Hassan, a 24-year-old nurse who paid just over a dollar an hour to chat on the computers.

The Internet has also become a powerful organizing tool. The Women's International League for Peace and Freedom (WILPF), inspired by the process that led to the Security Council's adoption of Resolution 1325 on Women and Peace and Security, has created a website called PeaceWomen.org to "nurture communication among a diversity of women's organizations by providing an accessible and accurate information exchange between peace women around the world and the UN system."

One of the largest of the women's international information and communication networks is the International Women's Tribune Centre (IWTC), established in 1976 following the UN International Women's Year World Conference in Mexico City. IWTC, whose constituency exceeds 25,000 women in 150 countries (94 per cent in the global South) is widely recognized for its innovative, pioneering efforts to link women and the means of communication.

Many people — members of the media included — say we have entered an "information era." Whether this is true or not, there is no doubt that the information the media spreads around the world affects war and peace as never before. We need to put women into the picture — both as producers of media information and as subjects of it. Otherwise, women's role in peace-building will continue to be ignored, and the primary images we get from conflict zones will be ones of despair.

8

RECOMMENDATIONS

1. Increased donor resources and access for women to media and communications technology, so that gender perspectives, women's expertise and women's media can influence public discourse and decision-making on peace and security.

2. UN, government, private and independent media to provide public information and education on the gender dimensions of peace processes, security, reconciliation, disarmament and human rights.

3. Hate media, under any circumstances and particularly when used for direct and public incitement to commit crimes against women, to be prosecuted by national and international courts.

4. Donors and agencies to support the training of editors and journalists to eliminate gender bias in reporting and investigative journalism in conflict and post-conflict situations, and to promote gender equality and perspectives.

5. A panel of experts to undertake an assessment of the relevance and adequacy of standards on the military use of "psychological and information warfare" and its impact on women.

6. The Special Rapporteur on Freedom of Opinion and Expression of the Commission on Human Rights to carry out a study on gender, media and conflict.

East Timorese celebrate independence, May 2002.

THE
INDEPENDENT
EXPERTS'
ASSESSMENT
ON

prevention

In Kosovo we met Zlata who told us that when she saw arms caches growing in early 1998, she realized that armed conflict was imminent. But she had no one to tell and doubted that her concerns would be taken seriously. "At a certain point, the boys — young men I suppose, my own nephew also — went up into the hills and got trained," she said. "That was the beginning. Then there were guns, first only some, which is usual, but then a lot of weapons being talked about. I didn't see them, but I heard about them. We knew all this, but still nobody was watching or listening to us in Kosovo."

Sometimes, women have nowhere to turn with their information. A young woman in Sierra Leone named Amy told us that in her village, "we knew roughly where and when the RUF were planning something big against the peacekeepers. My friend and I, we wanted to tell someone, but it was hard, we were watched, it would take a long time to walk in the night, and it was dangerous. It was a big pity too, because the RUF took the guns and the pride of the UN that day, but it took our hope too. We were scared again, which is exactly what they wanted."

Over and over on our journey we heard stories such as Zlata's and

Amy's — stories that appear to be about women's helplessness and marginalization. But gradually we learned to listen to these narratives differently, and to appreciate that they were a signal — of the potential escalation of hostilities — that had been ignored. Preventing deadly conflict is as much about knowing the signs as it is about acting on them. Women have much to offer but their analysis is often devalued and their solutions deemed irrelevant. Because women are disconnected from what are considered "high politics" and the "seats of power," there are few opportunities for information from and about them to inform preventive actions. Yet throughout our visits we saw impressive, though generally small scale, actions by women working to build peace and resolve conflicts. Ultimately, we came to view women's experiences and perceptions as an untapped set of resources to prevent deadly conflict and its resurgence.

In November 1999 United Nations Secretary-General Kofi Annan urged the international community to move from a culture of reaction to a culture of prevention.[1] The United Nations, regional organizations, non-governmental organizations (NGOs) and women's peace groups have taken concrete steps towards establishing systems of early warning and response.[2] The European Union (EU), the Organisation for Security and Cooperation in Europe (OSCE) and the African Union (AU),[3] groups such as the G8 representing the major economic powers, and NGOs have all begun to recognize that deadly conflict can be prevented and are re-examining what it takes to do that. Addressing the root causes of conflict and investing in development is the first step.

Processes such as disarming and demobilizing the warring factions, or transforming a corrupt or crumbling police force, are not only part of ending a war but also a way of preventing future wars. Whether through preventive deployment, grass-roots reconciliation or security sector reform, we are convinced that women's contribution to these processes can make a difference.

GENDER, INFORMATION AND EARLY WARNING

Formal early warning systems monitor potential crisis situations, collect information and generate analyses that will give decision makers a way to assess risk and find openings for preventive action. Preventing an incipient armed conflict requires time — time to gather and analyse information, time to build political support for action and time to design and implement preventive strategies. The signs of potential conflict or resurgence are as many as the methods for collecting them. Some organizations collect and report data on human rights violations; others carry out case studies on specific conflicts or broadcast information about drought, diseases, famine and other potential causes of conflict. The Centre for Documentation and Research of the UN High Commission for Refugees (UNHCR) monitors and analyses information to predict refugee flows, while the Global Information and Early Warning System (GIEWS) run by the Food and Agricultural Organization (FAO) provides alerts of imminent food crises. The early warning system of the North Atlantic Treaty Organization (NATO) is structured to foresee a different range of threats and crises, leading to both non-military and military response options.

In the eyes of many early warning experts, the system is working well except for some deficits in information analysis and response. But from our perspective, one of the major problems is that women and gender issues have been left out. By and large, early warning systems do not consider information about what is happening to women or what they are doing. In their "Preliminary Framework on Gender and Conflict Early Warning," Eugenia Piza-Lopes of the NGO International Alert and Susanne Schmeidl of the Swiss Peace Foundation suggest that incorporating gender-sensitive indicators may fine-tune existing approaches to information collection and analysis. They argue that previously overlooked signs of instability at the grass-roots level provide early warning signals of impending conflict.[4]

Preliminary research suggests that the status of women is associated with a country's level of stability.[5] Countries with very low percentages of women in parliament or with high rates of domestic violence are considered more prone to repression and violent conflict. Afghanistan under the Taliban, with its massive human rights violations against women, is one such example. Other "gendered" violations, including rape, trafficking and military-related prostitution, are also indicators.

Although always context specific, other indicators that are often overlooked in early warning and information collection systems include:

- propaganda emphasizing hyper-masculinity
- media scapegoating of women, accusing them of political or cultural betrayal
- sex-specific refugee migrations
- engagement of women in a shadow war economy
- sex-specific unemployment
- resistance to women's participation in peace processes and negotiations
- lack of presence of women in civil society organizations
- growth of fundamentalism
- increase in female-headed house-holds[6]

The indicators of potential conflict are often visible in the routines of daily existence. Espionage and high tech surveillance methods are not always the best tools; the signs of potential conflict may be as obvious as the operating time of markets or the price of a gun. In Sierra Leone one woman told us, "As the war was brewing, women were up and about very early in the morning, getting all of their business done as quickly as possible. The markets were only open for a few hours because people were afraid. When the market was open for longer, it was a sign that things were getting back to normal." In Burundi according to another woman, "In the morning, if we see women coming down from the mountain, then we know it is safe to send our children to school. If we don't see women, we know that something may happen. They have been sent back by the men for a reason, and it is very possible that it is not safe."

Women's efforts to prevent and resolve conflicts are equally as important as the information they gather as they go about their day. Women's peaceful protest can also reveal new opportunities for non-military preventive action.

Though successful in the short term, women's often bold and creative efforts at peace-building

are rarely followed up or supported, despite the plethora of opportunities to do so. When receiving information about potential conflicts, for example, the UN Secretary-General can alert the Security Council and initiate fact-finding missions; he has also been asked by the Security Council "to include information on gender mainstreaming throughout peacekeeping missions and all other aspects relating to women and girls" in his reports on country and thematic issues. But very little information has been made public, except for reports from Kosovo, the Democratic Republic of the Congo, East Timor and Sierra Leone, where gender units or advisers have been part of peacekeeping operations. This lack of information is partly due to the fact that information collection systems are not broken down by sex, and partly because of a lack of expertise.

The absence of information about and from women has been signalled in recent UN resolutions and reports, including the Secretary-General's July 2001 report on conflict prevention, in which he called on the Council to make protecting women's human rights part of conflict prevention and peace-building, and urged it to include a gender perspective in its work.[7] The Security Council reaffirmed this, in its Resolution 1366 on conflict prevention, which calls for greater attention to gender perspectives in the implementation of peacekeeping and peace-building mandates as well as in conflict prevention.[8] While the importance of gender is well recognized, concrete measures to improve the flow of early warning information from and about women have not been put in place. If preventive visits and fact-finding missions to areas of potential conflict were to routinely include gender expertise and consultations with women's organizations, systematic and useable information about women could be collected and analysed. Only then could "gender perspectives" be turned into concrete early warning indicators.

The 2001 statement by the Foreign Ministers of the G8 industrial nations on "Strengthening the Role of Women in Conflict Prevention" describes the opportunities available for supporting and identifying local women who represent an influential voice for peace, and delineates the resources needed to carry this out.[9] The G8 statement emphasizes the importance of the systematic involvement of women in the prevention and resolution of conflicts and in peace-building, as well as their full and equal participation in all phases of conflict prevention, resolution and peace-building. It also encourages the participation of all actors of civil society, including women's organizations, in conflict prevention and conflict resolution, and encourages the sharing of experiences and best practices.[10] Now, a reporting mechanism is needed to monitor their progress on implementing these commitments.

At the NGO level, there are many regional organizations that recognize the importance of women's input. The European Platform for Conflict Prevention and Transformation is an open network of some 150 European NGOs that are involved in the prevention and/or resolution of violent conflicts in the international arena. It facilitates the exchange of information and experience among participating organizations, including women's organizations.[11] The African Centre for the Constructive Resolution of Disputes (ACCORD), founded in 1991, is one of many African NGOs focused on conflict prevention that has devoted considerable energies to exploring gender and African women's role in prevention and peace-building.[12] The Global Action Plan to Prevent War was launched by a large coalition of international and national groups in 1999 and also focuses on women's role in conflict prevention throughout the world.[13]

DISARMAMENT, DEMOBILIZATION AND REINTEGRATION (DDR) — THE KEY TO KEEPING THE PEACE

During the post-conflict period prevention of new violence depends not only on early warning systems, but on the willingness of armed groups to lay down their arms, disband military structures and return to civilian life. If armed groups or warlords do not put down their weapons, peace will never be possible. When weapons remain in circulation, they combine with trauma, poverty and lawlessness to turn neighbourhoods and homes into war zones, heightening the lethality of crime and of domestic and political violence. If dis-

armed ex-combatants become "restless" — as officials in Sierra Leone describe the 30,000 former fighters awaiting reintegration — the peace is fragile at best.[14] This is why disarmament, demobilization and reintegration (DDR) programmes need to be thoughtfully planned, and adequately funded with a long-term commitment to see the process through.

Each of the DDR processes involves and has implications for women, whether they participated in combat, have family members who did, or are members of a community trying to integrate former combatants. While some women joined armed groups of their own free will, large numbers were abducted into combat and/or forced to become sexual and domestic slaves. But no matter how they came to military groups, almost all of them are neglected during the DDR process. El Salvador, where female ex-combatants were effectively excluded from the reintegration programme is just one example.

Disarmament

Disarmament is the most essential and most frequently neglected component of the DDR effort. In Mozambique because of the small weapons left in circulation after the civil war, crime took on an added danger: women were raped at gunpoint and homes were robbed by armed thieves.[15] Unless soldiers feel safe without their weapons and can survive by means other than violent crime, disarmament programmes are doomed to fail.

Successful disarmament depends on sufficient resources to effectively disarm, destroy, store and guard weapons caches. Although the responsibility for disarmament rests with the government and is often supported by a peacekeeping force, transitional authority or regional organization, these resources are rarely available. Rather than sit by and do nothing, humanitarian staff or women from the local community may, by default, attempt to collect weapons. In Cambodia a local activist described the situation that has forced women to take action: "There are so many weapons left over from the war. Almost every house has them. Accidental deaths are happening all the time: in domestic arguments; guns are pulled out at traffic jams; even to round up the cows, guns are used. Too many women were getting hurt so we started a campaign to collect them." In the Democratic Republic of the Congo women demanded disarmament on International Women's Day 2001, because they understood it as a first step towards peace. Liberian women organized a weapons collection and destruction campaign before elections in 1997. In many sites we visited we met women who, because of their efforts towards disarmament, were accused of treason by their governments and by rebels for whom the AK-47 symbolized liberation.

Women most affected by guns often have the best ideas about how to remove them from the community. The "Weapons for Development" collection instituted in Albania by the UN Development Programme (UNDP), owes a great deal of its success to women supported by UNIFEM. In Gramsche women went door to door collecting weapons and preaching the danger of small arms under the slogan, "One Less Weapon, One More Life." In Elbasan women collected 2,332 weapons and 1,801 tons of ammunition.[16] In Diber 65 women of various ages, professions, occupations and organizations collected 2,407 weapons and 855 tons of ammunition. And in a district of Tirana women's associations distributed questionnaires on the issue of disarmament. "While [they were] filling out the questionnaire we talked to many women," one of the organizers said. "They spoke about anxiety about the arms they had in their houses. The general feeling was that the arms are a great danger for every family. There were some women who considered arms as necessary for defence because of the weak police force. If the state would better defend people and help them feel safe, then arms would not be needed in the home."[17]

The media, the schools and society in general can play an important role in showing that weapons do not provide security. Operation Essential Harvest, a NATO mission to disarm ethnic Albanian groups in Macedonia, was supported by public service announcements on television and radio, many of which focused on women and

home safety. According to Major Jeffrey White, responsible for NATO Southern Region Psychological Operations, "We found this theme to resonate very powerfully with women, and contrary to our first thoughts, even with many men. I would say it is demonstrably the best approach overall to these types of efforts."[18]

Demobilization

Aisha is from a village near Baidoa, Somalia. Her husband, brother and children were all killed in an attack on her village. Since all of their belongings were looted, she arrived in Baidoa without any

> "As the war was brewing, women were up and about very early in the morning, getting all of their business done as quickly as possible. The markets were only open for a few hours because people were afraid. When the market was open for longer, it was a sign that things were getting back to normal."

clothes. Aisha told us that she decided to join the fight against the militia that had attacked her village out of a desire for revenge and became part of a group of 50 militia women. But life in the military was mainly a struggle for survival. "We walked for 5 days in the bush without food and without water. Mostly we supported the young boys by taking care of the wounded and by bringing them water when we found some. Often I had to walk 350 to 380 kilometres carrying ammunition and food. I also used to cook for them."

Sarah in Sierra Leone spent three years with the Revolutionary United Front (RUF), a rebel group known for its brutality towards civilians. Unlike Aisha, she did not join of her own accord. "I was taken by the RUF when I was 14 years old," Sarah told us. "Now I am 17. I was made to be the 'wife' of a man for nearly two years. That is quick to say, two years, but every day felt like a year to me. I feel like an old woman now. Nobody will ever want me. I don't want to face my family because they know what happened. I will never love."

Aisha and Sarah represent two examples of the ways in which women become part of armed groups. Some join voluntarily as combatants, and perhaps even larger numbers are abducted and enslaved. What they have in common is the experience of war and the likelihood of being excluded from demobilization programmes, when former combatants are offered assistance to help meet their immediate basic needs, and are discharged and transported to their home communities. In some cases experienced troops are recruited into a new, unified military force.

Since many demobilization programmes base eligibility on a "one-man, one-gun" model and since most women forced into combat or support functions do not own weapons – even if they used them – they are often excluded from these programmes. According to a woman ex-combatant in Sierra Leone, "Unless you were a fighter with a weapon to lay down, you are not eligible to join the programme." The situation in East Timor was similar. Male Failintil fighters were offered the option of joining the new East Timor Defence Force; those who chose not to received the equivalent of US$100 along with language and computer training. Nothing comparable was offered to the women who had performed support functions throughout the struggle. In Somalia there is currently no DDR programme at all. Women's groups have identified at least 420 female ex-combatants, most of who were attacked and raped by opposing forces before joining a militia. Most are illiterate and eager to be educated.

Demobilizing women means more than providing vocational alternatives; it also means overcoming the difficulties women face in everything from receiving financial payments when they do not have bank accounts to making autonomous decisions about their future. During the demobilization phase, abducted women need private spaces where they can speak confidentially with staff to tell them if they are being held against their will, or to ask for reintegration and training. If the women do leave their captors, they may need special arrangements to protect them from reprisals.[19]

Reintegration

All combatants find it difficult to reintegrate into civilian communities, but it is especially challenging for women, who usually receive less support than men do, even from their families. Some of the challenges faced by former combatants are social. The rules of war – or the lack of rules, as in many local wars – do not apply in civilian life, and readjustment can be hard. Women who voluntarily joined armed groups face an extra layer of alienation because in many cultures their decision violates traditional expectations. This means that communities may be suspicious of women returning from battle, and that the women themselves may no longer feel they fit in. This may be due to the new responsibilities and skills they have acquired during conflict, or it may be related to their struggle to deal with abuses they have survived, or both.

Many women who participate in combat have lived through violent battles and experienced brutal sexual violence, both of which can lead to post-traumatic stress disorder. They often refuse to speak about what happened to them for fear of being mocked or ostracized or further violated. While the isolation that accompanies this silence is in some ways self-protective, it also makes it harder for women to settle down to a new life.[20]

Despite their clear needs, women are not included in most reintegration programmes and are typically excluded from veterans' associations. Their wartime experiences do not bring them the status and social roles accorded to male combatants; their voices and experiences tend to disappear when peace processes begin,[21] and they are rarely looked to as leaders during reconstruction. Too often former combatants, women and men alike, find themselves in competition for scarce resources with non-combatants, such as returning displaced persons. Tensions frequently occur between former combatants, returnees and those who did not take up arms when one group perceives the other as receiving more privileges. Although reintegrating ex-combatants is central to creating a secure post-conflict society, all such initiatives should be designed to take into account the needs of combatants as well as receiving communities.

SECURITY SECTOR REFORM

Security does not just mean the end of war, it means the ability to go about your business safely, in a safe environment, to go to work, to go home, and to travel outside your home knowing that your family is safe and will not be harmed.

— Lakhdar Brahimi
Special Representative of the
Secretary-General, Afghanistan[22]

When an armed conflict ends, maintaining the ceasefire and preventing further violence depends on reform within the military, the police and the justice system. Former combatants are generally united into one military, military and police functions are separated, and the rule of law is re-established. But security sector reform is also about civil society regaining faith and democratic control of all those organizations that have authority to use or threaten force. This goal can't be achieved without building a security sector that protects and involves women.

Women will never be safe if those who committed crimes during conflict are not held accountable. In Rwanda one woman asked us, "How can we be expected to believe that men in the uniform of our new government will protect us when so many of them were themselves our brutalizers?" Often the military and police who committed abuses in the past are still in place after a ceasefire. At the public hearing on crimes against women held in Tokyo in December 2000, a 19-year-old Burundian woman described what happened after she had been kidnapped and raped by rebels:

"One day, after their normal 'homework' of raping me, they told me that they would take me to my brothers. Brothers meaning the government soldiers...They pulled me to a certain point and told me to walk by myself towards a government military position...I walked toward the place shown to me and called for help. I mentioned that the rebels brought me there and that I had no guns. Immediately after that, one strong man caught me from the back as if I were a criminal, put me down on the floor and touched me everywhere as if look-ing for guns and ammunitions, identity cards and so on...I wanted them to tell me that I was now in good hands. That I was going to see a doctor and my family. That I'm not pregnant and I don't have AIDS...I was left with one person who asked me to have sex with him. He threatened that if I did not, he would take me back to the rebels. I refused and told him that I'm going to die. He then tied me up like the previous group of people, forced himself on me and raped me. He left me there soon after and disappeared in the bush. The second person came and did the same, and the third person...Like the first group of rebels, the government soldiers too asked me to keep it secret and said nobody will believe me anyway."[23]

Making sure that the police, military and judiciary protect women and guarantee their legal rights requires specialized training and mandates that make these new functions explicit. Community policing – collaboration between civil society and the police to identify security risks – holds promise for increasing women's security. In

Women's organizations have been at the forefront of researching and protesting the enormous resources devoted to war, asserting that the ability of military violence to achieve its stated aims is routinely over-estimated, while the extent of its costs are overlooked.

Bosnia and Herzegovina and Cambodia, UNIFEM-supported women's groups organized training for police and community leaders to help them respond appropriately to violence against women. In Bosnia and Herzegovina local police created special teams to ensure privacy and protection for women who bring charges of violence committed against them. After the Cambodian training police began efforts to combat domestic violence and trafficking.

Human rights monitoring is another way to reintroduce standards of law and humanity, particularly in societies traumatized by violence. An international human rights presence can also lay the foundation for a local human rights structure.

UN Missions such as those in El Salvador or Guatemala have supported emerging human rights and security institutions at the national level.

Addressing gender bias within the judiciary — the very institution that determines how equality is achieved in society — is essential. Sensitizing judges about women's human rights and about gender equality can help mitigate bias. Support services and programmes should be provided to ensure that legal aid is available and that women witnesses and complainants are treated fairly. Legal literacy programmes are urgently needed.

Setting quotas to address the extreme gender imbalance in the security sector is also important.[24] Different security priorities are likely to emerge when women participate in all sectors. Priorities for mine clearance, for example, may shift from clearing military bases to agricultural areas or transportation routes. Women's participation in police forces often means that crimes against women are taken more seriously, but women must be present in all areas of police work. Currently, although their numbers are growing around the world, they are typically assigned only to areas dealing with violence against women and female prisoners.

Security sector reform also requires that the police, military and judiciary are open and democratic. Civilian control of the armed forces, through parliamentary and governmental oversight, must be the fundamental starting point for security sector reforms, but in many conflict and post-conflict situations, the veil of secrecy over national security prevents civilian oversight. This is doubly true when security sector functions are privatized, as is happening in many countries.

Private organizations and mercenaries increasingly play roles once considered the preserve of governments, and have been engaged in the conflicts in Angola, Papua New Guinea and Sierra Leone. Private groups are also often hired to provide security to humanitarian workers and training for police and military forces. They sell arms and take up combat roles in wars. Central to the concern about these companies is the lack of accountability and absence of any legislation to regulate their activities, including their treatment of women.[25]

Ultimately those entities that fight for financial gain are a dangerous threat to the sovereignty of states and are anathema to the broader requirements of transparency and good governance that are the basis for democratic security sector reform. The international community first condemned the use of mercenaries in 1968. In 1989 the General Assembly strengthened its position when it adopted the International Convention against the Recruitment, Use, Financing and Training of Mercenaries, and a recent UN Expert Panel recommended that a monitoring mechanism be established to improve the accountability of private security and military companies.[26]

THE COST OF INVESTING IN WAR RATHER THAN PREVENTION

For 87 years the Women's International League for Peace and Freedom has insisted that wars are preventable. Ever since 1915, we have signalled developments that unless managed quickly would develop into violent conflict and war. We reject the idea that war is inevitable and is part of human existence. It is the deliberate investment in and preparation for war, pursued under the guise of "defence," that makes armed conflict inevitable. If we are serious about preventing war, we must support the United Nations and proceed with systematic disarmament – disarming militaries, economies, cultures and lives. This is what will save future generations from the scourge of war.

— Edith Ballantyne, Women's International League for Peace and Freedom

Increased military spending has not increased world security. Women's organizations have been at the forefront of researching and protesting the enormous resources devoted to war, asserting that the ability of military violence to achieve its stated aims is routinely over-estimated, while the extent of its costs are overlooked.[27] The U.S. military budget for fiscal year 2003 alone is $396.1 billion,[28] which is more than the combined spending of the next 25 biggest military spenders.[29] While recognizing a country's right to defend itself from violent aggression, women's organizations are overwhelmingly calling for an international condemnation of first strike policies. In 1997, 99,000 women signed their names to the

Women's Peace Petition presented to the General Assembly.[30]

This petition called for at least 5 per cent of national military expenditures each year over the next five years to be redirected towards health, education and employment programmes.[31]

Research suggests that just one quarter of the world's approximately US$839 billion in military spending[32] would allow nations to provide decent housing, health and education to their citizens. It would also allow governments to provide energy, clean up the environment, stop global warming, ease the debt burden, disarm nuclear weapons and de-mine the world.[33]

As the World Bank has pointed out, excessive levels of military spending divert scarce resources and impede good governance. The Bank cites the potential benefits of reducing global military spending for balancing economic disparities — which are the root of many conflicts — and for improving environmental conditions. Yet so far, very few governments have acted to reduce their military spending. The military establishment is one of the few sectors that is exempt from trade regulations established by the World Trade Organization.[34] The Security Council has yet to act on Article 26 of the United Nations Charter calling for it to formulate a plan "for the least diversion for armaments of the world's human and economic resources." Meanwhile, the Permanent Five Security Council members face a clear conflict of interest: they are the main purveyors of the international arms trade and reap 85 per cent of its billions of dollars in profit.[35]

Article 33 of the UN Charter calls on parties to any dispute to "first of all seek a solution by negotiation, enquiry, mediation, conciliation, arbitration, judicial settlement, resort to regional agencies or arrangements, or other peaceful means of their own choice." The reality could not be further from this: Instead, governments have chosen to go to war dozens and dozens of times since 1945, leaving millions dead, and millions more injured and displaced.

Despite the selective implementation of the UN Charter, it provides a clear mandate and formula for conflict prevention. Through its calls for early warning, preventive action, disarmament and demilitarization, it delineates the path for "saving succeeding generations from the scourge of war." It is time to recommit to this goal with renewed determination and with the benefit of the energy and efforts of the world's women.

9

RECOMMENDATIONS

ON THE PREVENTION OF CONFLICT THE EXPERTS CALL FOR:

1. The Secretary-General to systematically include information on the impact of armed conflict on women and women's role in prevention and peace-building in all of his country and thematic reports to the Security Council. Towards that end, the Secretary-General should request relevant information from UN operations and all relevant bodies.

2. The systematic collection and analysis of information and data by all actors, using gender specific indicators to guide policy, programmes and service delivery for women in armed conflict. This information should be provided on a regular basis to the Secretariat, Member States, inter-governmental bodies, regional organizations, NGOs and other relevant bodies. A central knowledge base should be established and maintained by UNIFEM together with a network of all relevant bodies, in particular the Department of Political Affairs (DPA).

3. The Security Council to formulate a plan for the least diversion for armaments of the world's human and economic resources. Sixty years after being assigned the task, the Security Council should implement Article 26 of the United Nations Charter, taking into account the Women's Peace Petition which calls for the world's nations to redirect at least 5 per cent of national military expenditures to health, education and employment programmes each year over the next five years.

4. The UN Development Programme (UNDP), as a leading agency in the field of security sector reform, to ensure that women's protection and participation be central to the design and reform of security sector institutions and policies, especially in police, military and rule of law components. UNDP should integrate a gender perspective into its country programmes.

5. Operational humanitarian, human rights and development bodies to develop indicators to determine the extent to which gender is mainstreamed throughout their operations in conflict and post-conflict situations and ensure that gender mainstreaming produces measurable results and is not lost in generalities and vague references to gender. Measures should be put in place to address the gaps and obstacles encountered in implementation.

6. Inter-governmental and regional organizations to strengthen and expand women's role in conflict prevention and peace-building. To this end, the UN together with regional organizations should convene an Expert Group Meeting to improve collaboration, share information and develop expertise.

7. In cooperation with relevant UN bodies, UNIFEM to develop and test a set of gender-based early warning indicators for mainstreaming into the UN Early Warning Framework and explore use of such indicators with regional organizations.

8. Disarmament, Demobilization and Reintegration (DDR) initiatives to equitably benefit women ex-combatants and those forced into service by armed groups. Resettlement allowances and other forms of support should be provided on a long-term basis.

9. The UN to conduct a "lessons learned" study on the gender aspects of DDR processes in which it has been involved.

Two women carry wood salvaged from ruined homes in Sarajevo, Bosnia and Herzegovina.

reconstruction

We entered through a small wooden doorway into the dimly lit room. There was no electricity. Slowly our eyes adjusted and we could make out the faces of 15 women sitting in a half-circle around the room. At first no one spoke. In the amplified silence we heard the buzzing of flies and outside the sound of uninterrupted hammering, as local villagers worked to rebuild their homes on the ruins of Liquica, East Timor.

One by one the women introduced themselves and began to tell us their stories. As each woman spoke the others sat quietly, hands folded in their laps. They described what happened in April 1999, when pro-Indonesia militia attacked the church in the centre of Liquica. Townspeople had taken refuge in the church, believing it was a safe haven. The militia found them there. They slaughtered the men and raped the women. Those who survived escaped to the capital, Dili, or to the mountains. One woman told us that she knew the killer of her husband who was hiding in a camp in West Timor. He was from one of the "specialized units" of the Indonesian national army — some specialized in rape, others in murder or burning villages or disposing of the dead. The women never learned what happened to the bodies of their husbands killed in the church.

The stories were shockingly familiar: rape, pillage, mutilation, torture, death. The women showed no agitation when they spoke of the horror and violence they had endured. But if they showed no anger, neither were they resigned. They had come together in a conscious and determined act of survival. These women of Liquica had returned to their village 18 months before and formed a cooperative. Together they built the small communal house we were seated in and use it to meet regularly, to organize community events, to make handicrafts and to sell produce. They share the workload and the profits. Several were farming small plots of land. They had succeeded in forming a tight unit that meets their immediate survival needs and provides social support. The women accomplished all this without outside support, resources or training. It was painfully obvious that, with assistance and guidance, with proper skills and tools, they could achieve much more.

Three months earlier we had visited the Balkans where women were struggling to claim their share of the resources being channeled for post-conflict reconstruction. Vesna, an activist from Mostar in Bosnia and Herzegovina, told us, "Woman has grown in wartime because she has carried the burden while the men were away fighting. She will therefore not settle for less now, after the war." But the reality is that women in countries emerging from conflict — in Bosnia and Herzegovina, Cambodia, East Timor and Sierra Leone — have not been given equal opportunities to work or take part in community and political life. Instead they have been marginalized, left to scrape together small earnings from cottage industries and to sell handmade items, the products of their domestic life.

Vesna told us how pleased she had been, initially, when she qualified for a small business loan. She worked single-handedly to build her own tailoring business but in the end was frustrated by the experience. "In order to receive a small credit of around US$100, women are expected to work day and night," she told us. "Those conditions drive women into the black market where they are exploited. If they are not smart enough to bribe the right people, they will find themselves under arrest."

In Guatemala we learned of similar frustrations. Niluz, who lived in a small village, told us that the economic benefits for women included in the peace agreement had been ignored while many of the policies that had been implemented were detrimental. Like the women of Bosnia, Niluz understood the implications very well: "The war was fought off women's backs and now the country is being rebuilt with their sweat," she said bitterly.

Women carry the burden of domestic work, and during conflict their unpaid labour becomes even more complex and demanding. Water, health care, transportation and other public services are hit first and hardest by war. Without these services, women are left to fend for themselves. They may spend hours hunting for firewood and carrying water. Very often they take on additional roles and responsibilities, performing "men's" work as well as their own. They farm land even though they cannot legally possess it. They build homes they are not entitled to own. When schools are closed or destroyed, they teach their children at home. They care for the sick and wounded. During the Taliban regime, women in Afghanistan drew maps to help each other locate community services, ran clandestine schools for girls, provided health care for women and set up home-based work to support their families.

Even after peace is declared, women are threatened by militarization and the culture of violence that persists in post-conflict situations. The collapse of governments and social fragmentation leave women exposed to physical attack and exploitation. But the devastation is lucrative for some. In many conflict situations warlords and profiteers create separate economies that thrive on the breakdown of social and economic order. They inflate the price of food and other necessities, sell arms and seize land, or steal humanitarian aid. They market diamonds, timber, gold and other natural resources, and illegal drugs. And they traffic girls and women. In North and South Kivu, in the Democratic Republic of the Congo

(DRC), militias attacked villages and abducted women to be forced labourers in mines. In Rwanda land and property were seized during the genocide. Illicit profit-making can come to dominate post-war economies, where instability creates a lawless environment. Secretary-General Kofi Annan pointed to the mounting international concern over this issue: "Despite the devastation that conflict brings, there are many who profit from the chaos and lack of accountability, and who may have little or no interest in stopping the conflict and much interest in prolonging it."[1]

But even in war economies, women find ways to cope. Their skills and capacities, which have been almost totally neglected, are one of the greatest untapped resources for stabilizing and rebuilding community life. After the genocide in Rwanda, village women created the Duhozanye Association — which translates, "Let's Console Each Other." The association's founder and president described how it began:

"After the genocide, the widows decided to get together. There were 310 of us ... At the first gathering it was mostly crying and some talking. We told each other what happened to us. Little by little we got accustomed to the situation — crying wasn't the solution. We thought of activities to do. We thought about getting lodging and getting houses ... A group of four or five would build for one, then go to another to build a shelter for her. If it was too difficult we would go to the local authorities and ask them to help build the house. In Rwanda women are not allowed to go on the roof. That is the man's job. At first we'd go out at night to repair our houses, so no one would see us. But then someone found out and gave us pants to wear. Then we decided it did not matter if anyone laughed. We went out during the day."[2]

Restoring community life after conflict is a long process that brings together a broad range of political, economic and social issues, many addressed elsewhere in this report. Several specific areas are examined in detail here.

TRANSITIONAL AID

In making a transition from war to peace, resources matter. Reconstruction provides a rare opportunity for women not only to help shape emerging political, economic and social structures, but to benefit from the large amount of funds pooled by bilateral and multilateral donors. How these resources affect women's lives will depend on many factors: the volume of aid, the channels for its distribution, the timing, its intended purpose and the conditions attached to it. Although women may benefit broadly from the positive forces of reconstruction, there is no doubt in our minds that the vast majority of aid for reconstruction and peace-building is not being directed to women. They certainly will not receive their fair share without deliberate planning and we see little evidence that this planning is taking place.

In Somalia members of women's groups told us that they were frustrated by the lack of international assistance. One woman spoke out frankly: "No one cares about us. The Somali Aid Coordination Body does nothing for women. The United Nations and the European Union are not interested in women's issues either. We are not invited to contribute to the donor discussions and decisions on reconstruction projects. How can we organize ourselves and be expected to participate in reconstruction and decision-making if we have no support?"

For women to benefit equitably from transitional aid, specific policy and programme strategies are needed. Data must be broken out by gender, so that those developing a transitional assistance plan can understand how it will affect women. Gender expertise must be available, and there must be follow-up, monitoring and reporting. We do not know of a single transitional plan that meets even one of these requirements.

Although the 2002 Needs Assessment for Afghanistan, prepared by the World Bank and the Asian Development Bank, made important gestures to improving women's status, it did not include women or gender issues as a specific sector. Only .07 per cent of funds were requested for women-specific projects in the $1.7 billion UN-sponsored Immediate and Transitional Assistance Programme for 2002.[3] We understand that this should not be taken as the only indicator to measure how reconstruction benefits women; there is no question that women will benefit from funds and programmes in other sectors. But the fact that gender remains one of the least funded sectors in a country where women's inequality was so central to the conflict is wholly unacceptable.

Similar data emerges from other transition plans. The World Bank Reconstruction and Development Programme in Bosnia and Herzegovina has no gender analysis and mentions women only once, in the micro-credit section.[4] The World Bank Group Transitional Support Strategy for Kosovo does not mention gender or women at all. Nor did the UN's Mission in Kosovo (UNMIK) Consolidated Budget for 2001, except for one gender-training project costing $31,000, or approximately .006 per cent of the total budget of $467 million. No money is committed to supporting this project after the initial funding.[5] In East Timor's draft national budget, the Office of Equality was given only 6 permanent staff out of a total of nearly 15,000 civil servants, and a budget of less than half of one per cent — $38,000 — of a total budget of approximately $77 million.[6]

"It is amazing," said one Kosovar woman working as a secretary in UNMIK,"that the international community cared only about Kosovar women when they were being raped — and then only as some sort of exciting story. We see now that they really don't give a damn about us. What we see are men, men, men from Europe and America and even Asia, listening to men, men, men from Kosovo. Sometimes they have to be politically correct so they include a woman on a committee or they add a paragraph to a report. But when it comes to real involvement in the planning for the future of this country, our men tell the foreign men to ignore our ideas. And they are happy to do so — under the notion of 'cultural sensitivity.' Why is it politically incorrect to ignore the concerns of Serbs or other minorities, but 'culturally sensitive' to ignore the concerns of women? I wish someone would explain this!"

Women miss out even before the spoils of peace are divided. Aid intended for reconstruction that has been vetted through humanitarian or emergency channels rarely takes account of women. Although the UN called for a gender perspective to be mainstreamed in humanitarian activities and policies by the year 2000, the April 2002 External Review of the Inter-Agency Consolidated Appeals, for example, while nearly 80 pages in length, makes no mention of gender except briefly in the context of the group's own working mechanism to support gender mainstreaming.[7]

Moreover, the Inter-Agency Standing Committee on Humanitarian Affairs (IASC) — the group of agencies that are involved in humanitarian situations — only recently admitted the United Nations Population Fund (UNFPA) as a member after a difficult negotiation. While the IASC has acknowledged that there is a need for greater involvement of UNFPA, UNIFEM and the Joint UN programme on HIV/AIDS (UNAIDS) when decisions are being made that affect women in emergency situations, currently the agencies most concerned with women's issues have little input into many of the humanitarian policies developed by the United Nations. A staff member from UNFPA who travelled to East Timor to provide basic supplies for safe birthing was asked by one staff person from the Office for the Coordination of Humanitarian Affairs (OCHA) why UNFPA was involved. "This is an emergency situation," he was told. "We are concerned with food and shelter right now. It is not time for what you do." The UNFPA staffer had to point out that even in emergency situations, women were still pregnant and delivering and that victims of sexual violence need immediate treatment.

Consolidated Appeals Process (CAPs) projects that focus on more subtle needs, such as women's vocational training, have rarely been funded by donors. One interpretation for this is that donors prefer to support higher priority concerns such as food and shelter. This is, of course, true — but sadly, even basic food, shelter and protection needs are not fully supported in the CAPs. In 2002 the World Food Programme (WFP) and the High Commission for Refugees (UNHCR) faced acute funding crises and had to cut programmes in many countries, leaving people without basic support. The Food and Agriculture Organization

(FAO) has been grossly underfunded for agricultural rehabilitation, as well. This has seriously affected women — the simple lack of food has led to sexual exploitation of women and girls in countries such as Angola, Liberia, Sierra Leone and Somalia. The provision of food is a basic necessity — no other investments can pay off if people do not have enough food.

Interestingly, international donors have been more receptive to the idea of establishing what is known as "women's machinery" — depending on the structure of the government, this could mean a Ministry for Women's Affairs, an office, or a bureau in the executive office. Women's machineries are considered a strategic way to bring a gender perspective into all aspects of government and processes of constitutional, legislative, policy and judicial reforms. However, while donors are willing to help these offices get up and running, they are often reluctant to take on the recurring costs. Donor support is critical for a women's machinery to function, but it can also create a dependence on external funding. If donors support a women's ministry, it is often less likely to be given priority in the national budget.

Understanding how donors and governments give priority to women in their budgets is often referred to as "gender budget analysis." Assessing the budget priorities of transitional assistance plans and national budgets from a gender perspective is one way to see how women will benefit from available resources. Gender budget analysis looks at direct allocations to women and the way in which other expenditures or priorities will have an impact on women's lives. It looks at specifics within and across sectors — spending on education versus spending on the military, or spending on commercial versus domestic water use, for example. It also looks at how each budget line will affect women: Will there be jobs and training for women in new public construction projects? Will new taxes fall more heavily on women than on men? Gender budget analysis is also an important training tool for women because it looks at the process of creating a budget. It allows them to understand governance

in a wholly new, hands-on way. It gives women a stake in setting the priorities for reconstruction. In South Africa, Tanzania and Uganda, women have used gender budget analysis as a way to hold their governments accountable for delivering on their pledges for gender equality, for health care spending and for the delivery of water. In Peru 40 municipalities included a gender perspective in their development planning, thanks to gender budget analysis.[8]

Can Micro-Credit Make a Difference?

Not only are women excluded from reconstruction funds and programmes, they rarely benefit from business opportunities generated by those funds. While international and regional business-

Vesna, an activist from Mostar in Bosnia and Herzegovina, told us, "Woman has grown in wartime because she has carried the burden while the men were away fighting. She will therefore not settle for less now, after the war." But the reality is that women in countries emerging from conflict have not been given equal opportunities to work or take part in community and political life.

es are profiting from large-scale contracts, women are more likely to be offered micro-credit — small loans for start-up businesses — which is being hailed as a way to overcome the feminization of poverty.

In some cases micro-credit has helped women, especially when it is designed with a very careful understanding of the local context. In Rwanda micro-credit programmes for displaced and widowed women were among the first kinds of assistance made available during reconstruction. The loans helped support activities such as agriculture, animal farming and home-based enterprises. They strengthened business networks among women and increased their confidence. Micro-finance has also been linked with education in innovative ways. "Credit with Education" programmes combine lending with training in public health or vocational and business skills. These programmes include everything from family planning to HIV/AIDS prevention to literacy and nutrition. Many Rwandan women told us that the programmes had literally saved their lives. In Uganda the Foundation for Credit and Community Assistance offers village banking along with micro-credit and education.

But micro-credit is no panacea. Lucretia, the training officer of a local non-governmental organization (NGO) in the DRC, does not think much of traditional micro-credit programmes. "We have been visited by a number of international groups who say they want to help us — and it seems as if they all have the same Bible — micro-credit! They come and say that they can provide a little money to get materials for women to make baskets and sell them. I always ask — who do you think will buy these baskets? No one here has any money. Some people haven't seen a bank note in two years! And it isn't as if we are getting a planeload of tourists every day. If we lend a woman money, how will she pay it back? I know that micro-credit can work in places like Bangladesh, but they have an economy there. People have jobs and can buy things. We would love to be like Bangladesh. But we are more like hell, I am sorry to say. Some of these agencies can't see the difference."

There is a small but growing body of literature that indicates women are falling into a "microfinance ghetto." Small loans limit them to small purchases, such as a sewing machine or one or two farm animals. These purchases can generate immediate income but, without larger loans, the businesses cannot grow. And the persistent cultural bias that perceives women as supplementary wage-earners, rather than as entrepreneurs, often keeps them stalled at the level of household and cottage industries. Even in Bangladesh, where micro-credit has been heralded as a success, women have found that a small increase in income from a home-based business may come at the expense of much heavier workloads and repayment pressures. In some instances women have been charged interest rates as high as 20 per cent. In another instance a study of four micro-credit programmes showed that 39 per cent of the women interviewed had little or no control over their loans, and that their male family members actually controlled the money. It is important to put this in context, however: As Helen Todd, from CASHPOR, a network of micro-credit programmes, said in an interview at the Micro-Credit Summit, "Thirty-nine per cent having little or no control means that 61 per cent have partial or full control. That is a lot better than the kind of powerlessness with which these women begin."[9]

Ultimately, micro-credit programmes must address the root causes of women's poverty. Otherwise, rather than break the cycle of poverty that locks women into the domestic sector and out of larger financial markets, micro-credit can actually reinforce women's marginalization, as Mary, an entrepreneur, told us in Liberia:"Why is it that it is only men's companies that get the contracts for these World Bank and other projects? Because they have the connections and because they are more established. Well, of course they are more established! But if we can't win contracts, how can we become established? It seems like the deck is always stacked against us. Men have made this war and men are profiting from this war. I guess we are supposed to just pick up the pieces."

Women need to be equipped to operate within the broader economy. But in order to take advantage of larger opportunities, women need to learn non-traditional skills and new technologies. They also need access to financial markets and institutions. Some groups have already begun looking at strategies that can make a difference, such as better networking and information-sharing, and access to larger loans and to financial infrastructure as well as to technology and lower insurance and interest rates.

STRENGTHENING PUBLIC SERVICES

Everywhere we visited, whether in the midst of conflict or after peace agreements were signed, we met women spending hours of unpaid labour to provide basic necessities such as water, fuel and food for themselves and their families. In the DRC we met displaced women from the hills and forests of Masisi and Walikali outside Goma. They were able to earn a little income by carrying loads of firewood to sell, but many who were pregnant suffered miscarriages because of the physical strain of carrying heavy loads of wood on their back. In Somalia some of the women we spoke to had to walk for three or four days to fetch 20 litres of water, becoming easy prey for bandits and rapists.

In mountainous Rwanda we visited widows living on a hilltop laced with soil erosion who told us how they struggled to collect water. A woman in her late sixties, who lost her husband and children in the genocide, said: "Look at me, I am an old lady. I cannot go down to get water and walk up again. I therefore have to ask a neighbour's child to fetch water for me. When the child is not available, I have to look for money in order to buy water. I do not work, where do I get the money from?"

Women also provide health care at home. During conflict and emergencies, when public health services are not available, nursing the sick and injured puts an enormous strain on women. In nearly 40 per cent of households surveyed in the occupied Palestinian territories, women on average were found to dedicate 10 hours a day to caring for injured family members. In many countries, particularly in sub-Saharan Africa, women are at the centre of the growing HIV/AIDS crisis and have become virtual slaves in a care economy that deprives them of their mobility, and their right to work and go to school. The impact of HIV/AIDS is compounded by poverty and the destruction of social and health systems during armed conflict. It is no coincidence that 13 of the 17 countries with over 100,000 children orphaned by AIDS are extremely poor countries and either in conflict or threatened by conflict.[10]

In a visit to a clinic in Bas Congo, DRC, we were astounded to see a list of fees on the door. In an attempt at "cost recovery" — so heavily emphasized in structural adjustment programmes — the Ministry of Health has had to establish fees for health services such as antenatal care, immuniza-

tions and family planning. In a country virtually without a health budget, these fees are supposed to help pay the salaries of those who work in the clinics. But very few people can pay the fees, which means that many are going without services. It also means that health workers are going without salaries — which has led in turn to an increase in fees. The situation is untenable. We heard of cases where families tried to pay bills with radios or chickens.

Because of the DRC's debt situation, and because of donor distrust, government ministries are receiving limited direct financial support. The fledgling government cannot pay salaries and basic services are lacking even in the most prosperous areas, such as Bas Congo and Kinshasa. In war-torn regions the situation is even more desperate, but donors and the international assistance community still speak about "sustainability," "cost recovery" and "breaking dependence." How can such a destitute population pay for services? How can services be sustainable when there is no infras-

In Sierra Leone a remarkable woman named Juliana has established a programme for young women forced to sell sex to survive. It offers literacy and vocational training combined with treatment for sexually transmitted infections (STIs). The 'Woman in Crisis' project has provided sorely needed moral support for hundreds of destitute women, but many told us that in the evening, after they attend their training, they still have to prostitute themselves to get enough food to eat.

tructure and the economy is in shambles? Sustainability is an excellent goal, but it is still a dream in the DRC. First, there has to be peace and people have to get on their feet again.

In Sierra Leone a remarkable woman named Juliana has established a programme for young women forced to sell sex to survive. The "Woman in Crisis" project offers literacy and vocational training combined with treatment for sexually transmitted infections (STIs). It has provided sorely needed moral support for hundreds of destitute women, but many told us that in the evening, after they attend their training, they still have to prostitute themselves to get enough food to eat. Others sell their bodies to be able to pay for transportation to the drop-in centre. Juliana is hoping to add a lunch programme and get a bus to bring women there. Cheap public transportation could help the women tremendously. If they could get one meal a day for their children and themselves, they could avoid the dangerous sexual interactions they have each evening. But basic services are not on the agenda. As one UN officer said:

"Donors seem to think that now that there is peace in this country, everything is fine. They have all jumped on the fad of supporting 'governance' — the Special Court, the Peace and Reconciliation Commission, the training of police, even the reconstruction of the houses of the traditional chiefs — but no one seems very interested in supporting basic services such as health, sanitation, clean blood supply, education. The UN agencies here and the NGOs are trying — but our budgets are so small that we can't make a dent. I wonder if the donor community realizes that if people don't get some basic needs met, this peace will not hold. It costs US$2 million a day to maintain the peacekeeping force here — a fraction of that should have been spent earlier to educate people, to develop the economy and provide jobs so that the poor didn't feel so oppressed and forgotten. Development could have prevented this war. Only development now will ensure the peace."

Restoring basic public services will lessen the burdens on women. But reconstruction efforts of the past decades have neglected, by design, that essential task. Instead, aid for reconstruction has stuck to a rigid framework that requires public sector downsizing, reduced government and the expansion of a free-market economy.[11] This has had negative effects on women and the entire peace process. In East Timor these policies led international lenders to demand a reduction in state agricultural assistance, which severely limited

opportunities for women to advance from subsistence to larger-scale farming, and accelerated the trend from national self-sufficiency to dependence on agricultural imports. In an agricultural economy, with so much money being spent to import food, the transitional government quickly needed additional donor funds.[12]

Women are the most affected by structural adjustment policies that reduce government's ability to provide health care, education, water, transportation, energy, housing and sanitation.[13] While seemingly gender-neutral, every policy decision made in these sectors will drastically affect women's lives since they are precisely the sectors in which women provide the majority of their unpaid labour. The privatization of electricity, water and land is particularly devastating for women, who generally do not have the means to purchase land[14] and are unable to afford market rates for electricity and water. We met women in Sierra Leone who spent days in the forest without tools, breaking firewood off with their bare hands and carrying it out on their backs. Some who came back empty-handed were beaten by their husbands.

In many rural communities, water is a life and death issue, yet a private owner sells water only to those who can pay for it. Giving priority to commercial rather than domestic needs for water can deepen the spiralling poverty of women and their families, who will have even less access to this precious resource. Currently private corporations own or operate water systems globally that bring in about $200 billion a year. But this accounts for the water use of only 7 per cent of the world's population, leaving an enormous potential market to be privatized at great profit.[15] Despite the perilous price increases that have already put safe water beyond the reach of poor women in many developing countries, many international institutions promote the privatization of water.

In general, the rush to privatize public services, which has dominated recent macroeconomic approaches and is often the basis for international loans, has created new grievances in post-conflict societies. When a government sells public resources and services to private investors, those resources — and the profits they generate — become concentrated in the hands of a few investors, typically the same people who benefited from pre-existing inequalities. Decisions about where, and to whom, water or electricity should go are made on a purely cost/profit basis.[16] Priority must be given to strengthening public services during reconstruction. This is the only way to create a space for women to play an active role in rebuilding their communities.

LAND AND LIVELIHOOD

"I work this land every day. I know each and every hill and rock and tree as well as I know my own children. How dare anyone tell me that this land has to belong to my dead husband's brother now?" Janet in Liberia asked us. "This land feeds my family. What if he wants to sell it? How will we survive? How can anyone think that this is fair? I will fight for my land even if I have to die. Because if I lose this land my whole family will die."

For many women in countries emerging from conflict, agriculture is their primary source of income and food. Access to land also provides access to critical resources such as water, forest products and property to graze livestock. Most important, having land means having a place to call home. Yet in many countries women don't have the right to own or inherit property. They may have lived on communal land before the conflict, but the destruction of community structures and land seizure by warlords, combatants or local merchants can leave women homeless and impoverished.

In Rwanda the government needed to deal with the staggering number of landless female heads of households after the genocide. A gender desk was established in Parliament supported by UNIFEM in collaboration with the Forum of Women Parliamentarians, and reviewed laws that discriminated against women. The desk successfully argued that women should be given the right to inherit property from their parents or husbands and that widows should be able to reclaim property from male relatives of their deceased husbands. While the process was successful in institutionalizing support for women's rights, the new law granting property rights to women has been difficult to implement at the local level. Traditionalists are loathe to alter centuries-old customs, and Rwandan women's rights activists warn that, without a nationwide education campaign to inform women about their new rights, the law will not be implemented.

Even in countries where women have traditionally been allowed to own land, transactions are likely to be negotiated by men. That means that when land is available for purchase, widows and single women who are without a male relative may be unable to obtain credit, capital and other necessary resources. In Cambodia the indifference of local authorities and the low social status of widows have created enormous obstacles to gaining possession of land. In Bosnia and Guatemala women can inherit property from their spouses, but other family members can and often do prevent widows from claiming their inheritance. In Peru, where widows comprise 26 per cent of displaced families in specially designated *zonas de repoblamiento* or resettlement areas, they report that men control the access to fertile land.

EMPLOYMENT

In post-conflict situations a shortage of male labour caused by deaths in conflict — as high as a third or more of working-age men in some areas[17] — encourages and sometimes forces women to seek employment outside the home, often for the first time in their lives. Women typically find work based on their domestic skills, such as cooking, sewing and hairdressing, or they end up in the so-called unprotected sector, where they may be harassed and forced to work at the whim of an employer. Some may hire themselves out as day labourers on plantations or farms. Others start small-scale gardens to have something to take to market. In Sudan women have been imprisoned for illegally brewing and selling liquor.[18] As became clear to us in our travels, the paid work most available to women is prostitution. In Pakistan Afghan women refugees, who could not even walk outside their home in Afghanistan without a male escort, are now forced to roam the streets for clients. Many have succumbed to drug addiction.[19]

Even for women who find work in the industrial sector the terms and conditions are usually discriminatory, with less pay than men receive and longer working hours.[20] In places like the Balkans, where women have traditionally worked outside the home, they still suffer employment discrimination and shoulder the double burden of caring for families while holding down a full-time job. Large state-owned manufacturing industries, which were traditionally dominated by women, have been closed down, leaving women jobless. The UN Mission's ombudspersons in Sarajevo and Banja Luka told us that the majority of workplace discrimination complaints there come from women. The International Confederation of Free Trade Unions (ICFTU) has responded by providing free legal advice for women employees on workers' rights in Bosnia and Herzegovina, along with training for women to participate in political bargaining and decision-making.

Many women, searching for paid employment, turn to small businesses and self-help projects — risky ventures, especially in post-conflict economies. In Africa, for example, traditional industries run by women, including small-scale agriculture, food processing, textiles and weaving, are bankrupted by cheap imports that flood the market as a result of trade liberalization. This liberalization was supposed to attract foreign investment, but if and when this comes, the new jobs it offers are likely to be low-paying, with long-hours and poor working conditions. It is important to examine the policies promoted by the World Bank and the International Monetary Fund (IMF) to ensure a gender perspective is present in all areas. Privatization policies should take into account the care economy of women, and in the case of public employment, policies should not create a situation in which women are the first to be let go because of spending reductions.

In the face of these enormous challenges, some women — many more than we could have imagined — have overcome the obstacles and created thriving, successful work projects that provide income for themselves and their neighbours. And, in some cases, women are creating new role models. In Somalia we met women making and selling bricks. In Côte d'Ivoire and Ghana UNIFEM provided Liberian refugee women with skills training in non-traditional sectors like construction and brick-making. These women have built their own houses, schools, dormitories and even women's centres in the refugee camps. In East Timor women, trained as *tais* or ceremonial cloth weavers, received very low wages for their many hours of work. Now, with support from UNIFEM, they are forming a regional collaboration to focus on a more strategic and market-oriented approach to cottage industries, which are expected to be a significant source of export earnings.

The International Labour Organization (ILO), through its INFOCUS programme, has developed an extremely practical set of interventions which can help women to develop cooperative ventures and to get the skills which are appropriate to the local situation. UNFPA has helped Eritrean deportees from Ethiopia re-establish a sanitary towel factory. A multitude of NGOs, including the Chamber of Commerce, have supported efforts to empower women entrepreneurs — but there are too few of these efforts. In order for projects like these to succeed and for women to enter the paid workforce with a modicum of success, they need what women the world over need: basic social support, including childcare; legal protection against workplace discrimination; access to jobs with adequate pay; and wage parity. In post-conflict situations, they also need jobs in civil service, construction and other sectors where employment is most abundant. The UN has a unique ability to play a lead role in this. With more developed skills and better access to decision makers, women could share in and contribute to economic growth and reconstruction.

EDUCATION AND TRAINING

Investing in "human capital" is generally not a priority of transitional aid. Yet for most countries emerging from conflict, and certainly among the women we met, rebuilding the education system is a key priority. On every continent, in rural and urban areas, and across all affiliations, women pleaded for education — for themselves and for their daughters. The displaced women we met in Colombia, the farmers in Central Africa and the prostitutes in Cambodia all saw education and training as their key to economic independence and their full participation in political and decision-making processes. Women should not serve as "decoration" they told us, but must be supported to "make a difference in their country's future." Somali women wanted education to help them understand their rights, voice their problems and identify their priorities. Every woman we met in Rwanda saw access to land and education as the bridge to her own future and that of her children.

This came as no surprise. After all, even in non-conflict situations, women and girls have less access to education than men and boys. Of the more than 110 million children not in school, two thirds are girls. Of the world's nearly 960 million illiterate adults, two thirds are women.[21] In Somalia women speak of a "lost generation" who never had a chance to go to school because their education was interrupted by ten years of war. Today it is estimated that 87 per cent of Somali women are illiterate.

The focus of education during reconstruction is almost wholly directed at primary school children. Women are more than ready to sacrifice their own schooling so their children can attend class, even though they know that better skills and education are precisely what they themselves need. Women are eager for education and information that will equip them to start businesses and find better jobs. In Rwanda we met Jane, a widow with five children of her own, who had adopted 20 more children orphaned by war. "It is hard to take care of 25 children by myself," she told us. "I have no education and I am not employed. But what can I do? These children have no parents. Somehow I have to feed and clothe them, and send them to school."

Women should not have to choose between their own education and their family's survival. In Eritrea the WFP and the National Union of Eritrean Women (NUEW) launched a pilot programme to help illiterate women learn to read and write. The Food for Training programme offers oil, cereals, salt and pulses each month to women, and some men, who attend two hours of literacy lessons each day. The food parcel is intended to compensate women for the time they would oth-erwise spend preparing food for their families. WFP and NUEW also plan to offer food for women who attend vocational training courses.[22]

In Costa Rica UNHCR provided support for refugee women from El Salvador and Nicaragua who chose not to repatriate. Women were hired to staff UNHCR offices and to help organize workshops that focused on human rights and gender issues as well as literacy. One literacy project had flexible hours and provided childcare. It also trained participants to become literacy instructors.[23] In Bosnia and Herzegovina Medica Zenica has established an education centre for traumatized women and girls whose education was interrupted during the war. They are offered individual counselling and the opportunity to complete their high school education or a vocational skills-training course.

But these are not the norm. Typically, training for women during post-conflict reconstruction supports occupations that are the least prestigious and most poorly paid. Programmes emphasize domestic functions, such as sewing, knitting and cooking, and rarely take into account skills that women may have learned during conflict.[24] The women we met in Somalia told us, "Our country took the step directly from the Middle Ages to the IT-age and we want to be a part of it. Give us the training." Women in the DRC asked for computers and technical training. If women do not obtain marketable skills or education, poverty is likely to be increasingly feminized and they will be even more vulnerable to exploitation and trafficking.

To increase women's participation in post-conflict economies, particularly in the formal sector, education and vocational skills training need to be geared towards long-term, sustainable employment. That means teaching women more than basic literacy. In fact, many countries combine workshops on entrepreneurship, gender equality, human rights and peace education with literacy classes. Some countries emerging from conflict are starting to recognize the need for women trained at secondary and university levels, so they can qualify for jobs as government workers and professionals in the new economy. Education and job training can be tailored to existing and potential employment and economic opportunities, as the ILO has pointed out and as women's centres supported by UNIFEM in Afghanistan have illustrated. These centres will bring women out of their homes and provide training in a variety of areas with a goal of linking women to employment opportunities.

Men alone cannot rebuild war-torn societies. Too often women are given new roles and responsibilities when emergency relief is underway, and then excluded once the structures of governance are re-established. As countries emerge from the rubble of war, women must be equal partners in rebuilding. Supporting women's participation in reconstruction means giving women access to the rooms where decisions are made. Those rooms tend to be reserved for two groups of people: those with private capital and those with political power. When we met with Winnie Byanyima, a Ugandan parliamentarian, she gave us her assessment: "Women see that private interests are shaping the situation of conflict. We need to think creatively about what women can do to leverage the interlocking of private interests and political interests."

International financial institutions, donors and the United Nations can help ensure that gender equality is a part of governance programmes and economic reforms. When funding reconstruction — building roads and supplying transportation systems, power, telecommunications, housing, water and sanitation — these institutions can insist on policy and structural reforms that are responsive to women's needs and can create entry points for their participation.

Post-conflict reconstruction and peace-building must support a society's transition while also addressing root causes of conflict. This process — neither strictly humanitarian nor developmental in character, but an amalgam of both — cannot take place without involving women. There is no doubt in our minds that reconstruction and peace-building require specific strategies to support women, and that women can be engaged in all phases of the transition to a peacetime economy. Indeed, investing in women may be one of the most effective means for real, sustainable development and peace-building.

10

RECOMMENDATIONS

1. Gender budget analysis of humanitarian assistance and post-conflict reconstruction to ensure that women benefit directly from resources mobilized through multilateral and bilateral donors, including the Consolidated Appeals Process, the Bretton Woods Institutions and donor conferences.

2. Establishment of macroeconomic policies in post-conflict reconstruction that prioritize the public provision of food, water, sanitation, health and energy, the key sectors in which women provide unpaid labour. Special attention should be paid to the consequences for women of decentralization policies.

3. A lead organization to be designated within the United Nations for women's education and training in conflict and post-conflict situations. This lead organization, together with the United Nations Educational, Scientific and Cultural Organization (UNESCO), UNHCR and UNICEF, should ensure that all education programmes for displaced persons provide for women as well as girls.

4. The World Bank, bi-lateral donors, UNDP and all other relevant UN departments, funds and agencies to integrate gender analysis in needs assessments for post-conflict reconstruction and throughout the planning, design, implementation of and reporting on programmes.

5. International organizations and governments to introduce affirmative measures that give local women priority in recruitment during emergencies and post-conflict reconstruction.

6. Affirmative measures to be adopted to guarantee women's socio-economic rights including employment, property ownership and inheritance and access to UN and public sector procurement in post-conflict reconstruction.

7. The International Labour Organization (ILO) to expand vocational and skills training for women in post-conflict situations including in non-traditional, public and private sectors, in a manner that is sustainable and responsive to the local and national economy.

RECOMMENDATIONS BY CHAPTER

I

ON VIOLENCE AGAINST WOMEN THE EXPERTS CALL FOR:

1. An international Truth and Reconciliation Commission on violence against women in armed conflict as a step towards ending impunity. This Commission, to be convened by civil society with support from the international community, will fill the historical gap that has left these crimes unrecorded and unaddressed.

2. Targeted sanctions against trafficking of women and girls. Those complicit must be held accountable for trafficking women and girls in or through conflict areas. Existing international laws on trafficking must be applied in conflict situations and national legislation should criminalize trafficking with strong punitive measures, including such actions as freezing the assets of trafficking rings. Victims of trafficking should be protected from prosecution.

3. Domestic violence to be recognized as systematic and widespread in conflict and post-conflict situations and addressed in humanitarian, legal and security responses and during training in emergencies and post-conflict reconstruction.

4. The UN, donors and governments to provide long-term financial support for women survivors of violence through legal, economic, psychosocial and reproductive health services. This should be an essential part of emergency assistance and post-conflict reconstruction.

2

ON REFUGEE AND DISPLACED WOMEN THE EXPERTS CALL FOR:

1. Strengthening of United Nations field operations for internally displaced women and of those bodies that support a field-based presence. Protection officers from all relevant bodies, including the Office of the High Commissioner for Refugees (UNHCR), the Office of the High Commissioner for Human Rights (OHCHR), the Office for the Coordination of Humanitarian Affairs (OCHA), the United Nations Children's Fund (UNICEF) and the International Committee of the Red Cross (ICRC), should be deployed immediately if a state cannot or will not protect displaced populations or is indeed responsible for their displacement. Resources should be made available for this purpose.

2. Governments to adhere to the UN Guiding Principles on Internal Displacement, and incorporate them into national laws to ensure protection, assistance and humanitarian access to internally displaced persons within their territory.

3. Refugee and internally displaced women to play a key role in camp planning, management and decision-making so that gender issues are taken into account in all aspects, especially resource distribution, security and protection.

4. Women to be involved in all aspects of repatriation and resettlement planning and implementation. Special measures should be put in place to ensure women's security in this process and to ensure voluntary, unhindered repatriation that takes place under conditions of safety and dignity, with full respect for human rights and the rule of law.

5. All asylum policies to be reformed to take into account gender-based political persecution. Women, regardless of marital status, should be eligible for asylum and entitled to individual interview and assessment procedures.

ON WAR AND WOMEN'S HEALTH THE EXPERTS CALL FOR:

1. Psychosocial support and reproductive health services for women affected by conflict to be an integral part of emergency assistance and post-conflict reconstruction. Special attention should be provided to those who have experienced physical trauma, torture and sexual violence. All agencies providing health support and social services should include psychosocial counselling and referrals. The United Nations Population Fund (UNFPA) should take the lead in providing these services, working in close cooperation with the World Health Organization (WHO), UNHCR, and UNICEF.

2. Recognition of the special health needs of women who have experienced war-related injuries, including amputations, and for equal provision of physical rehabilitation and prosthesis support.

3. Special attention to providing adequate food supplies for displaced and war-affected women, girls and families in order to protect health and to prevent the sexual exploitation of women and girls. The World Food Programme (WFP) and other relief agencies should strengthen capacities to monitor the gender impact of food distribution practices.

4. Protection against HIV/AIDS and the provision of reproductive health through the implementation of the Minimum Initial Services Package (MISP) as defined by the Interagency Manual on Reproductive Health for Refugees (WHO, UNHCR, UNFPA, 1999). Special attention must be paid to the needs of particularly vulnerable groups affected by conflict, such as displaced women, adolescents, girl-headed households and sex workers.

5. Immediate provision of emergency contraception and STI treatment for rape survivors to prevent unwanted pregnancies and protect the health of women.

ON HIV/AIDS THE EXPERTS CALL FOR:

1. All HIV/AIDS programmes and funding in conflict situations to address the disproportionate disease burden carried by women. Mandatory gender analysis and specific strategies for meeting the needs of women and girls should seek to prevent infection and increase access to treatment, care and support.

2. HIV/AIDS awareness and prevention programmes to be implemented during conflict and in post-conflict situations, with care and support provided whenever there is access to affected populations. National governments, national and international NGOs, and UN agencies should incorporate HIV/AIDs prevention into all humanitarian assistance. Donors should strongly support these interventions.

3. Vulnerability assessments to be carried out in each humanitarian situation to determine links between conflict, displacement and gender. Information and data collection should be strengthened in order to document this relationship and to guide appropriate responses. Governments and agencies should work together to document vulnerabilities.

4. Clear guidelines for HIV/AIDS prevention in peacekeeping operations. All troop-contributing countries should make available voluntary and confidential HIV/AIDS testing for their peacekeeping personnel. Counselling and testing should be provided for all contingent forces and civilian personnel participating in emergency and peace operations before and during deployment on a regular basis. HIV prevention as well as gender training should be provided in all missions, to all personnel.

5. The Inter-Agency Standing Committee (IASC) Reference Group on HIV/AIDS in Emergency Settings to develop clear policy guidelines for HIV prevention and care in humanitarian situations and application of these guidelines to be supported by national authorities, humanitarian agencies and donors.

6. The Global Fund to Fight AIDS, Tuberculosis and Malaria to make special provisions for support of HIV/AIDS programmes in conflict situations, including in countries without the government capacity to manage the application process. In such cases NGOs and UN agencies should be eligible to submit proposals. Further, we encourage the systematic consideration of gender issues in all programme funding.

7. Institutions and organizations to address HIV prevention in conflict situations. In particular, the New Partnership for Africa's Development (NEPAD) should take a leadership role in that region.

8. The development and enforcement of codes of conduct for all UN and international NGO staff to protect against abuse and exploitation of women and girls. All such staff should received training in prevention of sexual and gender based violence, as well as reproductive health information, including STI and HIV/AIDs prevention.

ON PEACE OPERATIONS THE EXPERTS CALL FOR:

1. Gender experts and expertise to be included at all levels and in all aspects of peace operations, including in technical surveys and the design of concepts of operation, training, staffing and programmes. To this end, a Memorandum of Understanding should set out the roles and responsibilities among the Department of Peacekeeping Operations (DPKO), the Department of Political Affairs (DPA), the United Nations Development Fund for Women (UNIFEM) and the Division for the Advancement of Women (DAW).

2. A review of training programmes on and approaches to the gender dimensions of conflict resolution and peace-building for humanitarian, military and civilian personnel. United Nations entities active in this area should lead this process with support provided by the Special Advisor on Gender Issues and Advancement of Women and the Task Force on Women, Peace and Security with a view to developing guidance on training policy and standards.

3. All UN peace operations to include a human rights monitoring component, with an explicit mandate and sufficient resources to investigate, document and report human rights violations against women.

4. The improvement and strengthening of codes of conduct for international and local humanitarian and peacekeeping personnel and for these codes to be consistent with international humanitarian and human rights law and made compulsory. An office of oversight for crimes against women should be established in all peace operations. The office should regularly monitor and report on compliance with the principles set forth in the IASC Task Force on the Protection from Sexual Exploitation and Abuse in Humanitarian Crises.

5. No exemptions for peacekeepers from prosecution by international tribunals, the International Criminal Court and national courts in the host country for all crimes committed, including those against women. All States maintaining peacekeeping forces should take necessary measures to bring to justice their own nationals responsible for such crimes, as called for by the Security Council (S/RES/1400 (2002).

6. UN peace operations to improve opportunities for collaboration with women's groups to address gender issues in a peacekeeping environment.

7. Member States and DPKO to increase women's representation in peace operations, including through the recruitment of police, military and civilian personnel.

6

ON ORGANIZING FOR PEACE THE EXPERTS CALL FOR:

1. The Secretary-General, in keeping with his personal commitment, to increase the number of women in senior positions in peace-related functions. Priority should be given to achieving gender parity in his appointment of women as Special Representatives and Envoys, beginning with the minimum of 30 per cent in the next three years, with a view to gender parity by 2015.

2. Gender equality to be recognized in all peace processes, agreements and transitional governance structures. International and regional organizations and all participating parties involved in peace processes should advocate for gender parity, maintaining a minimum 30 per cent representation of women in peace negotiations, and ensure that women's needs are taken into consideration and specifically addressed in all such agreements.

3. A United Nations Trust Fund for Women's Peace-building. This Trust Fund would leverage the political, financial and technical support needed for women's civil society organizations and women leaders to have an impact on peace efforts nationally, regionally and internationally. The Fund should be managed by UNIFEM, in consultation with other UN bodies and women's civil society organizations.

4. UNIFEM to work closely with DPA to ensure that gender issues are incorporated in peace-building and post-conflict reconstruction in order to integrate gender perspectives in peace-building and to support women's full and equal participation in decision-making; and for the UN

Population Fund (UNFPA) to strengthen its work in emergency situations in order to build women's capacity in conflict situations. UNIFEM and UNFPA should be represented in all relevant inter-agency bodies.

5. Peace negotiations and agreements to have a gender perspective through the full integration of women's concerns and participation in peace processes. Women's peace tables should be established and enabled through financial, political and technical assistance.

6. The UN and donors to invest in women's organizations as a strategy for conflict prevention, resolution and peace-building. Donors should exercise flexibility in responding to urgent needs and time-sensitive opportunities, and foster partnerships and networks between international, regional and local peace initiatives.

7. National electoral laws and international electoral assistance to establish quotas to achieve gender parity in decision-making positions, beginning with a minimum of 30 per cent, to ensure voter registration and education for women, to increase the ratio of women in electoral commissions and observer missions and to provide training for women candidates.

ON JUSTICE THE EXPERTS CALL FOR:

1. The Secretary-General to appoint a panel of experts to assess the gaps in international and national laws and standards pertaining to the protection of women in conflict and post-conflict situations and women's role in peace-building.

2. States parties to the Statute of the International Criminal Court to undertake national law reform to ensure compatibility with the Statute as a matter of priority, with particular attention given to the substantive and procedural provisions regarding crimes against women.

3. National legal systems to penalize and remedy all forms of violence against women in conflict and post-conflict situations. Specially trained police units should be established to investigate crimes against women and law enforcement officials, including judges, police and armed forces, should be sensitized about such crimes. Women's access to justice should be ensured through legal literacy programmes, support services and legal aid.

4. Gender equality in constitutional, legislative and policy reforms. The principle of gender should be integrated into all relevant constitutional clauses, reaffirming the principles of non-discrimination, equality, affirmative action, freedom and security. Special attention should be given to family, civil and labour laws and land reforms.

5. Rapid establishment by the UN of interim judicial systems capable of dealing effectively with violations against women by family members and society at large. Rape and sexual violence should be addressed by post-conflict truth- and justice-seeking mechanisms at national and local levels. The treatment of crimes against women in traditional mechanisms should be consistent with international standards.

8

ON MEDIA AND COMMUNICATIONS THE EXPERTS CALL FOR:

1. Increased donor resources and access for women to media and communications technology, so that gender perspectives, women's expertise and women's media can influence public discourse and decision-making on peace and security.

2. UN, government, private and independent media to provide public information and education on the gender dimensions of peace processes, security, reconciliation, disarmament and human rights.

3. Hate media, under any circumstances and particularly when used for direct and public incitement to commit crimes against women, to be prosecuted by national and international courts.

4. Donors and agencies to support the training of editors and journalists to eliminate gender bias in reporting and investigative journalism in conflict and post-conflict situations, and to promote gender equality and perspectives.

5. A panel of experts to undertake an assessment of the relevance and adequacy of standards on the military use of "psychological and information warfare" and its impact on women.

6. The Special Rapporteur on Freedom of Opinion and Expression of the Commission on Human Rights to carry out a study on gender, media and conflict.

9

ON THE PREVENTION OF CONFLICT THE EXPERTS CALL FOR:

1. The Secretary-General to systematically include information on the impact of armed conflict on women and women's role in prevention and peace-building in all of his country and thematic reports to the Security Council. Towards that end, the Secretary-General should request relevant information from UN operations and all relevant bodies.

2. The systematic collection and analysis of information and data by all actors, using gender specific indicators to guide policy, programmes and service delivery for women in armed conflict. This information should be provided on a regular basis to the Secretariat, Member States, inter-governmental bodies, regional organizations, NGOs and other relevant bodies. A central knowledge base should be established and maintained by UNIFEM together with a network of all relevant bodies, in particular the Department of Political Affairs (DPA).

3. The Security Council to formulate a plan for the least diversion for armaments of the world's human and economic resources. Sixty years after being assigned the task, the Security Council should implement Article 26 of the United Nations Charter, taking into account the Women's Peace Petition which calls for the world's nations to redirect at least 5 per cent of national military expenditures to health, education and employment programmes each year over the next five years.

4. The UN Development Programme (UNDP), as a leading agency in the field of security sector reform, to ensure that women's protection and participation be central to the design and reform of security sector institutions and policies, especially in police, military and rule of law components. UNDP should integrate a gender perspective into its country programmes.

5. Operational humanitarian, human rights and development bodies to develop indicators to determine the extent to which gender is mainstreamed throughout their operations in conflict and post-conflict situations and ensure that gender mainstreaming produces measurable results and is not lost in generalities and vague references to gender. Measures should be put in place to address the gaps and obstacles encountered in implementation.

6. Inter-governmental and regional organizations to strengthen and expand women's role in conflict prevention and peace-building. To this end, the UN together with regional organizations should convene an Expert Group Meeting to improve collaboration, share information and develop expertise.

7. In cooperation with relevant UN bodies, UNIFEM to develop and test a set of gender-based early warning indicators for mainstreaming into the UN Early Warning Framework and explore use of such indicators with regional organizations.

8. Disarmament, Demobilization and Reintegration (DDR) initiatives to equitably benefit women ex-combatants and those forced into service by armed groups. Resettlement allowances and other forms of support should be provided on a long-term basis.

9. The UN to conduct a "lessons learned" study on the gender aspects of DDR processes in which it has been involved.

1. Gender budget analysis of humanitarian assistance and post-conflict reconstruction to ensure that women benefit directly from resources mobilized through multilateral and bilateral donors, including the Consolidated Appeals Process, the Bretton Woods Institutions and donor conferences.

2. Establishment of macroeconomic policies in post-conflict reconstruction that prioritize the public provision of food, water, sanitation, health and energy, the key sectors in which women provide unpaid labour. Special attention should be paid to the consequences for women of decentralization policies.

3. A lead organization to be designated within the United Nations for women's education and training in conflict and post-conflict situations. This lead organization, together with the United Nations Educational, Scientific and Cultural Organization (UNESCO), UNHCR and UNICEF, should ensure that all education programmes for displaced persons provide for women as well as girls.

4. The World Bank, bi-lateral donors, UNDP and all other relevant UN departments, funds and agencies to integrate gender analysis in needs assessments for post-conflict reconstruction and throughout the planning, design, implementation of and reporting on programmes.

5. International organizations and governments to introduce affirmative measures that give local women priority in recruitment during emergencies and post-conflict reconstruction.

6. Affirmative measures to be adopted to guarantee women's socio-economic rights including employment, property ownership and inheritance and access to UN and public sector procurement in post-conflict reconstruction.

7. The International Labour Organization (ILO) to expand vocational and skills training for women in post-conflict situations including in non-traditional, public and private sectors, in a manner that is sustainable and responsive to the local and national economy.

ENDNOTES

INTRODUCTION

1. Cynthia Cockburn, background paper for conference on "Gender, Armed Conflict and Political Violence," 10th and 11th June 1999, The World Bank, Washington, DC, http://www.worldbank.org/gender/events/

2. The UNDP Human Development Report 2002 documents that gender inequality is universal — that although the extent of the inequality varies significantly, no country on earth treats women as well as it treats men, p. 23.

3. Charlotte Lindsey, *Women Facing War,* Geneva: International Committee of the Red Cross, 2002, p. 40.

4. S/Res/1325 (2000), http://www.un.org/

5. Graça Machel, "War-Affected Children," The Machel Review 1996-2000.

6. Report of the Secretary-General to the Security Council on the protection of civilians in armed conflict (S/2001/331), 30 March 2001, http://www.un.org/

7. Cockburn, "Gender, Armed Conflict and Political Violence," op.cit.

8. Global Policy Forum, "UN Financial Crisis," http://www.globalpolicy.org/finance/

9. World military expenditure in 2001 was estimated at $839 billion, Stockholm International Peace Research Institute (SIPRI), *Yearbook 2002: Armaments, Disarmament and International Security,* London: Oxford University Press, http://www.sipri.se/

10. "Prevention of armed conflict," Report of the Secretary-General A/55/985 – S/2001/574, 7 June 2001, http://www.un.org/

11. Cynthia Enloe, *Bananas, Beaches and Bases: Making Feminist Sense of International Politics,* Berkeley and London: University of California Press, 2000.

12. General Assembly Resolution 54/136 of 17 December 1999, http://www.un.org/

13. Charlotte Bunch, "Transforming Human Rights from a Feminist Perspective," in Julie Peters and Andrea Wolper, (Eds.) *Women's Rights, Human Right: International Feminist Perspectives,* New York: Routledge, 1995. p. 11.

14. UNICEF, *Facts for Life,* New York, 3rd edition, p. iv, http://www.unicef.org

CHAPTER 1: VIOLENCE AGAINST WOMEN

1. "War-related Sexual Violence in Sierra Leone," Physicians for Human Rights with the support of the UN Assistance Mission in Sierra Leone, Massachusetts, 2002.

2. Organisation of African Unity (OAU) [currently African Union (AU)], "Rwanda, the Preventable Genocide," Report of the International Panel of Eminent Personalities to Investigate the 1994 Genocide in Rwanda and Surrounding Events, 2000.

3. "Report of the Special Rapporteur on Systematic Rape, Sexual Slavery and Slavery-like Practices During Armed Conflict," E/CN.4/Sub/2/1998/13, 22 June 1998.

4. Radhika Coomaraswamy, "Sexual Violence During Wartime," paper prepared for UNIFEM, January 2002.

5. UN General Assembly Resolution 48/104, 20 December 1993.

6. Sarah Maguire, "Researching a Family Affair: Domestic Violence in FRY, Albania," in Caroline Sweetman (ed.) *Violence Against Women,* Oxford: Oxfam, 1998.

7. Seth Mydans, "Sexual Violence as a Tool of War: Pattern Emerging in East Timor," *The New York Times,* 1 March 2001.

8. Sexual crimes are also committed against boys and men. Young boys and men have been raped or forced into prostitution; because of the stigma, many victims do not report these violations. During the conflict in Bosnia and Herzegovina, sons and fathers were forced to commit sexual atrocities against each other. Graça Machel, *The Impact of War on Children,* London: Hurst and Company, 2001.

9. Ibid., and see also Coomaraswamy, "Sexual Violence During Wartime," op. cit.

10. Coomaraswamy, "Sexual Violence During Wartime," op. cit.

11. Suzanne Williams and Rachel Masika, "Editorial," in *Gender, Trafficking, and Slavery,* Oxford: Oxfam, 2002.

12. Ibid.

13. "EU Toughens Line on Human Trafficking," *Financial Times,* London, 19 March 2001.

14. International Organization for Migration, "New IOM Figures on the Global Scale of Trafficking," *Trafficking in Migrants Quarterly Bulletin,* No. 23, April 2001.

15. Survey conducted in April 1995, cited in Human Rights Task Force on Cambodia, "Cambodia: Prostitution and Sex Trafficking: A growing threat to the human rights of women and children in Cambodia," 1996.

16. Ibid.

17. IOM, "New IOM Figures on the Global Scale of Trafficking," op. cit.

18. "Historic Trial Makes Rape a War Crime," 22 February 2001, http://www.CNN.com/WORLD

19. "Recommended Principles and Guidelines on Human Rights and Human Trafficking. Report of the United Nations High Commissioner for Human Rights to the Economic and Social Council," 20 May 2002, E/2002/68/Add.1.

20. Lindsey, *Women Facing War,* op. cit.

21. See also C. Zimmerman, "Plates in a Basket Will Rattle: Domestic Violence in Cambodia," Phnom Penh Project Against Domestic Violence, 1995.

22. David Meddings and Stephanie M. Connor, "Circumstances around weapon injury in Cambodia after departure of a peacekeeping force: prospective cohort study," *British Medical Journal* (BMJ), no. 319, 1999; Michael Markus, David Meddings, Sarah Ramez and Juan Luis Gutierrez-Fisac, "Incidence of weapon injuries not related to interfactional combat in Afghanistan in 1996: prospective cohort study," BMJ, no. 319, 1999; David Meddings, "Weapons injuries during and after periods of conflict: retrospective analysis," BMJ, no. 315, 1997.

23. Catherine Lutz and Jon Elliston, "Domestic Terror," *The Nation,* 14 October 2002.

24. "Household survey on domestic violence," Project Against Domestic Violence (PADV), Phnom Penh. The survey, published in 1996, was conducted by the Ministry of Women's Affairs and PADV. It covered six provinces and Phnom Penh, representing approximately 59 per cent of the Cambodian population. Another study in 1994 suggested that 75 per cent of Khmer women faced domestic violence, an increase from the pre-war period. *Seed for Peace Newsletter,* 1994, cited in the BRIDGE Cambodia case study report, 1995 http://www.ids.ac.uk/bridge/

25. Eileen Kuttab and Riham Bargouti, "The Impact of Armed Conflict on Palestinian Women," presented to UNIFEM/UNDP-PAPP, April 2002.

26. "Violence Against Women: An Issue of Human Rights," newsletter of the Office of Women in Development, Summer 1997, http://www.usaid.gov/; see also UNIFEM, "Progess of the World's Women 2002," vol. 2.

27. Lepa Mladjenovic, Email communiqué, 1 May 2002.

28. Report of the Secretary-General to the Security Council on the UN Transitional Administration in East Timor, S/2002/80, January 2002, and UNTAET press releases, 22 January 2002.

29. Helena Smith, "Rape Victims' Babies Pay the Price of War," *The Observer,* 16 April 2000.

30. Albert Gaylor, "The Legacy of Peacekeepers' Kids in Liberia," *Public Agenda,* Accra, 13 March 2001.

31. "East Timor's Children of the Enemy," *The Weekend Australian,* 10 March 2001.

32. E/CN.4/Sub.2/1998/13, para 111.

33. CCPR/C/21/Rev.1/Add.1.

34. Laurel K. Fain, "Unsafe Haven: Report on the findings of a baseline sexual violence survey among Burundian refugees," International Rescue Committee, http://www.rhrc.org/resources/

CHAPTER 2: WOMEN FORCED TO FLEE

1. Report of the Secretary-General to the Security Council on the protection of civilians in armed conflict, S/1999/957, 8 September 1999, p. 4, http://www.reliefweb.int/

2. Global IDP Project, http://www.idpproject.org/global_overview. In addition there are 3.9 million refugee and internally displaced Palestinians who live in camps and receive aid from the United Nations Relief and Works Agency (UNRWA).

3. Report of the Secretary-General on protection for humanitarian assistance to refugees and others in conflict situations, 22 September 1998, paragraph 12, http://www.un.org/

4. In the DRC, civilians have been trapped in the forests around Goma and Bafwasende for months at a time with no access to humanitarian assistance.

5. Andrew Mawson, Rebecca Dodd and John Hilary, *War Brought Us Here,* London: Save the Children-UK, 2000, p. 20.

6. Ibid., p. 21.

7. "Secretary-General Presents His Annual Report to the General Assembly," UN press release, 20 September 1999, SG/SM/7136-GA/9596.

8. Report of the Secretary-General on the work of the Organization, A/55/1, September 2000, http://www.un.org/documents/sg/report00/

9. The International Commission on Intervention and State Sovereignty, *The Responsibility to Protect,* Ottawa, Canada: International Development Research Centre, December 2001, p. xii.

10. Human Rights Watch, "Indonesia/East Timor: Forced Explusions to West Timor and the Refugee Crisis," December 1999, vol. 11, no. 7, http://www.hrw.org/reports/1999/wtimor/

11. Norwegian Refugee Council, Global IDP Project. http://www.idpproject.org/global_overview

12. Women's Commission for Refugee Women and

ENDNOTES

Children, "The Gender Dimensions of Internal Displacement: Concept Paper and Annotated Bibliography," Office of Emergency Programmes Working Paper Series, UNICEF, 1998.

13. World Food Programme (WFP) Emergency Report, no. 10, 10 March 2000, www.cidi.org/humanitarian/wfp/

14. Global IDP Project database, DRC country profile, 8 August 2002, p. 78, http://www.db.idpproject.org/Sites

15. Women's Commission for Refugee Women and Children, *A Charade of Concern: The Abandonment of Colombia's Forcibly Displaced,* May 1999, pp. 2-4.

16. "Agents of Displacement: Paramilitary groups (1994 –2002)," Global IDP Project, 22 August 2002, http://www.db.idpproject.org/Sites

17. Refugees International, "Displaced Women in West Kalimantan, Indonesia," 3 July 2002, http://www.refugeesinternational.org/

18. Note by the Secretary-General, "Internally Displaced Persons," A/56/168, 21 August 2001.

19. Ibid., pp. 6-8.

20. United States General Accounting Office, *Foreign Affairs: Internally Displaced Persons Lack Effective Protection,* GAO-01-803, 2001, pp. 21-22.

21. Ibid., p. 14.

22. Ibid., p. 17.

23. UNHCR/Save the Children-UK, "Sexual Violence and Exploitation: The Experience of Refugee Children in Liberia, Guinea, and Sierra Leone," 2002, pp. 2–5.

24. Ibid., p. 10.

25. Refugees International Bulletin, 26 June 2001, http://www.refugeesinternational.org/

26. Rosemary Barber-Madden et al., *Poverty, Violence and Health in the Lives of Displaced in Angola,* New York: UNFPA, 2001.

27. Women's Commission for Refugee Women and Children, *UNHCR's Policy on Refugee Women and Guidelines on their Protection: An assessment of ten years of implementation,* May 2002.

28. Human Rights Watch, "UNHCR at 50: What future for refugee protection?" p. 12, http://www.hrw.org/campaigns/refugees/

29. Women's Commission for Refugee Women and Children, *UNHCR's Policy on Refugee Women and Guidelines on their Protection,* op.cit.

30. Human Rights Watch, "UNHCR at 50" op. cit., p. 12, http://www.hrw.org/campaigns/refugees/

31. UNHCR, "Prevention and Response to Sexual and Gender-based Violence in Refugee Situations,"

Interagency Lessons Learned proceedings, 27–29 March 2001, p. 22.

32. ReliefWeb, UN OCHA Integrated Regional Information Network, "Burundi-Tanzania: Focus on sexual violence among Burundi refugees," 7 May 2002, http://www.reliefweb.int/

33. UNHCR, "Prevention and Response to Sexual and Gender-based Violence in Refugee Situations," op. cit., p. 31.

34. Press briefing, 9 May 2002, http://www.un.org/News/briefings/

35. Kari Karamé, "Improving the Security of Refugee and Displaced Women: Recommendations for Policy and Practice from International Experts," seminar at Norwegian Institute of International Affairs, Oslo, Norway, 24 January 2002.

36. IRIN News, "Food Supplies for Refugees Running Out," UN Office for the Coordination of Humanitarian Affairs, 24 May 2002, http://www.irinnews.org/report

37. Executive Committee of the High Commissioner's Programme, 31 May 2002, EC/52/SC/CPR/4, http://www.unhcr.ch/

38. Kari Karamé, "Improving the Security," op. cit.

39. cited by Corey Levine, "Gender Dimensions of Peace-building," NPSIA Conference, "Human Security: Policy Implications for the 21st Century," September 1999.

40. Correspondence with Alison Parker, Refugee Policy Review Fellow, Human Rights Watch, 31 July 2002. Ms. Parker conducted the research for Human Rights Watch.

41. Ibid.

42. Ibid.

43. Women's Commission for Refugee Women and Children, "Fending for Themselves: Afghan Refugee Children and Adolescents Working in Urban Pakistan," January 2002, pp. 1-2.

44. Save the Children-UK, *War Brought Us Here,* Summary, 2000, p. 11.

45. Women's Commission for Refugee Women and Children, "UNHCR Policy on Refugee Women and Guidelines on their Protection," op. cit., p. 26.

46. 1951 Geneva Convention on the Status of Refugees, Article 33.

47. Graça Machel, *The Impact of War on Children,* London: Hurst, 2001, p. 38.

48. Binaifer Nowrojeee in *World Refugee Survey,* 2000, p. 53.

49. UNHCR, "Guidelines on the Protection of Refugee Women," Geneva, July 1991, paragraph 63.

50. UNHCR, "First it was the Lost Boys of Sudan. Now it is the Lost Girls of Sudan," *Refugees*, vol.1, no.126, 2002, p. 8.

51. UNHCR Resettlement Handbook, Division of International Protection, Geneva 1997, p. 43.

CHAPTER 3: WAR AND WOMEN'S HEALTH

1. Dominique Legros and Vincent Brown, "Documenting Violence Against Refugees," *The Lancet*, vol. 357, no. 9266, 2001 www.thelancet.com

2. Centers for Disease Control, "Famine-affected, Refugee, and Displaced Populations: Recommendations for public health issues," *Morbidity and Mortality Weekly Report*, vol. 41, no. RR-13, July 1992.

3. For a recent overview of the data for deaths from conflict worldwide, see Christopher J.L. Murray et al., "Armed Conflict as a Public Health Problem," *British Medical Journal*, vol. 324, 2002, www.bmj.com

4. Ibid.

5. L. Roberts et al., *Mortality in Eastern Democratic Republic of Congo: Results of 11 mortality surveys*, New York: International Rescue Committee (IRC), 2001.

6. Organisation of African Unity (OAU). "Rwanda, the Preventable Genocide," Report of the International Panel of Eminent Personalities to Investigate the 1994 Genocide in Rwanda and the Surrounding Events, 2000, p. 176.

7. Presentation at UNDP/UNFPA Executive Board Annual meeting, June 2002.

8. Mauno Konttinen, "Postwar Health and Healthcare in Bosnia and Herzegovina," in *War or Health? A Reader*, London: Zed Books, 2002.

9. S.T. Baksaas, "Military Attacks against Ambulances and Health Personnel," *Tidsskrift for den Norske laegeforening*, vol. 122, no. 10, April 2002, p. 1055.

10. Marinkovic et al., "Trends in Mortality in Serbia Excluding the Provinces 1973-1994," *Srpski arkiv za celokerpuo lekarstvo*, vol. 128, no. 9-10, Sept-Oct 2000, pp. 309-315.

11. R. Garfield, "The Impact of Economic Embargoes on the Health of Women and Children," *Journal of the American Medical Women's Association*, vol. 52, no. 4, Fall 1997, pp. 181-184.

12. Ronald Waldman, "Prioritising Health Care in Complex Emergencies," *The Lancet*, vol. 357, no. 9266, 2001, www.thelancet.com

13. "Public Health Impact of Rwandan Refugee Crisis: What happened in Goma, Zaire in July 1994?" Comment in *The Lancet*, vol. 345, no. 8946, Feb. 1995, pp. 339-344, www.thelancet.com

14. Emanuele Capobianco, Akihiro Seita, Mohamed Abdi Jama, Letter to the editor regarding "Reconstruction of Health Care in Afghanistan," *The Lancet*, vol. 359, no. 9311, 23 March 2002, www.the-lancet.com

15. N. Andersson, S. P. da Sousa and S. Paredes, "Social Costs of Landmines in Four Countries: Afghanistan, Bosnia, Cambodia, and Mozambique," *British Medical Journal*, vol. 311, 1995, www.bmj.com

16. K.E. Rajab, A.M. Mohammed and F. Mustafa, "Incidence of Spontaneous Abortion in Bahrain Before and After the Gulf War of 1991," *International Journal of Gynaecology and Obstetrics*, vol. 68, no. 2, Feb. 2000, pp. 139-144.

17. Michelle Marble, "Women Reporting Health Problems Related to the Gulf War," *Women's Health Weekly*, 13 May 1996, pp. 9-10.

18. Maurice Eisenbruch, "From Post-Traumatic Stress Disorder to Cultural Bereavement: Diagnosis of Southeast Asian refugees," www.dinarte.es/salud-mental/

19. Angela Burnett, "Health Needs of Asylum Seekers and Refugees," *British Medical Journal*, vol. 322, 3 March 2001, pp. 544-547, www.bmj.com

20. M.K. Nock, J. Kaufman and R.A. Rosenheck, "Examination of Predictors of Severe Violence in Combat-exposed Vietnam veterans," *Journal of Traumatic Stress*, vol. 14, no. 4, Oct. 2001, pp. 835-841.

21. M.J. Toole, S. Galson and W. Brady, "Are War and Public Health Compatible?" *The Lancet*, vol. 341, no. 8854, May 1993, pp. 1193-1196, www.thelancet.com

22. Centers for Disease Control, "Famine-affected, Refugee, and Displaced Populations," op. cit. p. 16.

23. Nathan Ford and Austen Davis, "Chaos in Afghanistan: Famine, aid, and bombs," The Lancet, vol. 358, no. 9292, 3 Nov. 2001, www.thelancet.com

24. Cliff et al. "Konzo Associated with War in Mozambique," *Tropical Medicine and International Health*, vol. 2, no. 11, Nov. 1997, pp. 1068-1074.

25. WHO/UNICEF/UNFPA, "Maternal Mortality in 1995: Estimates developed by WHO, UNICEF, UNFPA," Geneva: World Health Organization, 2001.

26. Victoria Brittain, "What you get for backing a tyrant," *New Statesman*, 8 Oct. 2001.

27. Save the Children Fund-UK, http://www.savethechildren.org.uk/

28. Celia Palmer, "Rapid Appraisal of Needs in Reproductive Health Care in Southern Sudan: Qualitative study," *British Medical Journal*, vol. 319, Sept.

ENDNOTES

1999, pp. 743-748, www.bmj.com

29. B.C. Zapata, "The Influence of Social and Political Violence on the Risk of Pregnancy Complications," *American Journal of Public Health,* vol. 82, no. 5, 1992, pp. 665-670.

30. Family planning programmes have proved popular in a wide variety of refugee camp settings, in host countries such as Pakistan, Thailand and Tanzania, regardless of whether there were programmes in the countries of origin. Clearly there is a strong demand for such services by refugees.

31. Population Issues Briefing Kit 2001, p.17, http://www.unfpa.org/modules/briefkit/

32. P. Mayaud et al., "STD Rapid Assessment in Rwandan Refugee Camps in Tanzania," *Genitourin Medica,* vol. 73, no. 1, Feb. 1997, pp. 33-38.

33. WHO, *Health in Emergencies,* issue 10, June 2001.

34. Legros and Brown, "Documenting Violence Against Refugees," op. cit.

35. Physicians for Human Rights, "War-Related Sexual Violence in Sierra Leone: A Population-Based Assessment," 2002, http://www.phrusa.org/research/sierra_leone/

36. N. Bareslau, "Gender Differences in Trauma and Posttraumatic Stress Disorder," *Journal of Gender Specific Medicine,* vol. 5, no. 1, Jan-Feb. 2002, pp. 34-40.

37. C.L. Port, B. Engdahl and P. Frazier, "A Longitudinal and Retrospective Study of PTSD among Older Prisoners of War," *American Journal of Psychiatry,* vol. 158, no. 9, Sept. 2001, pp. 1474-1479.

38. United Nations, "Key Actions for the Further Implementation of the Programme of Action of the International Conference on Population and Development," A/S-21/5/Add.1, 1 July 1999, para. 29.

39. William Aldis and Erik Schouten, "War and Public Health in Democratic Republic of Congo," *The Lancet,* vol. 359, no. 9298, 15 Dec. 2001, p. 2088, www.thelancet.com

40. W. Van Damme, V. De Brouwere, M. Boelaert and W. Van Lergerghe, "Effects of a Refugee-assistance Programme on Host Populations in Guinea as Measured by Obstetric Interventions," *The Lancet,* vol. 351, no. 9116, May 1998, pp. 1609-13, www.thelancet.com

CHAPTER 4: HIV/AIDS, WOMEN AND WAR

1. Human Rights Watch, "The War Within the War: Sexual Violence Against Women and Girls in Eastern Congo," June 2002 http://www.hrw.org/reports/2002/drc/

2. UNICEF and WHO, "Health Sector Assessment Mission in Eastern Congo," http://www.who.int/eha/disasters

3. UNAIDS, "Report on the Global HIV/AIDS Epidemic 2002," report prepared for the XIV International Conference on AIDS, Barcelona, 7-12 July 2002, http://www.unaids.org/epidemic_update/report_july02/

4. B. Eshaya-Chauvin and R.M Coupland, "Transfusion Requirements for the Management of War Injured: The experience of the International Committee of the Red Cross," *British Journal of Anaesthesia,* vol. 68, no. 2, Feb. 1992, pp. 221-223.

5. UNAIDS, *AIDS and the Military,* Geneva: UNAIDS, 1998, http://www.unaids.org/publications/documents/sectors/military/

6. P. Songwathana, "Women and AIDS Caregiving: Women's work?" *Health Care for Women International,* vol. 22, no. 3, April-May 2001, pp. 263-279.

7. Overseas Development Institute, "HIV/AIDS and Emergencies: Analysis and recommendations for practice," HPN Paper, London: ODI, February 2002.

8. Tamar Renaud, *HIV/AIDS and Children Affected by Armed Conflict,* New York: UNICEF, 2001.

9. Interview with UNFPA representative, Freetown.

10. UNAIDS, *AIDS and the Military,* op.cit.

11. Pam DeLargy, interviews with soldiers in Eritrea.

12. W. Brady, P. DeLargy and L. Leon, "Controlling HIV/AIDS in Complex Emergencies and Post-Conflict Situations: Follow-up to Security Council Resolution 1308: Joint Agency Post-Conflict Assessment for Ethiopia and Eritrea," New York: UNFPA/UNAIDS, 2000.

13. *IRIN,* "Conditions Ripe for HIV/AIDS Explosion in DRC," 15 August 2001.

14. DIA/AFMIC, 1999.

15. Report of the Secretary-General on the Progress of the UN Mission to Eritrea and Ethiopia, 7 March 2001, http://daccess-ods.un.org/doc/

16. "Infected Troops Spread Scourge Worse Than War," *San Jose Mercury News,* 8 April 2001.

17. Albert Gaylor, "The Legacy of 'Peacekeepers' Kids in Liberia," *Public Agenda,* Accra, 13 March 2001.

18. U.S. State Department, "U.S. International Strategy on HIV/AIDS," July 1995.

19. James Bones, "UN Forces Play Deadly Role in Spread of AIDS, Ambassador Says: Condoms to be given to all peacekeepers." *Ottawa Citizen,* 10 March, 2000.

20. UN Security Resolution 1308 (17 July 2000)

emphasizes the need for member states to develop effective, long-term strategies for HIV/AIDS education, prevention, voluntary and confidential testing and counselling, and treatment of their personnel.

21. A. Wakhweya, C. Reilly, M. Onyango and G. Helmer, "HIV/AIDS, Gender and Conflict Nexus: The case of Sierrra Leone: The commoditization of girls and women," Boston University/UNFPA/UNIFEM, September 2002.

22. Todd Summers, "The Global Fund to Fight AIDS, TB, and Malaria: Challenges and opportunities," CSIS HIV/AIDS Task Force, Washington, DC, June 2002.

CHAPTER 5: WOMEN AND PEACE OPERATIONS

1. UN celebration of the first anniversary of Security Council Resolution 1325, UN, New York, 31 October 2001.

2. Bosnia and Herzegovina, the Democratic Republic of the Congo, East Timor, Kosovo, occupied Palestinian territories and Sierra Leone.

3. http://www.un.org/Depts/dpko/

4. Astri Suhrke with Kristian Berg Harpviken, Are Knudsen, Arve Ofstad and Arne Strand, "Peacebuilding: Lessons for Afghanistan," CMI Report R 2002:9, p. 108 http://www.cmi.no/

5. For the text of these documents, go to http://www.reliefweb.int/library/

6. Statement to the Security Council Open Meeting on Conflict, Peacekeeping and Gender, New York, 25 July 2002.

7. Coordination of policies and activities of specialized agencies and other bodies of the United Nations system related to the theme: Mainstreaming a gender perspective into all policies and programmes in the United Nations System, E/1997/L.30, 14 July 1997.

8. "Mainstreaming a Gender Perspective in Multidimensional Peace Operations," Lessons Learned Unit, DPKO, July 2000, p. iii.

9. Louise Olsson, "Mainstreaming Gender in Multidimensional Peacekeeping: A Field Perspective," *International Peacekeeping,* vol.7, no. 3, Autumn 2000, pp. 1-16.

10. Secretary-General's Bulletin on policies to achieve gender equality in the United Nations, ST/SGB/282, 5 January 1996.

11. Olsson, "Mainstreaming gender," op. cit., p.11.

12. UN press release, 22 October 2002.

13. UN Charter, Article 8, http://www.un.org/aboutun/charter/

14. Report of the Secretary-General on resource requirements for the implementation of the report of the Panel on United Nations Peace Operations, Addendum, A/55/507/Add.1, 27 October 2000, para 5.28.

15. Australia, Canada, Jamaica and New Zealand, Press Release, GA/AB/3509, Fifth Committee of the UN General Assembly, 21 May 2002.

16. Australia, Canada, Denmark (speaking on behalf of the European Union and CEE countries associated with the EU), France, Ireland, Jamaica, Japan, Nigeria, Norway, Republic of Korea and Russia, Security Council Open Meeting on Gender and Peacekeeping, 25 July 2002.

17. Report of the Secretary-General on resource requirements for implementation of the report of the Panel on United Nations Peace Operations, op. cit.

18. UNTAET, Report to DPKO on the Implementation of Security Council Resolution 1325, 25 May 2001.

19. Course materials are available at http://www.dfait-maeci.gc.ca/genderandpeacekeeping/

20. A/55/305–S/2000/809. For a comprehensive review of the question of peacekeeping operations in all their aspects, see paragraph 62, quoting the report of the Independent Inquiry into the Actions of the UN during the 1994 genocide in Rwanda (S/1999/1257) in support of basic UN principles and, as stated in the report of the Independent Inquiry on Rwanda, consistent with "the perception and the expectation of protection created by [an operation's] very presence."

21. UNTAET, Report to DPKO, op. cit.

22. UNMIK, Police Annual Report 2000, http://www.unmikonline.org/civpol/reports/; UNMIBH/OHCHR, "Report on Joint Trafficking Project of UNMIBH/OHCHR," May 2000. Between March 1999 and March 2000 UNMIBH and OHCHR intervened in 40 cases of trafficking and possible trafficking, involving 182 women. The report states that "In approximately 14 cases. . .there was compelling evidence of complicity by police, primarily local officers but also some international police, as well as foreign military (SFOR troops)."

23. Report of the Expert of the Secretary-General, Graça Machel, submitted pursuant to GA resolution 48/157, A/51/306, 26 August 1996.

24. Barbara Bedont, "International Justice: Implication for peacekeeping," unpublished paper, December 2001.

25. Michael Kaplan, "One Woman's War on Sexual Slavery," *Glamour,* May 2002 pp. 296-306.

ENDNOTES

26. Ibid.

27. Kirsten Ruecker, "Engendering Peace Building: Case studies from Cambodia, Rwanda and Guatemala," Peace Building and Human Security Division, DFAIT, Ottawa, Canada, January 2000, p. 20.

28. Kai Grieg, "War Children of the World," War and Children Identity Project, Bergen, December 2001, pp. 97-99, http://www.warandchildren.org/

29. Haxhere Veseli, Statement at an informal meeting with members of the Security Council, 30 October 2001, http://www.peacewomen.org/un/sc/

30. Ruth Pollard, "UN forces more at risk from HIV than war," *Sydney Morning Herald,* 11 July 2002.

31. 1946 Convention on the Privileges and Rights of the United Nations, Articles V and VI, and Model Status-of-forces Agreement for peacekeeping operations, A/45.594, 9 October 1990, para 15.

32. Bedont, op.cit., p. 4.

33. Model Status-of-forces Agreement, op. cit.

34. Bedont, op. cit., p. 11.

35. Secretary-General's Bulletin on Observance by United Nations forces of international humanitarian law, 6 August 1999, ST/SGB/1999.

36. HCHR, "Training Manual on Human Rights Monitoring," Chapter XXII, pp. 456-458.

37. Radhika Coomaraswamy, "Sexual Violence During Wartime," paper prepared for UNIFEM, January 2002.

38. Kaplan, *Glamour,* op. cit.

39. Daniel McGrory, "Women sacked for revealing UN Links with Sex Trade," *The Times,* London, 7 August 2002.

CHAPTER 6: ORGANIZING FOR PEACE

1. Marieme Helie-Lucas, "Introduction," *Public Hearing on Crimes Against Women in Recent Wars and Conflicts: A compilation of testimonies,* New York: Women's Caucus for Gender Justice, 11 December 2000.

2. "Major Battles of World War I," http://info.ox.ac.uk/departments/humanities/rose/

3. Jane Addams, Emily Greene Balch and Alice Hamilton, eds. "Resolutions Adopted at the Hague Congress," in *Women at The Hague: The International Congress of Women and Its Results,* New York: MacMillan, 1916, pp. 150-59, http://womhist.binghamton.edu/hague/

4. Addams shared the 1931 Nobel Peace Prize with Nicholas Murray Butler who promoted the Kellogg-Briand Pact.

5. Gertrude Bussy, *Pioneers for Peace: World International League for Peace and Freedom 1915-1965,* London: Allen and Unwin,
1965.

6. http://www.wilpf.int.ch

7. "Peace Inextricably Linked with Equality between Women and Men says Security Council, in International Women's Day Statement," Security Council press release SC/6816, 8 March 2000, http://www.un.org/women-watch/news/articles/

8. Association of Genocide Widows, http://www.avega.org.rw/

9. Email communication, 12 August 2002.

10. Jeremy McDermott, "Colombia's female fighting force," BBC News, 4 January 2002, http://news.bbc.co.uk/

11. Kvinna till Kvinna, "Engendering the Peace Process: A Gender Approach to Dayton and Beyond," Stockholm: Kvinna till Kvinna Foundation, 2000, http://www.iktk.se/english/

12. George Mitchell, lecture on "Preventive Diplomacy and Conflict Resolution in the United Nations: Integrating Theory and Practice," School of International and Public Affairs, Columbia University, 8 April 2002.

13. UNRISD, "War-torn Society Project Report: Women and Post-Conflict Reconstruction: Issues and Sources," Geneva: UN Research Institute for Social Development, 15 June 2000, www.unrisd.org/

14. REDE, "Women's Issues in East Timor," briefing paper to the Donors Meeting, prepared by the Timorese Women's Network (REDE), June 2001, http://www.pcug.org.au/

15. CIIR, "East Timor Constituent Assembly Elections: Update on Campaign for Quotas for Women," London: Catholic Institute for International Relations, 24 February 2001, http://www.pcug.org.au/

16. http://www.un.org/womenwatch/daw/cedaw

CHAPTER 7: JUSTICE

1. Not only do the Geneva Conventions protect civilians during international armed conflict by setting out the laws of war but, under Common Article 3 on internal conflicts, they also prohibit certain violations in all circumstances. Common Article 3 guarantees protection against: violence to life and person, in particular murder of all kinds, mutilation, cruel treatment and torture; committing outrages upon personal dignity, in particular humiliating and degrading treatment; taking of hostages; and the passing of sentences and the carrying out of executions without previous judgement pronounced by a regularly constituted court, affording all

judicial guarantees which are generally recognized as indispensable http://www.icrc.org/ihl.nsf/

2. Kelly Dawn Askin, *War Crimes Against Women: Prosecution in International War Crimes Tribunals,* The Hague: Kluwer Law International, 1997, supra note 27, pp. 8-9.

3. Women's Caucus for Gender Justice Action Alert, July 2002, http://www.iccwomen.org/

4. "Summary of Findings" of the Women's International War Crimes Tribunal on Japan's Military Sexual Slavery, December 2000, http://www.jca.apc.org/vaww-net-japan/. For more on the Tribunal, see Christine Chinkin, "Towards the Tokyo Tribunal," Women's Caucus for Gender Justice, http://www.iccwomen.org/tokyo/

5. Kelly Dawn Askin, "Comfort Women: Shifting shame and stigma from victims to victimizers," *International Criminal Law Review,* 2001, pp.7-8.

6. Articles 7 and 8 of the Statute (crimes against humanity and war crimes) list gender-specific crimes, including rape, sexual slavery, enforced prostitution, forced pregnancy, enforced sterilization and other forms of sexual violence of comparable gravity, http://www.un.org/law/icc/statute/

7. Theodor Meron, "Crimes under the Jurisdiction of the International Criminal Court," in Herman A. M. von Hebel, Johan G. Lammers and Jolien Schukking, (eds.), *Reflections on the International Criminal Court,* The Hague: T.M.C. Asser Press, 1999, pp.47-48.

8. ICTY Bulletin No. 14, the Erdemovic jurisprudence.

9. Article 36(8), The Rome Statute, http://www.un.org/law/icc/statute/

10. The ICTY and ICTR have upheld convictions of rape and other forms of sexual violence as instruments of genocide (*Akayesu*), crimes against humanity (*Akayesu, Kunarac*), war crimes (*Celebici, Furundzija*), forms of torture (*Kunarac, Celebici, Furundzija*), means of persecution (*Kvocka*) and forms and indicia of enslavement (*Kunarac*).

11. Women's Caucus for Gender Justice, "Testimony of Witness A," *Victims and Witnesses in the ICC,* Report of Panel Discussions on Appropriate Measures for Victim Participation and Protection in the ICC, July-August 1999, http://www.iccwomen.org/resources/

12. Women's Caucus for Gender Justice, "Summary of Statement by Hon. Elizabeth Odio-Benito, Former judge at ICTY," *Victims and Witnesses in the ICC,* Ibid.

13. Cited in Barbara Bedont and Katherine Hall Martinez, "Ending Impunity for Gender Crimes under the International Criminal Court," *Brown Journal of World*

Affairs, vol. 6, issue 1, pp.65-85.

14. Women's Caucus for Gender Justice, *Victims and Witnesses in the ICC,* op. cit.

15. Ibid.; See also Margaret Owen, *Abuse of Women Witnesses by the International War Crimes Tribunal of Rwanda,* London: Widows for Peace and Reconstruction, August 2002.

16. Statement by Wendy Lobwein, support officer at the Victims and Witnesses Unit, ICTY, *Victims and Witnesses in the ICC,* op. cit.

17. Agreement between the United Nations and the Government of Sierra Leone on the Establishment of a Special Court for Sierra Leone, Freetown, 16 January 2002, http://www.sierra-leone.org/

18. See, for example, Human Rights Watch, "Recommendations for the Sierra Leone Special Court: Letter to Legal Advisors of UN Security Council Member States and Interested States," 7 March 2002, http://hrw.org/press/2002/

19. Human Rights Watch, "East Timor," Human Rights Watch World Report 2002, http://www.hrw.org/wr2k2/asia5.html

20. In the case of crimes against humanity, genocide, and grave breaches and other crimes of universal jurisdiction, there is no amnesty under international law, i.e. *aut dedere aut judicare* principle. See also Geoffrey Robertson, *Crimes Against Humanity: The Struggle for Global Justice,* London: Penguin, 1999.

21. Second Kampala Declaration on Human Rights, Democracy and Development in Sudan, adopted at the meeting 'Human Rights, Democracy and Development in the Transition in Sudan,' Kampala, Uganda, 17-20 July 2000, http://members.tripod.com/SudanInfonet/

22. Interview in Helsinki, 10-11 March 2002.

23. The text of truth commissions can be found on the website of the US Institute of Peace, www.usip.org

24. Priscilla Hayner, "Truth Commissions," Paper presented at the conference on "Truth, Justice, Accountability and Reconciliation in Societies Emerging from Crimes Against Humanity," Peter Wall Institute of Advanced Studies at the University of British Columbia, 13-14 October 2000.

25. Priscilla Hayner, *Unspeakable Truths: Confronting State Terror and Atrocity,* London: Routledge, 2000.

26. Ibid., p. 79.

27. Ibid., p. 78.

CHAPTER 8: MEDIA POWER

1. Amnesty International, "Democratic Republic of Congo: Kisangani killings – victims need justice now,"

ENDNOTES

press release, 19 June 2002, http://www.peacelink.it/

2. http://www.un.org/womenwatch/daw/beijing/

3. International Women's Media Foundation, (IWMF), *Leading in a Different Language: Will Women Change the News Media?* Washington DC, 2000, www.iwmf.org/

4. Presentation by Ms. Sermet and Ms. Dzumhur, Women's International League for Peace and Freedom (WILPF), WILPF Congress, Helsinki, 1995.

5. Quoted in Larry Minear, Colin Scott and Thomas G. Weiss, *The News Media: Civil War and Humanitarian Action,* Boulder: Lynne Reiner, 1996.

6. Richard Holbrooke, " No Media – No War," presentation at 'Between Past and Future' conference, Central European University, Budapest, Hungary, March 1999, http://www.ppu.org.uk/peacematters/

7. AOL/Time Warner, Disney, General Electric, News Corporation, Viacom, Sony, Bertelsmann, PolyGram, Seagram and TCI. Associated Press (AP) is the world's largest news organization, providing copy, photos and video for more than 1 billion people a day, serving 5,000 US radio and TV stations and nearly 9,000 subscribers in 121 countries.

8. Margaret Gallagher, *An Unfinished Story: Gender Patterns in Media Employment,* Geneva: UNESCO, 1995.

9. Annenberg Public Policy Center (APPC), "The Glass Ceiling in the Executive Suite: The second annual Annenberg Public Policy Center analysis of women leaders in communication companies," University of Pennsylvania, 2002, http://www.appcpenn.org/press/

10. Margaret Gallagher, *Gender Setting: New Agendas for Media Monitoring and Advocacy,* London: World Association for Christian Communication, 2001, http://www.wacc.org.uk/publications/

11. Cited in Danny Schechter, "Warring with the Coverage of War: Dissent disappears from media coverage," *Resist,* December 2001, http://www.resistinc.org/newsletter/

12. IWMF, "Leading in a Different Language," op. cit.

13. IMPACS, "The Media and Peace Building: A Roundtable Consultation," report of a consultation held by the Institute for Media, Policy and Civil Society, Vancouver, Canada, 8-9 April 1999, http://www.impacs.org/pdfs/media/

14. Organisation of African Unity, "Rwanda, the Preventable Genocide," op. cit., p. 7.

15. Media Network, "Counteracting Hate Radio," Radio Netherlands Wereldomroep, http://www.rnw.nl/realradio/dossiers/

16. Sasa Mirkovic, "Political Instrumentalisation of the Media: Examples from Serbia, France and Slovakia," http://www.ejc.nl/hp/rem/mirkovic

17. Radhika Coomaraswamy, "Sexual Violence During Wartime," paper prepared for UNIFEM, January 2002, quoting Catharine Mackinnon, "Turning Rape into Pornography: Post-Modern Genocide," *Ms.,* July/August 1993.

18. Steven Hurst, "Media, Power and Politics," Manchester Metropolitan University, United Kingdom, http://www.mmu.ac.uk/

19. Bill Kovach and Tom Rosenstiel, "Return to Normalcy? How the media have covered the war on terrorism," Project for Excellence in Journalism, http://www.journalism.org/

20. Peacecast III, 24 September 2001, Feminist International Radio Endeavour (FIRE) and Women's International News Gathering Service (WINGS) http://ww.fire.or.cr/oct01/

21. Kovach and Rosenstiel, "Return to Normalcy," op. cit.

22. BBC Newsnight, 16 May 2002, http://news.bbc.co.uk/

23. IWMF, "Leading in a Different Language," op.cit.

24. http://www.reportingtheworld.org/clients/

25. http://www.mediaaction.org/

26. David Zucchino, "Afghanistan's Female Pioneers in Print," *Los Angeles Times,* 9 May 2002.

27. FIRE, "Jornadas por la Paz, la Justicia Social y los Derechos Humanos," October 2001 http://www.fire.or.cr/oct01/

28. http://www.j-c-w.org/; http://www.batshalom.org/

29. See International Women's Tribune Centre (IWTC) IWTC GlobalNet #202, http://www.iwtc.org/

30. E-mail communiqué, Maria Suarez, July 2002.

31. Michiel van Geelen, "The Role of the Media in Conflict Prevention, Conflict Management and Peace Building: An Overview of Theory and Practice," IMPACS, February 2002, http://www.impacs.org/

CHAPTER 9: PREVENTION

1. UN Press Release, SC/6759, 29 November 1999.

2. The UN Preventive Deployment Force in the Former Yugoslav Republic of Macedonia is an often-cited example of formal intervention.

3. In 1997 the EU established a Policy Planning and Early Warning Unit in the Amsterdam Treaty. The precursor to the AU, the Organisation of African Unity (OAU), established its Mechanism for Conflict Prevention, Management and Resolution in 1993. See

Monde Mayangwafa and Margaret A Vogt, *An Assessment of the OAU Mechanism for Conflict Prevention, Management and Resolution 1993-2000,* New York: International Peace Academy, November 2000.

4. Susanne Schmeidl, with Eugenia Piza-Lopez, "Gender and Conflict Early Warning: A Preliminary Framework," Swiss Peace Foundation and International Alert, July 2002 http://www.international-alert.org/women/

5. Mary Caprioli, "Gendered Conflict," *Journal of Peace Research,* vol. 37, no.1, 2000, pp. 51-68 as cited on p. 11 of Schmeidl, with Piza-Lopez, Ibid., http://www.international-alert.org/women/

6. Schmeidl, with Piza-Lopez, "Gender and Conflict," op. cit.

7. Report of the Secretary-General to the Security Council on Conflict Prevention, A/55/895 – S/2001/574, 7 July 2001, http://www.un.org/Docs/sc/reports/2001/

8. Security Council Resolution 1366, 30 August 2001, http://www.un.org/Docs/scres/2001/

9. Conclusion of the meeting of the G8 Foreign Ministers, Attachment 2, G8 Roma Initiatives on Conflict Prevention, July 18-19 2001, Rome, Italy, "Strengthening the Role of Women in Conflict Prevention," http://www.g7.utoronto.ca/g7/foreign/

10. A recently published collection of 50 success stories reveals the strategies for prevention, conflict management and resolution that is now readily available from the NGO community, including women's organizations. See Dylan Mathews, "War Prevention Works: 50 stories of people resolving conflict," Oxford Research Group, September 2001, http://www.oxfordresearchgroup.org.uk/

11. European Platform for Conflict Prevention and Transformation, http://www.euconflict.org/

12. African Centre for the Constructive Resolution of Disputes (ACCORD), http://www.accord.org.za/

13. Global Action to Prevent War, http://www.globalactionpw.org/

14. UN Office for the Coordination of Humanitarian Affairs Integrated Regional Information Network, "Sierra Leone: Slow reintegration of ex-combatants causes concern," press release 28 June 2002, http://wwww.reliefweb.int/

15. Alcinda Antonio De Abreu, "Mozambican Women Experiencing Violence," in Meredith Turshen and Clotilde Twagiramariya (eds.), *What Women do in Wartime: Gender and Conflict in Africa,* London: Zed Books, 1998, p

76.

16. Jeta Katro Beluli, Women in Development Association, Albania, "Women Can Change Realities: The experience of Albania," in "In the Line of Fire: A Gender Perspective on Small Arms Proliferation, Peace-Building and Conflict Resolution," report of the WILPF International Women's Day Seminar 2001, Geneva, http://reachingcriticalwill.org/genderdisarm/

17. Izota Avduli and Kozeta Prifti, testimonies from "The Devastating Impact of Small Arms and Light Weapons on the Lives of Women: A Collection of Testimonies," International Action Network on Small Arms (IANSA) Women's Caucus, July 2001, p.13, http://www.peacewomen.org/campaigns/international/

18. Personal correspondence between Felicity Hill, UNIFEM and Major Jeffery White, NATO.

19. Vanessa Farr, "The Demobilisation and Reintegration of Women Combatants, Wives of Male Soldiers and War Widows: A Checklist," from "Gendering Demilitarization," forthcoming, Bonn International Centre for Conversion (BICC), http://www.bicc.de/demobil/

20. ILO, "Manual on Training and Employment Options for Ex-Combatants," Geneva: ILO, 1997, http://www.ilo.org/public/english/employment/recon/crisis/

21. Vanessa Farr, "Gendering Demilitarization as a Peace-building Tool," Paper 20, BICC, June 2002, p.7 http://www.bicc.de/general/

22. Press briefing, Kabul, 10 January 2002, on the occasion of the first meeting of the Interim Administration and the International Security Assistance Force (ISAF), http://www.un.org/apps/news/

23. Women's International War Crimes Tribunal on Japan's Military Sexual Slavery, December 2000, http://www.jca.apc.org/

24. Dorota Gierycz, "Women in Decision Making: Can we change the status quo?" in Ingeborg Brienes, Dorota Gieryzc and Betty Reardon, (eds.), *Towards a Women's Agenda for a Culture of Peace,* France: UNESCO Publishing, p. 27. According to research conducted by the UN Division for the Advancement of Women (DAW) only 1 per cent of those elected as Heads of State and Government are women, 7 per cent of those appointed as ministers are women (with even fewer women heading powerful departments such as ministries of foreign affairs, defence, the interior or finance) and some 11 per cent of those elected as parliamentarians are women.

25. Chaloka Beyani and Damian Lilly, "Regulating

ENDNOTES

Private Military Companies: Options for the UK Government," International Alert, UK, August 2001, http://www.internationalalert.org/

26. UN Press Release, "Expert Panel Recommends Amending UN Treaty for Clearer Definition of Mercenaries," 22 May 2002, http://www.unog.ch/news2/documents/

27. Carol Cohn and Sara Ruddick, "A Feminist Ethical Perspective on Weapons of Mass Destruction," unpublished paper.

28. Center for Defense Information, Highlights of the FY 2003 Budget Request, http://www.cdi.org/issues/budget/

29. In order of spending, Russia, China, Japan, UK, Saudi Arabia, France, Germany, Brazil, India, Italy, South Korea, Iran, Israel, Taiwan, Canada, Spain, Australia, Netherlands, Turkey, Singapore, Sweden, United Arab Emirates, Poland, Greece and Argentina, http://www.cdi.org/issues/

30. Women's Peace Petition, http://www.ngos.net/

31. "UNIFEM sponsors a press conference where a Women's Peace Petition with more than 99,000 signatures will be presented to the UN, UNIFEM Press release, 24 October 1997, http://www.unifem.undp.org/newsroom/

32. Stockholm International Peace Research Institute (SIPRI), *SIPRI Yearbook 2002: Armaments, Disarmament and International Security,* Oxford: Oxford University Press, 2002 http://editors.sipri.se/pubs/

33. See the World Game Institute's website http://www.osearth.com/resources/wwwproject/ or http://www.osearth.com/resources/wwwproject/ for the list of researchers and major sources that substantiate the findings of the World Game Institute.

34. See World Trade Organization site, http://www.wto.org/wto/english/

35. Bill Hartung, World Policy Institute, quoted in Harmoine Toros, 'With End of Cold War, Experts Say Arms Now Sold Like Commodities," Associated Press, http://www.globalpolicy.org/security/

CHAPTER 10: RECONSTRUCTION

1. Report of the Secretary-General to the Security Council and the General Assembly on the causes of conflict and the promotion of durable peace and sustainable development in Africa, 13 April 1999, A/52/871-S/1998/318.

2. Women's Commission for Refugee Women and Children, "Rwanda's Women and Children: The Long Road to Reconciliation," September 1997.

3. http://www.aims.org.pk/funding_updates/

4. http://www.worldbank.org.ba/ECA/

5. UNMIK Kosovo Consolidated Budget for 2000, http://www.seerecon.org/Kosovo/UNMIK/

6. The East Timor Combined Sources Budget 2002-2003, Budget Paper No.1, Draft (pending final clearance of text by Council of Ministers, 7 May 2002).

7. Toby Porter, "External Review of the CAP," commissioned by the Evaluation and Studies Unit, OCHA, April 2002.

8. Gender Workshop for Latin American and Caribbean Region, "Gender and Development in Latin America: A Story of Growing Prosperity but Increasing Inequalities," organized by the Inter-American World Bank, 26-27 October 2000, Quito, Ecuador.

9. Susy Cheston and Lisa Kuhn, "Empowering Women Through Microfinance," unpublished paper sponsored by UNIFEM.

10. Graça Machel, *The Impact of War on Children,* London: Hurst, 2001.

11. Astri Suhrke with Kristian Berg Harpviken, Are Knudsen, Arve Ofstad and Arne Strand, "A Decade of Peacebuilding: Lessons for Afghanistan," CMI Report R 2002:9.

12. Ibid.

13. Ibid.

14. Susana Lastaria-Cornhiel, 'Privatization of Land Rights and Access to Factor Markets: A Path to Gender Equity?' Agrarian Reform and Rural Development: Taking Stock, Conference sponsored by the Social Research Centre, American University, Cairo, October 2001.

15. John Tagliabue, "As Multinationals Run the Taps, Anger Rises Over Water for Profit," *New York Times,* 26 August 2002.

16. Susana Lastaria-Cornhiel, "Privatization of Land Rights," op. cit.

17. World Bank, "The Transition from War to Peace: An overview," http://lnweb18.worldbank.org/

18. Asma Halim Abdel, "Attack with a Friendly Weapon" in Meredith Turschen and Clothilde Twagiramariya, (eds.), *What women do in Wartime,* op. cit., pp. 89-90.

19. Women's Commission for Refugee Women and Children, "UNHCR Policy on Refugee Women and Guidelines on their Protection: An Assessment of Ten Years of Implementation," May 2002, p. 65.

20. ILO Employment Sector Crisis Response and Reconstruction Programme.

ELISABETH REHN

Elisabeth Rehn's distinguished career has included serving as Minister of Equality Affairs and Minister of Defence of Finland, Member of the European Parliament, UN Special Rapporteur for the Situation of Human Rights in Bosnia and Herzegovina, the Republic of Croatia, the Federal Republic of Yugoslavia and the Former Yugoslav Republic of Macedonia, and UN Under-Secretary-General, Special Representative of the Secretary-General in Bosnia and Herzegovina. She has also been a candidate for President of Finland.

Dr. Rehn is currently an Advisory Council Member of Intellibridge, an information management service in Washington DC, and a member of the UN Department of Peacekeeping Operations (DPKO) Review Board. She has been a member of the Court of Conciliation and Arbitration of the Organization for Security and Cooperation in Europe (OSCE) since 1994; a member of the International Steering Committee of Engendering the Peace Process and Chair of the Finnish Association for Education and Training of Women in Crisis Prevention since 1997; and Chair of the World Wildlife Fund, Finland since 2000. Previously, Dr. Rehn has served as Vice-chair of the Finnish Red Cross, Chair of the Standing Group of the National Committees of UNICEF, Vice-chair of the UN International Conference on Population and Development (ICPD), member of the UNFPA Advisory Committee for Implementation of ICPD decisions and Chair of the Youth Conference on Climate 2000.

Dr. Rehn's early memories of the Soviet invasion of Finland give her a personal understanding of the horrors of war. As Defence Minister, she was an advocate for those who wanted to do civil service rather than compulsory military service. However, says Dr. Rehn, it was in Bosnia as the UN Special Representative that she experienced first hand the gap between the decision-making level and those who are suffering on the ground.

Among the many awards and honours that Dr. Rehn has received are The Golden Charter of Peace and Humanism, 1998 (Sarajevo/US); Das Grosse Ehrenzeichen am Bande, 1994 (Austria); Commander of the White Rose of Finland, 1992 and several awards connected to her work in the area of defence. She was made an Honourary Member of Jaycees International in 1992, an Honourary Member of UNICEF Finland in 1994, and an Honourary Member of Zonta International in 1996.

Elisabeth Rehn (left), U.N. special envoy for Bosnia and Herzegovina, visited Bosnian Moslem refugees in the village of Sapna, August 6, 1998.

Dr. Rehn has two doctor of science degrees, one in politics and the other in economics. She has been married for 47 years and has four children.

ELLEN JOHNSON SIRLEAF

In a professional life that has spanned over thirty years, Ellen Johnson Sirleaf has held a number of prominent positions, including Minister of Finance of Liberia; President of the Liberia Bank for Development and Investment; Vice President of Citicorp, Africa regional office; Vice President of Hong Kong Equator Bank; and Senior Loan Officer of the World Bank. She was one of seven international eminent persons selected by the Organisation of African Unity in 1999 to investigate the Rwanda genocide.

Ms. Johnson Sirleaf is currently Chairperson of the Open Society Institute West Africa (OSIWA), part of the Soros Foundation Network. She also consults regularly for the UN Economic Commission for Africa as an External Advisor and is a member of the Advisory Board of the Modern Africa Growth and Investment Company (MAGIC); Senior Advisor and West/Central Africa Representative of Modern Africa Fund Managers (MAFM), which has offices in Washington DC, USA and Johannesburg, South Africa; and the Chair and CEO of Kormah Investment and Development Corporation (KODIC), a financial and management advisory consultancy firm incorporated in Liberia and Cote d'Ivoire. Additionally, she is the founder and key supporter of a community development NGO, Measuagoon, in Liberia.

A presidential candidate in the 1997 Liberia general elections, Ms. Johnson Sirleaf came second in a field of thirteen. Prior to that, she served for five years as Assistant Administrator and Director of the Regional Bureau for Africa of UNDP with the rank of Assistant Secretary General of the United Nations. She has represented Liberia on the boards of several international and regional financial institutions, including the International Monetary Fund, the World Bank and the African Development Bank.

Ms. Johnson Sirleaf has first hand experience of armed conflict. During the 1980 coup d'etat in Liberia she was one of only four government ministers who escaped assassination.

The recipient of numerous special honors, Ms. Johnson Sirleaf has been awarded the *Commandeur de l'Ordre du Mono* of Togo (1996), the Ralph Bunche International Leadership Award of the United States (1995), the Franklin D. Roosevelt Freedom of Speech Award of the United States (1988) and the Grand Commander Star of Africa Redemption of Liberia (1980).

Ms. Johnson Sirleaf holds a Master of Public Administration degree from Harvard University. She has four sons.

Presidential candidate Ellen Johnson Sirleaf walked with hundreds of supporters during a Women's Solidarity March, Monrovia, Liberia, July 15, 1997.